The History of Dive-bombing

By the same author:

NAVAL
Action Imminent
Arctic Victory
Battle of Midway
Battles of the Malta Striking Forces
Battleship *Royal Sovereign*
British Battle Cruisers
Cruisers in Action
Destroyer Action
Destroyer Leader
Eagle's War
Fighting Flotilla
Hard Lying
Heritage of the Sea
Hit First, Hit Hard
H.M.S. *Wild Swan*
Hold the Narrow Sea
Into the Minefields
Midway; Dauntless Victory
Pedestal; the convoy that saved Malta
Royal Navy Ships' Badges
Task Force 57
The Great Ships Pass
War in the Aegean

AVIATION
Close Air Support
Fairchild-Republic A10A Thunderbolt
North American T-6, SNJ, Harvard &
   Wirraway
Lockheed C-130 Hercules
Ship Strike
RAF Squadron Badges
T-6; the Harvard, Texan and Wirraway
The Sea Eagles
The Story of the Torpedo-bomber

MILITARY
Massacre at Tobruk
The Royal Marines: A Pictorial History
Per Mare, Per Terram
Victoria's Victories

DIVE-BOMBERS
Aichi D3A1/2 *Val*
Curtiss SB2C *Helldiver*
Dive-bomber!
Dive-bombers in Action
Douglas SBD *Dauntless*
Douglas AD *Skyraider*
Fist from the Sky
Into the Assault
Jungle Dive-bombers at War
Junkers Ju 87 *Stuka*
Luftwaffe Colours – Stukas – 1
Luftwaffe Colours – Stukas – 2
Petlyakov Pe-2 *Peshka*
Skua; The Royal Navy's Dive-bomber
Straight Down!
Stuka at War
Stukas over the Mediterranean
Stukas over the Steppe
Stuka Spearhead
Stuka Squadron
Vengeance!

The History of Dive-bombing

Peter C. Smith

Pen & Sword
AVIATION

Published in Great Britain in 2007 by
PEN & SWORD AVIATION
an imprint of
Pen & Sword Books Ltd
47 Church Street
Barnsley
South Yorkshire
S70 2AS

ISBN 978-1-84415-592-7

*First edition published as 'Impact!' in 1981
by William Kimber & Co Limited, London*

See all previous books by Peter C. Smith at www.dive-bombers.co.uk

Typeset by Concept, Huddersfield, West Yorkshire
Printed and bound in Great Britain by Biddles Ltd, King's Lynn

Pen & Sword Books Ltd incorporates the Imprints of
Pen & Sword Aviation, Pen & Sword Maritime, Pen & Sword Military,
Wharncliffe Local History, Pen & Sword Select,
Pen & Sword Military Classics and Leo Cooper.

For a complete list of Pen & Sword titles please contact
PEN & SWORD BOOKS LIMITED
47 Church Street, Barnsley, South Yorkshire, S70 2AS, England.
E-mail: enquiries@pen-and-sword.co.uk
Website: www.pen-and-sword.co.uk

For Pat, Paul and Dawn

This book, like everything else – is for you

Contents

Foreword

The story of the dive-bomber is a fascinating and complicated one in the overall history of military aviation. It is a subject that has intrigued me for many years, and when, almost five decades ago now, I first wrote a history of the famous Ju 87 Stuka, I was further drawn into research of its origins. To the best of my knowledge, no complete and detailed history of this type of aerial attack had ever been attempted in any depth, although some selected facts had received limited (and largely inaccurate) treatment in books and magazines. But to present the dive-bomber story as a complete and whole history proved to have been an insurmountable challenge, not for myself in presenting it, but for any publisher in choosing to present it in its entirety in the succeeding decades. When I conducted my research and study into this field I discovered that the story was far more complex and diverse than I had ever imagined. Moreover, minds were closed on the subject to a remarkable degree, and myth and legend were, and still are, reproduced in print and on film with scant regard to facts, despite my best efforts. My original completed manuscript in 1978 came out at more than half a million words and I have delved far more deeply since that time. I have had to accept that it is only in digestible chunks that this story will ever be presented. This book incorporates just some of the research material accumulated, but is valuable in that it contains many fascinating first-hand accounts from the men who had actually carried out such missions, rather than theorists proclaiming something of which they knew little by way of facts. These memories alone are worth recording for posterity, and they, in themselves, reflected the complete developments of dive-bombing and the dive-bomber.

The result is this book, in which the dive-bomber pilots themselves speak of their experiences and provide the background into many previously unrecorded and little-known incidents and are supplied from hitherto unculled documents and combat reports. This new edition has enabled me to add some fresh material and correct some of the errors that crept into the original typesetting. This then, is dive-bombing in peace and war – from the sharp end!

Acknowledgements

I would wish to thank and acknowledge the debt of gratitude due to the dive-bomber pilots themselves, who so patiently answered all my many, many questions all those years ago, and who allowed me to quote them in this book. All opinions expressed otherwise are my own interpretations, and the blame for any mistakes is purely mine, not theirs. Most have now passed on, but their legacy in partly contained in these pages. In alphabetical order these gentlemen were: Colonel F.D.G. Bird OBE, Royal Marines; Captain E.M. Brown, Royal Navy; Major V.B.G. Cheesman DSO, CBE, DSC, Royal Marines; Donald B. Cooney, US Navy; *Generale* B.A. Antonio Cumbat; *Ing.* Hans Drescher; Wing Commander Arthur Murland Gill, RAF (Rtd); Captain Halliday DSC, Royal Navy; Captain T.W. Harrington DCS, Royal Navy; Major L.A. Harris OBE, DSC, Royal Marines; Rear Admiral Paul A. Holmberg, USN; Lieutenant-Commander Mike Horndern, Royal Navy; Captain G.B.K. Griffiths, Royal Marines; George M. Lane, US Navy; *Oberst a. D.* Friedrich Lang; *Generalleutnant a. D.* Helmut Mahlke; Major Alan Marsh, Royal Marines; Lieutenant-Commander H.A. Monks DSC, Royal Navy; Major R.T. Partridge DSO, Royal Marines; Charles R. Shuford, US Navy; and Mr Dennis Young, RAF (Rtd).

Warmest thanks and best wishes are due to my friends who helped with information and photographs concerning their own nation's developments with translations – Alberto Borgiotti; Brian Gordon; Pierre Hervieux; Captain Claude Huan; Mrs Helga Hinsby; Nicola Malizia; Hans Obert; Giorgio Pini; Corrado Ricci; Hanfried Schliephake; Franz Selinger and Commander Sadao Seno. JMSDF (Rtd).

Gratitude and thanks go to the many individuals and departments that assisted me down the years and made available to me innumerable obscure documents and files – to Mr R. Simpson, Department of Archives and Aviation Records, RAF Museum, Hendon, London; Mrs E.W. Tink and the Fleet Air Army Museum, Yeovilton; W.A. Banner and HMS *Daedalus*, Lee-on-Solent; D.J. Hawkinge and the Naval Historical Branch, Ministry of Defence, London; Mr Haslam and E.H. Turner at the Air Historical Branch, Ministry of Defence, London; Fay Gould Lee, London; R. Marcham and the Patents Office, London;

E. Hine and the staff of Librarians at the Imperial War Museum, London; Mr F.F. Lambert at the old Public Record Office, London; Robert St John, Waldorf, MD; Lee M. Parsons, Operational Archives, Naval Air Systems Command, Washington DC; Dean C. Allard, Operational Archives Branch, Naval Historical Center, Washington, DC; G.M. Neufeld, History and Museums Section, US Marine Corps, Quantico, VA; Judy C. Endicott and Albert F. Simpson, Historical Research Center, Maxwell AFB, Alabama; George M. Watson, Officer of the Air Force Historical Center, Washington, DC; Robin Higham, Kansas State University, Manhattan, Kansas; *Capitaine de Vaisseau* Duval, *Etat Major Service Historique de la Marine*, Vincennes; Lieutenant-Colonel Nils Kindberg, *Flygvapnet*, Stockholm; Mannosake Toda, *Koku-Fan*, Tokyo; and Helene Thalnev, TASS, Moscow.

My thanks are also due to the following for permission to quote from published sources: George Harrap & Co and the authors for *With Rommel in the Desert* by Captain H.W. Schmidt and *Dive-bomber* by Robert A. Winston; William Kimber for *The Memoirs of Field Marshal Kesselring*; David Higham Associates Ltd for *Beaverbrook* by A.J.P. Taylor; Frederick Warne (Publishers) Ltd and the author for *Diary of a Desert Rat* by R.L. Crump; Collins Publishers and the authors for *The Turn of the Tide* by Arthur Bryant and *Years of Command* by Lord Douglas of Kirtleside; for extracts from *Two Block Fox: The Rise of the Aircraft Carrier, 1911–1929* by Charles M. Melhorn, copyright 1974, US Naval Institute, Annapolis, MD; Hodder & Stoughton Ltd and the Trustees of the author for *The Flames of Calais*, by Airey Neave; Cassell & Co for extracts from *The Second World War, Vol II* by Winston S. Churchill; Laurence Pollinger Ltd for *Zero!* by Masatake Okumiya and Horikoshi Jiro; Yale University Press for *History of United States Naval Aviation* by Turnbill and Lord; Hutchinson & Co (Publishers) Ltd for *Aviation Memoirs* by Owen Cathcart Jones and to Hans-Ulrich Rudel for extracts from his book *Stuka Pilot*.

Peter C. Smith, Riseley, Bedfordshire
January 2007

CHAPTER ONE

'I dove straight for the barge'

J ust about the only certain thing about the origins of the form of aircraft attack using bombs and a steep dive and known as dive-bombing is that nobody is certain just who originated it. Very few historians seem to agree about it, although the general consensus has been that it was the United States Marine Corps aviators in Central and South America who first brought this technique to a fine art.

While not wishing to detract one iota from the considerable achievements of those early pioneers, my own researches have led to the firm conclusion that *true* dive-bombing dates from earlier than this, from the latter years of the First World War in fact, and in particular from one attack by a British pilot on the Western Front, Harry Brown of No. 84 Squadron, RAF.

Much of the confusion and doubt as to the origins of dive-bombing stems from attempts to define clearly the angle of attack which could rightly be classified as dive-bombing, as distinct from glide or shallow bombing runs. Shallow glide-bombing has been defined as taking place when an aircraft is descending at angle of 20 degrees or less; steep glide-bombing when the aeroplane is descending at angles of between 20 degrees and 60 degrees. True dive-bombing is therefore seen by many to be confined to attacks wherein the aircraft approaches the target at an angle of 60 degrees or more.

While such a rule of thumb is convenient in its application, it cannot be made hard-and-fast and absolute. In the early days instrumentation was primitive and no particular record was kept of the angle at which an attack was made, save that it was in a steep dive. Furthermore, with the development of specialised dive-bombing aircraft many of the most important attacks which subsequently took place by these aircraft were made at angles of less than 60 degrees; they are none the less classic dive-bombing attacks by any normal reasoning. In fact, then, especially in the early years, dive- and glide-bombing are difficult, if not almost impossible, to classify separately.

Even before the outbreak of the Great War in Europe one early aviator from the United States could be said to have been pioneering

1

the basic technique. This was one Leonard W. Bonney. During the Mexican Civil War of 1913–15 Bonney was employed as an aerial scout seeking out enemy forces with his little Moisant aircraft. But as well as these types of mission he also carried special dynamite bombs rigged up by Mexican engineers, spherical devices which were fired by a rifle cartridge. He made his attacks at low level, and one contemporary description of his method is particularly relevant: 'Bonney drops his bombs himself at the end of a dive, before levelling out, and employs no sighting device.'[1]

Another early example can be found in the description of the French attack on German airship hangars at Metz in 1914. One of the pilots arrived over the target at 8,000 feet and his engine failed. 'Not wishing to fall before executing his mission, he volplaned [descended by gliding without use of the engine], and while doing so dropped his bomb with marvellous coolness.'[2]

A similar report came from an almost identical British aerial attack on the Zeppelin sheds at Dusseldorf on 8 October 1914 by Flight Lieutenant R.L.G. Marix of the Royal Naval Air Service, flying a Sopwith Tabloid. He attacked with 20 lb bombs in misty weather and was said to have 'dived to an altitude of only 6,000 feet ...' before releasing them to score direct hits. An assessment of this bombing raid noted 'that he found this to be necessary bears out the view that, for accuracy in bomb dropping, the aircraft must descend to an altitude that is very perilous.'[3]

Similarly three RNAS aircraft attacked the Zeppelin sheds at Friedrichshafen on 21 November 1914 with similar Cooper bombs, and again they made their bombing runs by diving from 1,200 to 700 feet before releasing their payload. Low-level attacks, which came to be termed 'strafing', played a great part in subsequent aerial operations not only on the Western Front, but further afield also. They were widely used on the Somme in 1916 with No. 43 Squadron in particular, and again at Ypres and Cambrai in 1917, while the Germans developed their own special *Schlachtstaffeln* for similar ground-level attacks. Two of the most classic uses of this method by the British were at Nablus in September 1918 against the Turkish Army and in the Kosturino Pass the same month against the Bulgarians. Spectacular as these attacks were, they were in no way dive-bombing attacks. They did, however, generate very severe losses among the aircraft and their crews from ground fire, and it was this factor, more than any other, that ultimately turned the RAF resolutely away from such methods, and also from true dive-bombing as well, in the years between the wars.

Attacking specific targets in a dive continued to be featured through-out the war in isolated incidents, as is reflected in numerous reports of 'nose-diving' in aviators' memoirs, and it was claimed that, 'If the aviator dives towards his target, accuracy of aim becomes easier and effective work can be done without scientific instruments.'[4]

One British magazine of the time examined this method, the writer stating:

> Tactically, the chances of direct hits are greatly enhanced by a nose-dive down on to the target, but probably the time available would preclude the making of detailed instrument adjustments during the precipitous descent, and for aiming the pilot would rely upon the judgement of the eye.[5]

Arthur Gould Lee, flying with No. 46 Squadron based at Izel-le-Hameau to the west of Arras at the end of November 1917, gives a vivid description of this type of attack and the risks involved. On 30 November he was dispatched armed with four 20 lb Cooper bombs to attack a specific house target at the village of Bourlon. Although instructed to make four separate attacks dropping one bomb at a time, he instructed his wingman to release all four bombs directly Lee himself dropped his first, and then to clear out to the rendezvous point over Havrincourt Wood. From a height of 4,000 feet Lee then made his attack.

> We dived steeply and I let go at 200 feet. It must certainly have been an important target, for a devil of a lot of machine-gun fire came up at us. As I pulled out of the dive in a climbing turn, I glimpsed Dusgate, also climbing, but then I lost him. I saw the smoke of our bombs bursting – mine was a miss, but his were quite near. But the house hadn't been hit. I had to try again.
>
> I honestly felt quite sick at the prospect. I felt I just hadn't the guts to dive down three more times into that nest of machine-guns, now all alert and waiting for me. I had to do it, but, I told myself, only once. And I did it, in a sort of numb indifference. If they got me they got me. I dived down, to 100 feet, and released all three bombs. Bullets were cracking round me. I swerved violently to the right, and skidded away at 20 feet, where they couldn't follow me. Whether I hit the damned house, I don't know. I wasn't interested in it any more. Marvellously, they hadn't hit me, but one bullet had broken the handle of the throttle control, and another had smashed in the Very pistol cartridges, which ought to have exploded and set me alight, but they didn't.[6]

Little wonder then that losses were high in such circumstances. In fact Lee was shot down that day, for the third time in his flying career, leading a strafing attack against the German counter-offensive at Cambrai.

So much for 'unofficial' claims to have originated dive-bombing, and there are many more to choose from. But the strongest claimant in my opinion for the first 'official' dive-bombing attack as such is held by Second Lieutenant William Henry Brown RFC, while serving with No. 84 Squadron in France in March 1918. Certainly this well-documented attack is a model of early combat experience and has the added attraction in that it was both successful and, with a bearing on the future, it was against a ship target.

No. 84 Squadron had been operating in France for several months prior to this mission, predominantly in its true scout or fighter role. Since August 1917 it had been mainly commanded by a Major W.S. Sholto Douglas MC DFC, a name to become famous in RAF history and one which we shall be meeting again in these pages.

The unit had continual changes of airfields behind the front, but the line at this time was fairly static. The squadron arrived at Flez airfield near St Quentin on 29 December 1917 and was equipped with SE5a fighters armed with a Vickers and a Lewis gun only.

If the SE5a appears an unlikely contender for the title of the first true dive-bomber then it must be remembered that it was fitted with both an Aldis and a ring-and-bead sight and that provision had been made under the fuselage for a quadruple 20 lb carrier. More than that it was an extremely agile and lively machine. One historian described it thus: 'The SE5a also earned a reputation for strength, and pilots were ready to dive it steeply and to pull it out of the dive on fairly small-radius curves without wondering if the wings would fall off.'[7]

No. 84 Squadron was already highly proficient at low-level strafing attacks and had been especially to the fore during the action on 3 May during the Third Battle of the Scarpe and later. But this mission was different.

From extracts from the unpublished memoirs of Lieutenant Brown it seems that the problems of carrying bombs on the SE5a to attack 'targets of opportunity' on their offensive patrols had been pre-occupying the squadron for some time. Offensive patrols formed the bulk by far of their normal day-to-day duties at this time, but chances frequently presented themselves for the opportunity to have a go at ground targets too large for the normal machine-gun strafing and too small for conventional bombing. Brown noted in his memoirs:

> As far as we knew, putting a load of bombs on the plane might be the same as asking a humming bird to carry a walnut around. He probably couldn't get off the ground and neither could we.[8]

It appeared that, in order to try out the bomb-carrying capacity of the SE5a, Harry Brown was chosen as the 'volunteer' because he was the lightest pilot in No. 84 Squadron at the time. He was provided with only a few days' practice before the first actual combat test. He noted:

> The following morning with a make-shift bomb rack we loaded four 25 lb wooden bombs on my plane .... My fellow officers had drawn a circle 100 feet in diameter near our field. I was told to fly at 1,000 feet and drop the bombs one at a time ... with no mechanical devices and only the use of my eyes for a bombing sight. I missed the circle with all four bombs.

The problem of accurately hitting the target circle was resolved after another pilot had put the question, 'We dive to strafe so why not drop a bomb at the end of a dive?' Following this suggestion, and with another four wooden practice bombs, Lieutenant Brown recorded that he hit the target all four times.

Further testing followed, and on 14 March 1918, his first real live target was allocated, ammunition barges on the canal near Bernot. A difficult enough target, but one which, if he should prove successful, would provide him with spectacular confirmation of his result!

Second Lieutenant Brown's dive-bombing attack is described in No. 84 Squadron's Combat Report as a 'Special Mission (Low bombing attack)' and is indeed, the only exclusively bombing raid listed, being tucked away in the middle of a mass of aerial combat reports more normal for a scout unit.

His SE5a (No. 5384) was prepared with four live bombs, but the day had dawned with a thick pea-soup fog that made an early mission impossible. Not until midday did his sluggish mount get airborne from Flez and drone off into the patchy mist. He was on his own and the fog was still thick enough to keep Brown initially at less than 100 feet. Even so, within twelve minutes of take-off he was over his target. He described his flight thus:

> On leaving the aerodrome I went as far as the Bois de Savy under the mist. Reaching here I started to climb, and got to a height of 5,000 feet. At this height I could just see the St. Quentin–Mont d'Origny road, which I followed. I missed, however, the aerodrome at Mont d'Origny, and started to follow the canal. At Bernot I found four barges.[9]

In his memoirs Brown remembered that his target was three barges being loaded with supplies, but he does not specify the fourth, which was probably already laden in mid-canal. He immediately went down and made his first attacks, but he could not dive straight down as planned because of the mist. 'I cursed the fog,' he wrote, 'for it prevented me from getting sufficient height for a real dive.'

His first and second bombs missed the barges, as did his third, one bomb hit the canal bank and the other two dropped harmlessly into the water.

> The fog lifted slightly ... I dove straight for the barge. As I pulled up and looked back I could feel the effect of the explosion. I had hit the middle barge square amidships.

In this final dive Brown released his bomb at a height of 500 feet. Not content with this success he went on:

> I then climbed, and, turning, dived on the barges firing a drum of Lewis and about 50 rounds from the Vickers. My Vickers jammed. On the way back I saw about three or four motor cars on the roads, which I shot at (about 30 rounds). There were no troops or other traffic.

Thus ended an historic mission. Was it the first 'true' combat dive-bombing attack? Well, one authority seemed convinced. *Aerospace Historian* concluded that, 'Within a week all SE5 Scout planes in his squadron were equipped for carrying bombs and a new word was added to the vocabulary of aerial warfare ... dive-bombing.'

The subsequent almost total opposition to dive-bombing by the Royal Air Force has tended to obscure this important milestone. Indeed, as early as 1936 Oliver Stewart was having to remind British readers that, 'Dive-bombing is often thought of as a post-war development, but actually the statistics upon which the method is based were obtained with a [Sopwith] Camel in 1917.'[10]

But the Sopwith Camel was not the only aircraft to be use in this role. Lieutenant Brown's exploit with his SE5a in March may or may not have been the first 'real' combat dive-bombing, but the use of this particular scout in dive-bombing tests actually pre-dated his action by several significant weeks.

Whatever the arguments already germinating, and indeed bearing first fruit, in the top echelons of what was soon to be the RAF on the emotive subject of dive-bombing as a result of these ground-attack missions, it can certainly be claimed with complete confidence that it was they who authorised the first tests of this new method under carefully controlled conditions at the RAE Armament Experimental Station at Orfordness in Suffolk early in 1918.

To carry out these dangerous experiments into a still relatively unknown method of attack, which subjected these still fragile flying machines to unknown stresses and tensions, officers of considerable experience were selected. But their combat and flying hours were not to a universal standard, because what the team, under Lieutenant-Colonel A.C. Boddam-Whetham, Commandant of the Experimental

Station, was trying to establish was a range of findings based on pilots of widely differing backgrounds and skills.

Both the SE5a and the Camel were used in these tests, which were made with a series of single attacks against a small yellow flag planted in the shingle. Dives were made from about 1,500 feet, with release between 800 and 1,000 feet. But, as the official report confessed: 'It was found to be difficult to lay down hard-and-fast rules on the operation as each pilot had his own way of doing the job, but a little practice enabled four pilots to make quite good shooting.'[11]

On the SE5a trials the report stated, rather obviously, that, 'The lower the machine is before the bomb is released the more accurate is the shooting.' But their overall conclusions were quite unfavourable. 'The proposed method of diving a Camel at 160 mph at a target and releasing the bomb at low height is *quite unsafe* for average pilots and the results expected are *not worth the expenditure in machines and trained pilots.*'[12]

From this attitude the official RAF line was formulated, and it was hardly to budge an inch from it in the next thirty years. Although testing of dive-bombing continued in the RAF, as we will see, the bias against the method had already been established in 1918 and was to remain deep seated, indeed ingrained, in the Air Ministry mindset.

* * *

Across the Atlantic the division of two trains of thought, Navy pro-dive-bombing, and Army Air Corps anti-dive-bombing, did not emerge so quickly as in Great Britain. On the contrary it was the US Army Air Corps that, in a modest way, was to provide the spark that rekindled the whole dive-bomber fire. France followed a similar pattern, although in the initial stages of post-war development she at one period led the world in the application of dive-bombing attacks against warships. The other major powers also concentrated their efforts more on the development of ground-strafing than true dive-bombing, and Italy, the Soviet Union and Poland followed this route at first, while Japan and Germany were dormant, although the former was eager to learn, and the latter had a huge well of expertise left over from the war.

In Great Britain it was the Fleet Air Arm fighters of the Royal Navy that continued experimenting with dive-bombing, but only as an additional role for their more normal duties. Diving attacks on major warships with very small bombs was a spectacular part of their training, but this was mainly with a view to suppressing the anti-aircraft fire of the warships while the real attacks were delivered by torpedo-bombers. This meant that in the Royal Navy dive-bombing attacks in the 1920s involved the Nieuport Nightjar (1922–4), the

Parnell Plover (1923–4) and the Fairey Flycatcher, and with these small fighters limited British dive-bombing continued to develop its chosen lines with the famous 'converging attacks' with four 20 lb bombs on carriers below the wings. By 1928 exercise in the Mediterranean had shown that the 'natural' targets for such light dive-bombing attacks at sea were the aircraft-carriers of the enemy fleet, and this continued to be their role into the 1930s.

France, along with the UK and the USA, carried out the only real dive-bombing work during this period, albeit for a limited time before shortage of funds stifled it. These French Navy experiments are very interesting, and indeed, although the French claim to have 'invented' dive-bombing is of course totally false, they do have a good case for being credited with the first serious application of the dive-bombing technique against warships at sea, in *advance* of the United States.

Credit for the earliest French experiments with this objective in mind go to Lieutenant Pierre Henri-Clément La Burthe, who, in 1918, while working as an artillery observer in *Escadrille* F50 of the Army Air Force at Dunkirk, propounded the diving attack for achieving the greatest accuracy, planning the bomb direct on the target, 'like a hand'.

La Burthe's ideas were adopted, with considerable modification, but enthusiasm later by *Lieutenant de Vaisseau* Teste, who conducted a series of trials in 1930–31 in which dive-bombing was utilised. The hazardous nature of such tests, revealed in the Orfordness Trials, was fully endorsed by Teste's experiences. In a letter written to the Commander of the St Raphael school, he described his experiences thus:

> As reported from Order No. 33, as soon as I returned to base with ACI Squadron, I set off alone with the HDR 39 to carry out a rapid bomb-attack exercise on the battleship *Bretagne* using the undersea bomb*.
>
> I attained an altitude of 1,600 metres on the port side of the ship, dived at an angle of 30 degrees and, after a horizontal flight of 100 metres level with the water, released. The bomb fell about 30 metres beyond the axis of the ship. I realised that my approach must have been too long.

It can be seen from this that Teste was not using true dive-bombing, but merely using the dive-in approach to get to the target quickly, and then dropping the bomb in level flight. However, he continued his experiments with a steeper angle, in true dive-bomber style. 'I began my attack again at an angle of 70 degrees down to a height of 600 metres, but I didn't have time to press the bomb release and I didn't

---

* An early French equivalent of the British 'B' Bomb.

fire.' On the third pass he attacked at an angle of 30 degrees from a height of 600 metres.

> Having positioned myself level to the water, I opened up the throttle, but the engine wouldn't open up. I backtracked to 50 metres, putting myself into the wind. I landed about 200 metres from *Bretagne*. The plane capsized and sank a few minutes later.

Fortunately he was rescued unharmed and the accident didn't dampen his enthusiasm. He concluded that:

> From the point of view of the drop the manoeuvre is very simple. It is practically certain that with training the average pilot would acquire great precision, and that the dropping zone would not exceed the size of a battleship of 23,000 tons. These tests are worth continuing.'[13]

His C-in-C, Admiral Salaun, agreed, writing: 'The methods of attack used appear interesting ... in spite of the very short training the lieutenant has succeeded, for the first time, in obtaining an interesting result, which can be improved on.'

These tests were carried on at St Cloud, the *Commission d'Etude pratiques d'Aviation* conducting them; their method, *Attaque à bout portant* (Attack at point-blank range) was described later thus:

> A fast plane carrying a bomb with a delayed-action device flying at a high altitude dives down in front of a target surface ship and releases its bombs on passing level with the water in front of the ship. The bomb is detonated by the shock of hitting the water, and with its four-second delay explodes against the target underwater.[14]

A special plane was designed for the French Navy but its development languished and they continued to employ the antique Levasseur PL7 for experiments until the late 1930s saw a change.

American Army aviators returned from the Western Front much influenced by British methods, and naturally dive-bombing was one idea they picked up. In late 1919, Lieutenant Lester B. Sweeley carried out a special test in vertical bombing at the Aberdeen Proving Ground, and followed it with another in September. He used a DH4B fitted with a 300 lb bomb, diving from 4,000 to 1,000 feet before release.

A more extensive and lastingly practical use was made by the Third Attack Group engaged in patrolling the uneasy border with Mexico during 1919–21. Commanded by Major (later Lieutenant-General) Louis H. Brereton, and flying old DHs of First World War vintage, it employed methods which were described later by Lieutenant Tourtellot of the USAS to Marine pilot 'Rusty' Rowell.

Although no one would believe that the wing structure of that type of plane could withstand the strains of dive-bombing, they used DH-ABs. By avoiding excessive speeds they were entirely successful, as no DH was ever lost, to my knowledge. They had installed the bomb releases in the pilot's cockpit, which was a new arrangement for a two-seater. They used the then latest type of external bomb rack developed just after World War I, an American rack designated Mark A-III. The plane carried ten bombs in racks on each wing.

Typical dive-bombing methods of delivering attacks were the rule, using a sighting point over the engine. Each pilot, depending on the height of his eye above the seat, would select some projection on the engine section as the current line of sight, would dive at an angle of approximately 60–70 degrees and release by visual judgement. The accuracy of their bombing was most impressive to me and I immediately visualised that certain naval employment of such tactics where accuracy against small moving targets is paramount.[15]

The US Marine Corps was also moving on similar lines, albeit more primitive. From March 1919, the 4th Air Squadron under Captain Harvey B. Mims was stationed inside Haiti, on the island of Hispaniola, flying operations against the 'Caco' terrorists in the interior. They were also fitted with the DH-4B/2B aircraft, which did not have bomb-sights. Level bombing proved highly inaccurate, and Lieutenant S.H. Sanderson therefore developed his own method of gaining the required precision by diving onto the target, and devised a means of launching the bomb safely, which was described as follows:

A large canvas mail sack of sufficient strength to hold the bomb was procured and one end of this sack was fastened securely to the bottom of the fuselage. A large bomb was placed in the sack and then the rear end of the sack was closed with a draw rope and the sack raised up to a horizontal position. The rear end of the sack was then tied to the rear cockpit with a rope system so that the rear end of the sack could be released while in flight.

On the next flight across enemy territory the plane was put into a dive and at the right moment the rear end of the sack was released, causing the sack to fall downward with the result that the bomb fell down and out. The force of gravity, plus the start of the pull-out and the shallowness of the dive, changed the bomb's course just enough to clear the de Havilland's propeller.[16]

The angle of dive employed was about 45 degrees, and to achieve accuracy with such a method Sanderson had to come down to about

250 feet! Such a primitive method was obviously OK against the kind of opposition the 'Cacos' could muster, but would hardly stand up to more realistic defences. But this is the method that is frequently held up by many historians who should know better, to represent the 'invention' of dive-bombing!

Off Virginia Capes in the summer and autumn of 1921 Billy Mitchell of the USAS conducted a series of tests with bombers against warships which received wide publicity. These attacks were almost all of the high- or medium-level type, but one test deserves more than passing mention. This was an attack carried out by 'Turk' Tourtellot, and he, in describing it to Rusty Rowell, claimed that it, in fact, constituted the first dive-bombing!

> He stated that he had attacked the ship with Cooper 25-pounders, carried on the single bomb rack attached under the fuselage of a British SE5 fighter plane. He told me in detail the method he used, stating that he had bomb releases in the cockpit and used a system identical with that which I had seen employed by the Attack Group at Kelly Field.[17]

Rusty Rowell was much impressed by what he had witnessed, and on assuming command of Marine Squadron VO-1-M in the late summer of 1924, he decided to train this force, based at San Diego with DH4Bs, as a dive-bomber unit, holding to his theory that his method would prove invaluable on counter-insurgency operations.

> As a preliminary training measure we attached miniature racks of the Navy type to the fuselages and connected them to the new type of bomb release in the pilot's cockpit. At a later date we received the Type A-3 bomb racks and conducted some experimental bombing tests using the standard type of Navy practise bombs then in use.
>
> We organised a show consisting of a demonstration of formation flying, combined with dive-bombing exhibitions, using smoke bombs, and with this program we participated in several airport dedications. It is my impression that some naval air officers who witnessed these early demonstrations of dive-bombing were impressed with the naval possibility of that form of manoeuvre. At all odds very shortly after that period the Navy Air began to practice dive-bombing with nearly all squadrons of Fleet Air shore-based at North Island.[18]

It may indeed have been like that, but it is certain that the Navy ran the Marines very close second in this period of experimentation. Another extremely valuable first-hand account of this vital formative period comes from Admiral F.D. Wagner, then one of the pioneer Navy pilots.

He recalled how in 1925 Captain Joseph Mason Reeves assumed command of Aircraft Battle Force and obtained permission to concentrate all Pacific Fleet aircraft at North Island, San Diego, for the summer of 1926 in order to develop new tactics. On Reeves' staff was Lieutenant F.W. Weed, and between these two questions were propounded to the various aircraft squadrons on how the squadrons would perform various missions. These questions formed a large mimeographed pamphlet which became known as Reeves' Thousand and One Questions. Admiral Wagner recalled how, on reporting to Reeves in June 1926 in command of VF-2 equipped with Curtiss F6C fighters, one of the questions was how to repel a landing force endeavouring to land on a beach. Strafing proved poor for accuracy and was dangerous. Wagner discovered that:

> The answer to the problem lay in approaching at high altitude (above 10,000 feet) to attain surprise and to avoid anti-aircraft gunfire, before diving at a steep angle (70 degrees plus) to attain very high speed in the dive and to obtain the optimum of accuracy in hitting and in changing the emphasis from machine-gun to bombs.
>
> The squadron knew it had developed a very important form of attack that would be effective against the strongest of targets and one that *in no way resembled the old strafing conception of attack*. We also appreciated the fact that attacks must not all be made from the same direction and that the formation from which the attack started must be a flexible one so that entry into the dive would be made promptly after sighting a target. Accordingly, the Vee of echelon and the ABC formations were developed.

Full of enthusiasm at their 'discovery', the squadrons carried out prolonged tests and trials in the back country of San Diego that summer. Once having satisfied themselves that they had perfected their art, the young pilots were eager to give a more practical demonstration in the hope of convincing their superiors. In a trial run they persuaded Captain Reeves to take up position in the centre of the attack zone and present himself as 'target'. The resulting demonstration made a firm and lasting impression on him and those assembled with him, including Vice-Admiral Felix Stump. So impressed was he that Reeves had no hesitation in giving his squadrons permission to utilise their new tactic in front of a more glittering audience, the US Pacific Fleet. On 22 October 1926, the F6Cs flew off to Long Beach, California. The fleet was due to sail from San Pedro for tactical exercises at sea, and they planned to join in. Admiral Wagner himself described the result:

> The attack was delivered from above 12,000 feet; the targets were the battleships. The attack was delivered on the instant of the schedule time, of which the battleships had been previous

informed. The squadron's approach was not detected until the planes actually were in the final phases of their almost vertical dives. The squadron recovered from the dives at low level and were landing at Long Beach about the time the battleships were sounding to general quarters![19]

It was a stunning debut. Wagner added:

This was the first dive-bombing, as such, that we had ever heard of and the reactions of the battleship commanders were most interesting. If you can find their reports in the archives forwarded by Commander Battleships through Commander Battle Force, you will find that the general consensus as that 'there was no defense against it!'

Unknown to either, the new tactics of the Pacific Fleet squadrons were being duplicated on the East Coast by the then Rear Admiral A.C. Davis and Lieutenant George Cuddiby with VF-2s. They had sent in their own independent reports of dives against destroyer targets with gun cameras carried in the aircraft to record estimated hits. These attacks were led by Lieutenant O.B. Hardison, while Lieutenant-Commander Davis, with the Bureau of Aeronautics, contributed much to the technique by rewriting the rules for gunnery practice and by arranging for the purchase of better bomb racks and improved equipment for the planes involved.

The dive-bomber had reappeared with a bang, and many old rules had to go overboard as a result. Admiral Wagner again: 'Prior to 1926 there had been no question about dropping bombs from fighters because, as you say, there was at the time a prescribed bombing practise for fighters in their gunnery exercises in the year 1926–7 during which, using the diving tactics as opposed to gliding tactics, the squadron made a very high score.' As Lee M. Parson stated in his classic summary of the pre-war dive-bomber in the U. S. Navy:

Early tests proved that this kind of attack gave unparalleled accuracy to machine-gun fire and bombing attacks. Where there had been great reluctance to interrupt scheduled training to experiment with the new tactics, now there was enthusiasm. The advantages of dive-bombing against destroyers and carriers with gas, demolition and fragmentation bombs, in sizes up to 100 lb, were immediately perceived, and there were even some proponents of dive-bombing against other aircraft.[20]

This new-found doctrine was expounded in a lecture delivered to the Naval War College by Lieutenant-Commander B.G. Leighton in 1928, in which he stated:

The diving form of attack is now being extended to use of heavier bombs up to 500 lb weight. We are now putting into the fleet a new type of two-seater machine to replace the old two-seater observation machines.[21]

The new era had dawned.

Notes

1. Jones, E.L., *Bomb Dropping with Carranza* (*Aeronautics*, London, Vol IX, 1 December 1915).
2. *Aircraft and the War* (*Flight*, 21 August 1914).
3. *Bomb Dropping from Aircraft* (*Aeronautics*, London, October 1914).
4. Supplement, *Scientific American*, dated 22 April 1916.
5. *The Elements of Bomb Dropping* (*Flying Magazine*, issue dated 10 October 1917).
6. Gould Lee, Arthur, *No Parachute* (Jarrold, London, 1968), pp. 187–8, quoted with special permission of Mrs Fay Gould Lee to the Author, 19 February 1977.
7. Stewart, Major Oliver, MC, AFC and Bridgman, Leonard, *The Clouds Remember* (Gale & Poulden, London, 1936).
8. Extracts from W.H. Brown's *Memoirs*, published in *Aerospace Historian, The Heritage of Flight*, Volume 16, No. 2, Summer, 1969 (Kansas State University, Department of History, Manhattan, Kansas).
9. Combat Reports of No. 84 Squadron, National Archives, Kew, London (AIR/1/1797).
10. Stewart & Bridgman, *The Clouds Remember*, op. cit.
11. Low Height Bombing from Scouts, Report, dated 18 May 1918. G/49. National Archives, Kew, London (AIR/1/1200/04632).
12. Bombing from Sopwith Camel using Aldis Sight, Report, dated 27 May 1918. G/50. National Archives, Kew, London (AIR 1/1200/04632).
13. Letter from *Lieutenant de Vaisseau* Teste, *Commandant l'Aviation d'Escadre* to *Capitaine de Frégate* Commandant le C.A.M. de Saint-Raphael, dated 11 November 1921.
14. Duval, *Capitaine de Vaisseau, Chef du Service Historique de la Marine*, to the Author, dated 27 July 1977.
15. Statement by Major Norbert Carolin to Major Ernest L. Jones, AC/AS, Intel, in 1943.
16. For a full description of these operations see: Hinkle, Stacy C., *Wings Over the Border* (University of Texas, Texas Western Press, South-Western Studies Monograph No. 26, El Paso, 1970) and Larkins, William T., *The Evolution of Naval Dive-bombing* (*Flight*, 1943).
17. These tests were described in *Aviation and Aircraft Journal*, Volume II, No. 14, issue dated 25 July 1921.
18. Interview given by Major-General Ross Erastus Rowell, USMC, to the Aviation History Unit, dated 24 October 1946. An invaluable source.
19. Letter from Admiral F.D. Wagner to Lieutenant-Commander H.M. Dater, USNR, Office of the Chief of Naval Operations (Op-501-D), Washington, DC, dated 30 December 1948.
20. Parson, Lee M., *Dive-bombers: The Pre-War Years* (Naval Aviation Confidential Bulletin, July 1949) See also – VF Squadron Two – Individual Battle Practice (light bombs) – Report of scores, dated 28 December 1926. (BuAer to CNO, Aer-M-156-MV, BuAer General Files A5-1, Vol 1) and 15 July 1926 (Aer-M-20 –MV, A16-3, Vol 2).
21. Lecture given to Naval War College, *The Relation between Air and Surface Activities in the Navy*, Leighton, Lieutenant-Commander B.G., delivered on 23 March 1928, copy Author's files.

CHAPTER TWO

'One developed one's own technique'

The Leighton lecture was also important as it answered, in 1928, the main criticisms against the dive-bomber, which were still being levelled against it some fifteen years later by the RAF.

It may seem to you at first sight that a machine which approaches so close to its target before releasing its bomb will be running into almost certain destruction, but a careful study of the conditions which obtain, taking into account the high speed and manoeuvrability of the planes, the short period during which they are within close range (a matter of seconds), the difficulty of gun-laying at high angles of fire and the considerable element of surprise and unavoidable haste which is always present, the danger to the planes, at least from any anti-aircraft defenses that are now provided or seriously proposed on ships in our navy, is very low indeed. Experimental practices with camera guns have been held which tend strongly to confirm this view.[1]

Further live combat experience seemed to confirm this viewpoint, and this, once again, came from the US Marine Corps. The Marines had been employed in Nicaragua in the 1920s, but in the middle of that decade the forces of Moncada rose up against the rule of Diaz, and to preserve the status quo under the Monroe Doctrine the Senate sent in the Marines again in January 1927. To support the ground forces Rowell's VO-I-M suddenly received orders to proceed there, and by the end of February they had set up their base at Managua on the local baseball park, still equipped with their old DHs. Complete anarchy reigned, and the Marine troops held fourteen strongpoints along the vital linking railway, interposing themselves between the two rival factions. Later reinforced by VO-4-M, these two units combined to form an aircraft squadron under Rowell's command until the Armistice. But in June, as they were preparing to move out again, rebel officers under Augusto Sandoni refused to accept the peace agreement as valid and took to the northern mountains to continue the fight, and on 15 July they launched an attack with several hundred men on the tiny outpost

15

of Octoal, which was held by thirty-seven Marines under Captain Hatfield. An estimated 700–800 rebels cut them off and their fate seemed sealed as no reinforcements could reach them by land within ten to fourteen days. Rowell's airmen first discovered Hatfield's plight at 1010 hours the next morning. The five available DHs were at once dispatched to help them. As Rusty Rowell later recalled:

> As I mentioned previously, all the pilots had been trained in dive-bombing and that was the kind of attack that I planned to employ. As I made the approach on the town, we formed a bombing column. We were fired upon as we flew over the outposts along the river, but at 1,500 feet did not suffer any particular damage from rifle fire.

On reaching Octoal Rowell made a circuit to assess the situation. A tropical storm was building up as they approached and Rowell knew he would have to act quickly to do any good.

> I led off the attack and dived out of column from 1,500 feet, pulling out at about 600 feet. Later we ended up diving in from 1,000 feet and pulling out at about 300 feet. Since the enemy had not been subjected to any form of bombing attack, other than the dynamite charges thrown from the Laird Swallows of the Nicaraguan Air Force, they had no fear of us. They exposed themselves in such a manner that we were able to inflict damage which was out of proportion to what they might have suffered had they taken cover.

It was estimated that Sandino's forces suffered casualties of between fifty and two hundred men, and of these, the dead were given as between forty and eighty from this one attack.

> This attack was highly successful and followed by a great many similar types of air action through the following two years. There was *never* an occasion when this form of attack failed to disperse the enemy with losses.[2]

One writer has claimed that this constituted 'the first organised dive-bombing attack and possibly the first low-altitude attack ever launched in support of ground troops,'[3] which of course is absurd. But Rowell's attack at Octoal was of major significance in the progression of the method, for it proved that dive-bombing against unprepared troops was as effective in the confusion and disarray it caused as in its material damage effects.

> There was another formation attack, which I led [wrote Rowell]. It consisted of only four planes because we were reduced to that number due to operational and normal casualties. It was one of the first occasions when we used the new Corsairs, just received.

This show was in January 1928, and was directed at Sandino's famed stronghold on Chiptoe Mountain, following some rather disastrous ambushes of our ground troops. In this attack we made the approach from downwind over a layer of overcast clouds and delivered the assault from an *almost vertical dive*.* This attack was also successful in inflicting losses and resulted in wide dispersal of the main body of the enemy. That was the first time we used the 50 lb demolition bombs.[4]

Development proceeded apace after the first impetus, although at first a large variety of differing aircraft types were produced. But gradually these crystallised into a basic two-seater carrying bomb loads of up to 1,000 lb. With regard to accuracy the first tests had been impressive, and in each further dive-bomber trial further improvement was shown. The Curtiss F8C claimed a hit rate of 67 per cent on target compared with the horizontal bomber average of 30 per cent, while Lieutenant-Commander Wagner once claimed his squadron scored 100 per cent hits on a battleship target.[5]

With regard to the ships' defences the first feelings were that they had little or no chance of stopping a committed dive-bomber by gun-fire alone, and Captain Leahy of the Board of Ordnance was recorded as stating that this method of attack had 'great possibilities'. As Melhorn dryly pointed out, however:

Harmony of views on this matter by BuAer and BuOrd was short-lived. By 1931 they were divided into an 'air-camp' and a 'gun-camp', the latter holding that it had a weapon to knock down the dive-bomber before it reached the release point, but had no way of proving it since a diving target could not be provided.[6]

However, perhaps the most devastating examples of that accuracy in bombing were being demonstrated by the dive-bomber pilots for the other side of the argument, as Turnbill and Lord later recorded:

In the 1931 war games the important feature had been the efficient training, and this was shown by the dive-bomber attacks against radio-controlled *Stoddert* and the destroyers *Marcus* and *Sloat*. The vulnerability of such small craft became particularly plain when they were raked from close overhead with .50 caliber machine-guns whose shots penetrated decks and bulkheads; when 30 lb demolition bombs smashed searchlights, boats and torpedo tubes. The conclusion was that bomber attacks delivered with the viciousness of which the Navy's pilots were now capable could be stopped only by much better shooting from many more anti-aircraft guns than were mounted by small, or even larger ships.[7]

* Author's italics.

In the Royal Navy the main interest still continued to be in the Fleet Air Arm, and Lieutenant Owen Cathcart-Jones gives this description of what it was like to dive-bomb in a Flycatcher aircraft in 1927.

> Carrying four practice-bombs beneath the fuselage, just above the main undercarriage, our original method of bombing was to take up a position about 2,600 feet immediately above the target, pull the nose up into a gradual stall and then let the machine drop in a vertical dive onto the target. While in the dive we aligned our sights on the target and released the bomb. This system was carried out quite successfully for some time until one after another of us had the experience of the small practice-bomb hitting the undercarriage on release, owing to the fact that our dive and the line of release of the bomb corresponded and the undercarriage fittings were directly in the way.
>
> Shortly after this a new and far more accurate method of bombing was introduced. It was known as converging bombing. To perform this we made a very steep dive from about 2,000 feet straight at the target and continued it until about 150 feet off the ground, keeping the target in our sights throughout the dive. When we reached the base of our dive we pulled the aircraft up in a steep zoom and bank, releasing the bomb about three seconds after commencement of the climb. With practice, this method became very accurate. We obtained excellent results, our bombs always fell within a very short radius of the centre of the target, and direct hits were more frequent than misses.
>
> For practice our flights were subdivided into sections, each of three aircraft, and during converging bombing we split up and took our position round the target equidistant from each other. The leader would signal by slightly rocking his wings and then commence the exercise by diving at the target. When he was nearing the base of his dive, No. 2 would start from another direction, followed by No. 3 from the opposite side. By the time No. 3 was finishing his dive No. 1 had already got into position again and commenced his second dive, with the result that there was always one machine diving at the target.[8]

The incidents of the bomb hitting the undercarriage noted by Sweeley in 1919 and by Cathcart-Jones in 1927 were finally brought to a head in Britain by a tragic accident in 1932 at the Sutton Bridge range at Holbeach Marsh, when Flight Lieutenant Henry Maitland-King was killed when his Flycatcher exploded in mid-air through this cause. This made the already luke-warm RAF, which at this time controlled the Fleet Air Arm, react strongly until some method of prevention could be found. Air Vice-Marshal Dowding sent a secret telegram to Air Marshal Sir John Steel in India:

> An accident has occurred in which a live 20 lb bomb released from the fuselage rack on a Flycatcher in a steep dive hit the axle and exploded. CAS does not wish to hamper your operations but orders prohibiting diving bombing from fuselage racks with live bombs on single engined aircraft are being issued to other Commands.[9]

In Germany military aviation was still forbidden, but between 1925 and 1932 the Junkers firm operated in Sweden and developed aircraft with military potential. Karl Plauth designed a low-wing monoplane fighter, the K-47, and experiments began, including fitting it with bomb racks on sloping struts. From such humble beginnings germinated the seed that was to lead to the Ju 87, or the dreaded Stuka. Japan, too, was having to decide on how to close the gap in battleship strength between herself and the United States and Great Britain. Frozen by the Washington Treaty to ten such ships against the other nations' fifteen each, she sought other avenues to redress the balance, and was much impressed by the dive-bomber explosion taking place across the Pacific. In 1931 she placed an order with the German firm of Heinkel for a two-seater plane, stressed for diving, capable of carrying a 500 lb bomb, This was the He50aW, and after tests, development of their own version, built by Aichi, the D1A1 Type 04 carrier-bomber, commenced in 1931.

However, it was still in America that the fastest development continued and the greatest enthusiasm remained. By the eve of war the Vindicator two-seater monoplane was the latest in a long development line, with others on the drawing board, and the dive-bomber was an integral part of the Navy's armament. By contrast, the US Army had completely lost interest. Rear Admiral Holmberg described to the author his initiation to the dive-bomber when he was a young ensign in 1940:

> My introduction to dive-bombing flight profile occurred as an Ensign, while attached to the *Saratoga*. I 'hitched' a ride in one which was part of her Air Group in training, flying off the West Coast of California in 1940. In a simulated attack against a 'target' (a spar towed by a ship) my pilot executed a standard dive on the target, releasing a miniature practise bomb at the right time before 'pulling out' of the dive and regaining horizontal flight a few hundred feet over the water.
>
> This model dive-bomber I rode in was the Curtiss-Wright Aircraft Company's model SBC and nicknamed the 'Helldiver'. It

was a biplane and made a lot of noise (with its struts and braces) as it flew at a relatively high speed in a dive. The physical sensation while making a dive was exhilarating to say the least and the pull-out put a force several times the force of gravity on the pilot's body, enough, on one occasion, to cause the blood to drain from the head, resulting in the pilot's inability to see until the force is relieved.[10]

By this date, then, the dive-bomber was the main backbone, with the torpedo-bomber, of the US Navy and Marine Corps air components. More importantly, the Americans *believed* in dive-bombing and they practised hard at it. In the RAF it was a very different picture. Tests had been conducted at Martlesham Heath in 1934 with a specially adapted Hawker Hart utilising angles of dive between 50 and 70 degrees. Dives were commenced at 5,000 feet, so this was 'high' dive-bombing compared with the US Navy methods of the same time.

The conclusions were that: 'In all these tests the pilot automatically becomes the bomb aimer directing the aircraft towards the target.' It was noted that there was a 'strong tendency considerably to overestimate the angle at which the aircraft was being dived' and the conclusion was that dive-bombing depended entirely on the judgement of the pilot to select the correct moment to enter the dive and his own skill at holding the plane on target. Once committed he could not take his eye off the target without affecting accuracy.[11]

Hawkers were developing a dive-bomber prototype at this time, the PV4. An even more promising design by the same company resulted from specification P4/34 in which the Air Ministry called for a light bomber for Army support. An all-out dive-bomber design was still shunned by the RAF, but it was asked for that the aircraft be fully stressed for diving. This resulted in the Hawker Henley, a dive-bomber superior to most foreign types, but by the end of 1935 the RAF had again lost interest, and although 200 were built they were used as target-tugs! Other designs by Fairey went the same way. Only Blackburn continued with what was to become the Skua, but the original specification still only called for a hybrid, a fighter/dive-bomber, albeit that the dive-bomber part was originally to be its *main* role.[12] These, however, were destined for the Fleet Air Arm, and not the RAF.

A specialised dive-bomber for the RAF was therefore abandoned, and a series of lectures delivered by Wing Commander Slessor reflected the official Air Ministry line in 1934, his main thesis being that 'the aeroplane is not a battlefield weapon', and that special classes of 'assault' aircraft were 'uneconomical'.

Further tests followed, and in April 1936 a report was submitted that concluded that, 'Some very accurate bombing was obtained in these trials, and it would appear that angles of dive between 30 degrees and 65 degrees *should cover all contingencies of attack in the future**.[13]

It further stated that, '... with great reluctance, that in diving attacks, aircraft of clean aerodynamic design will reach too high a velocity to make recovery from 1,500 feet reasonably safe and certain, and that it will be necessary to apply some form of air-brake to check speed.' It did admit that, 'The steeper the dive, within reason, without a substantial increase in speed, the better the sighting view, which in turn tends to increase the accuracy of the bombing.'

An interesting comment was made in a minute of December 1937:[14]

I cannot visualise such attacks being made in war with much enthusiasm unless there is little or no opposition in the way of enemy anti-aircraft fire [it began]. I am afraid our pilots have not yet developed the Oriental desire to greet Allah.

It continued:

I think that dive-bombing attacks will only take place as such when:
(a) There is little chance of encountering enemy aircraft after the formation has broken up.
(b) When ground defences are not troublesome.

It concluded: '... if aircraft are to bomb at 1,500 to 2,000 feet then they should make their get-away at ground level (I would hate to be in the last flight).'

Leighton apart, the difference between this attitude and the enthusiasm of the American pilots recorded earlier is educational.

In a final pre-war meeting to consider the dive-bomber held in September 1938 a committee on the subject came to the following conclusions regarding dive-bombers in the RAF:

1. That steep dive-bombing should not at present be regarded as a requirement for modern RAF aircraft ....
2. That shallow dive-bombing should be continued without special devices and sights ....
3. That the dive-bombing type trials of new aircraft done at A&AEE Martlesham Heath were sufficient and that no special dive-bombing armament trials are required.[15]

Finally, as if to pretend the subject did not exist, an ostrich-type approach was adopted and it was recommended that 'this type of bombing should in future be termed 'Losing Height Bombing'.

*   *   *

* Author's italics.

Despite the obsession by the RAF with the long-range heavy bomber, not everyone in that service was of a like mind. One report stated that, 'I know unofficially that Air Ministry think dive-bombing is a thing of the past, whereas I am of the opinion that this policy is wrong and that those officials who think so are probably not aware of the capabilities or possibilities of dive-bombing ....' Yet another squadron leader wrote in a memo in November 1938 that:

> (i) Dive-bombing is valueless, except at really low altitude, unless the angle of dive is at least 45 degrees.
> (ii) The overwhelming advantages of steep diving from 6,000 feet are as great to warrant its retention provided a suitable aircraft is available.[16]

It was all too late. One senior Royal Air Force officer much, much, later revealed a tinge of remorse at Air Ministry policy in the years 1932–9. In his memoirs Sholto Douglas wrote: 'I could not help feeling with the deepest regret that it would have been so much better if, some years earlier, we had developed a dive-bomber along the lines of Ernst Udet's Stuka, instead of devoting so much of our resources to the design, development and the production of those wretched [Fairey] Battles.'

The Royal Navy, though far more enthusiastic, was hampered by the fact that it did not have the power over the Fleet Air Arm itself until 1939. In a minute on the growing power of the Japanese Navy in November 1933, the DNAD (Director Naval Air Division) wrote that, 'In general, sufficient evidence is available to indicate that dive-bombing is likely to be far more effective than high-level bombing against any target ...',[17] and continued, '... there is little doubt that dive-bombing with SAP bombs should form the main part of the attack.'

The meeting held at the Air Ministry in November 1934 was to provide such a plane, which was termed a 'fighter-dive-bomber', a terminology resembling that mythical hybrid of incompatible parts – the Hippogriff! The Air Ministry representatives stated that the Admiralty had asked it to be emphasised that the new aircraft should combine both duties, but that, '*the first of these is dive-bombing** [this very clear stricture when discussing the Skua's merits or otherwise has been consistently ignored by air historians ever since] against hostile carriers, the second is the attack of enemy aircraft in the air.'[18] The Admiralty representative reinforced this emphasis also, stating the Navy '... would prefer a good dive-bomber, with reasonable efficiency as a fighter, to a good fighter with moderate efficiency as a dive-bomber.'

* Author's italics.

Thus was the genus of the Blackburn Skua. When she appeared she was the first low-wing monoplane to serve with the fleet. Dive-bombing in the Royal Navy in the 1930s was conducted by aircraft like the Flycatcher, which continued until 1935, the Hawker Nimrod and Osprey and then by the Swordfish, which was designed primarily as a torpedo-bomber. But it was the former two aircraft, and later the Skua, that the bulk of the Royal Navy's dive-bomber pilots trained on pre-war.

> Checking through my log-books and diaries I can only trace a modest amount of very elementary practice in Harts and similar. Basically this consisted of diving at the target at an angle of 45 degrees using the gunsight for aim – at about 500 feet you pulled out of the dive, counting three as the target disappeared, and then released the bomb. One developed one's own technique by practice.[19]
>
> In Ospreys and Nimrods [wrote another officer], the Navy versions of the Hawker Hart and Fury, we used the ring-and-bead sight provided for the guns. Let the target disappear under the wing root and then stall turn onto the target, trimming the nose-down during the dive. In Skuas we had the gunsight throwing an illuminated ring-and-bead onto the front armoured glass. The Swordfish did a pretty good dive-bomb too you know, as well as level and torpedo-bombing roles. Too rapid levelling off had been known to take the wings off the 'Stringbag', though, as we saw in *Illustrious* on occasion.

Major R.T. Partridge gave the author a detailed account of his experiences at this period, some of which are as follows:[20]

> I qualified as a Fleet Air Arm pilot in September 1934, having been trained during the previous year at RAF Leuchars, Scotland. At that time the Hawker Nimrod single-seater was the naval fighter aircraft, having succeeded the Fairey Flycatcher. The squadrons included Hawker Ospreys as sub-flight leaders. These were two-seater fighters and carried an observer for navigation over the sea.
>
> All pilots were trained to use these aircraft in the normal fighter role and also as dive-bombers. Using them as dive-bombers an experienced and skilled pilot could get reasonably accurate results, but the bomb load carried was quite inadequate for attacking enemy warships.

Major Partridge went on to describe the various ranges used in the training of dive-bombing and the methods in common usage at that period:

At these ranges, practice bombs were dropped and their fall marked by markers on the ground, so one knew the results of our accuracy. This was often pretty good, four bombs frequently averaging 15–20 yards. These ranges were: **Leuchars**. The range was nearby at Tentsmuir and it was here that naval pilots received their initial front gun firing and dive-bomber training from the RAF. **Sutton Bridge**. Naval Air Squadrons, when stationed in England or in Home Fleet carriers, used to pay an annual visit to Sutton Bridge for armament training lasting a week or two. This training included front gun and dive-bombing. Range markers, etc., were provided by the RAF but the training and exercises were organised by the squadrons concerned. This of course, at that time, could have meant command by either a Lieutenant-Commander RN or a Squadron Leader RAF. All RN officers flying had a temporary commission in the RAF and at this time I was therefore a lieutenant, Royal Navy, a major, Royal Marines and a flying officer, Royal Air Force.

I also recall the following gun firing and dropping ranges, all RAF, to which the remarks in the foregoing applied: Amyria near Alexandria in Egypt; Delimara near Hal Far, Malta; a range whose name I cannot recall, near Seletar, Singapore; possible a range near Kai Tak, Hong Kong; and RAF Calshot, near Southampton.

You will see from what I have already said that the FAA paid a lot of attention to attaining and maintaining efficiency in dive-bombing aircraft, in spite of the fact that Naval dive-bomber aircraft could not carry a useful bomb load. In my view their only useful roles as dive-bombers were firstly, to carry out diversionary attacks against enemy ships' AA crews while the torpedo-bombing aircraft were attacking, and secondly in support of landing parties during amphibious operations.

It must be remembered that naval fighter aircraft at this time were all modified RAF fighter aircraft, and as far as I know the RAF had no special aircraft for dive-bombing. It follows from that that their dive-bombing capabilities were similar to the FAA. I can't remember any very special formations or techniques used except rather obvious ones dictated by weather conditions, such as strong crosswinds, cloud extent and height, position of sun, etc. For example, if conditions were clear and good a squadron of twelve aircraft would probably try and carry out a continuous attack with sub-sections of three attacking bow, stern and port and starboard beams. If, however, it was going to be advantageous to attack out of a rising or setting sun, then the whole squadron might attack in line astern.

Optimum height for start of dive was about 8,000–10,000 feet, height for start of dive about this, with release at around 1,000–700 feet.

The arrival of the Skua in the fleet at least gave the FAA pilots and crews a bombing capability to enable them to do some real damage to warships of cruiser size and below, and, more important, to the enemy aircraft-carrier decks. The following are some Navy and Marine pilots' opinions of the Skua, and it should be noted that they, in strict contrast to most historians, who never flew them, were enthusiastic about her, as a dive-bomber at least!

In March 1939, No. 800 Squadron was flying twelve Hawker Ospreys, having changed from nine Nimrods and three Ospreys because the Nimrod's wings did not fold and the lifts of the parent ship, *Ark Royal*, would not take a Nimrod. At the end of that month we were re-equipped with twelve Skuas, three of which were later replaced by Rocs, which had a four-gun turret in the rear cockpit.

The Skua was described as a fleet fighter/dive-bomber and was the Navy's first monoplane. As a fighter it belied its title, being too heavy and unmanoeuvrable for that role, but as a dive-bomber it was well designed and steady in the dive. Visibility for the pilot was good for both dive-bombing and deck landing.

Bombs were carried on external bomb racks under each wing and the method of attack was to approach from up-sun, half rolling into a dive of between 70 degrees and 80 degrees. If the sun offered no advantage four flights of three aircraft each would approach the target in four clover-leaf patterns synchronised to arrive in succession from directions 90 degrees apart.

When re-equipping with Skuas the squadron was stationed at Worthy Down, which had operated RFC bombers in the First World War. There was a target in the middle of the grass airfield and quadrant positions on the perimeter. We used to do a good deal of practice bombing with small practice bombs which we also used when embarked to bomb a target towed by the carrier or by her attendant destroyer.

The bomb for use in earnest which we have cause to remember was called a 'Cooper'. For all that it was worth it could well have originated from a marmalade factory in Dundee. Most of its puff went upwards, to the undoing, I believe, of Thurston and Griffiths, two Skua pilots of No. 803 Squadron, who attacked a U-boat off Scapa early in September 1939 and, damaged by their own bombs, force-landed in the sea.[21]

Captain Griffiths, Royal Marines, despite this experience, has fond memories of the Skua:

> The Skua was a very good dive-bomber, being the first British aircraft to be designed with proper dive-brakes, and in an almost vertical dive reached its peak speed, and could be 'aileron-turned' to follow its target as it turned. The Skua originally started life as a single-engined single-seater project, very fast, rather like the Vickers Jockey, then it became a two-seater in order to have a navigator over the sea. Finally, as the RAF needed the engines for the Blenheim, it was given the new sleeve-valve Perseus of 800 hp, and a longer nose to balance it, as it was lighter, As a result to see properly for deck landings, the screen and canopy were raised, and by now its performance had suffered.

This pilot recalled its first testing.

> In 1939, when I visited North Weald, Squadron Leader Donaldson asked to try it, and flung it across the skies as if it were one of his Hurricanes, even though it was sadly underpowered. I found it a very pleasant aircraft to fly: it landed easily, and was absolutely rock steady in a dive, and had airbrakes which you could put down at any speed, and this probably startled many a Me 109 pilot in Norway, who overshot his Skua prey.
>
> The Skua, like the Ju 87, had a superb pilot's view, and was the first British aircraft to be a dive-bomber, with real dive-brakes, and its central bomb was carried clear of the propeller by two arms, when we were diving at 80 degrees. The lever for putting the air-brakes on and off was on the right of the pilot's seat.
>
> We practised with 12 lb Cooper bombs, either on rings painted on the airfield or buoys in harbours, or when we went to armament camps, on beach targets. At sea we practised (without bombs) on ships moving at high speed and used camera guns to evaluate our success.[22]

Captain Harrington provided me with another viewpoint on the Skua:

> I see from my log-book that the final pre-war dive-bombing training was on 9 February 1939 in one of the old Hart variants. By April that year at practice camp, I achieved a grouping of 29 yards with eight practice bombs, which seemed to satisfy the experts at Sutton Bridge. I do recall we all used to cheat a bit by going down as low as we dared (from both the Range Safety Officer's view-point, as well as from a personal view!) This habit was to exact a nasty penalty in war conditions. The military objectives of doing

this dive-bombing was simply that it was then the best method of achieving accuracy. The exchange rate of aircraft vulnerability was recognised generally, but what was not very widely foreseen were the limitations imposed by the bombs available then and the methods that would be needed to achieve target destruction. Here I have in mind the differing needs of any heavily armoured target (capital ship or fortification) or just of personnel or even very slightly constructed targets (merchant ships, small bridges and radar systems).

In a personal war sense, I was appointed to No. 801 Squadron of Skuas in May 1940, having been operationally trained in the torpedo-bomber and seaplane roles, but converted to the fighter role in March 1940. I had of course flown the Skua in October 1939, and see the remark 'very nice' in my log-book. The Skua, once you could get to the target in the conditions necessary for a successful outcome to the particular dive-bombing you were trying to achieve, was a good dive-bombing tool; the main problem was to get there and, you hoped, to get back. All these elements were tied up in what range (power, fuel and speed) you were operating within, the defensive opposition you were up against and the type of target you were trying to destroy (a function of heights and dive entry and to the pull-out above the target and the type of bomb and its fusing arrangements – instantaneous or delayed to allow penetration of target).

The Skua had a characteristic in long steep dives that, as the speed built up, the aircraft tended to rotate around its axis. This was easily controlled and was caused by the setting of the ailerons being adjusted for normal flight conditions. One countered this by the controls plus laying one's sighting to let a natural creep take place. The old girl also had a bomb-throwing crutch which took the main bomb on the belly clear of the propeller, an essential for a steep dive.[23]

Finally, Major Partridge again:

As a fighter it was sadly deficient in speed, rate of climb and manoeuvrability; it only had about a ten-knot advantage of speed over, say, an He 111. On this score, in spite of this, it must not be forgotten that it was a Skua that shot down the first [confirmed] enemy aircraft of World War II by a British aircraft.

But if it wasn't really a fighter it was certainly a very good dive-bomber. It had very large, strong flaps, and when these were down it could be put into a beautiful 65–70-degree controlled dive and a well-trained pilot could bomb with great accuracy.

This then was the aircraft with which the Royal Navy went to war. But what of their principal opponents?

Notes

1. Lecture to the Naval War College, Leighton, op. cit.
2. Interview by Major-General Rowell, op. cit.
3. Sherrod, Robert, *History of Marine Corps Aviation in World War II* (Combat Forces Press, Washington, 1952).
4. Interview, by Major-General Rowell, op. cit.
5. Letter from Admiral F.D. Wagner, op. cit. See also *Information Pertaining to the Development of Dive-bombing 1910–1930* (USAAF Historical Division Research Studies Institute, Maxwell Air Force Base, Alabama, May 1956), Original compilation by Major Ernest L. Jones, AC/AS Intel; 7 July 1943. I am grateful to the USAF Historical Division for making these papers available to me for study. They note themselves that these are not comprehensive, but that they are useful, '... because so little material for the years 1910-1920 is available'.
6. Melhorn, Charles M., *Two Block Fox; The Rise of the Aircraft Carrier, 1911-29* (Naval Institute Press, 1974).
7. Turnbill, Captain A.D. and Lord, Lieutenant-Commander C.L., *The History of United States Naval Aviation* (Yale University Press, 1949).
8. Cathcart-Jones, Lieutenant Owen, *Aviation Memoirs* (Hutchinson, 1934).
9. Telegram dated 5 October, 1932 (National Archives, Kew, London, AIR 2/655/S31592, *et seq.*).
10. Holmberg, Rear Admiral Paul A., to the Author, 27 March 1977.
11. *Hart K-2466 Diving Bombing Trials, Report,* dated February 1934 (No. M/512.k) Aeroplane and Armament Experimental Establishment, Martlesham Heath, Suffolk. (National Archives, Kew, London, AIR 2/655/831592) and *Hart K-2967 Diving Bombing Trials,* dated March 1934 (M/512.1.) Aeroplane and Armament Experimental Establishment, Martlesham Heath, Suffolk. (National Archives, Kew, London, AIR 2/655/831592 08862).
12 Dive-bombing Technique with High Speed Aircraft of clean Aerodynamic Design, OR, dated 2 April 1936 (National Archives, Kew, London, AIR2/1655/5/36709) See Peter C. Smith, *Skua! the Royal Navy's Dive-bomber,* Pen & Sword, Barnsley, 2006.
13. Memo from Wing Commander Training, dated 18 December 1937. (National Archives, Kew, London, AIR 14/181/IIH/241/3/406).
14. *Meeting to Consider Dive-bombing,* held at Room 467, York House, Kingsway, WC2, on 19 September 1938. (National Archives, Kew, London, AIR 2/1787/04811).
15. Memo, Squadron Leader Ops, dated 16 November 1938. (National Archives, Kew, London, AIR 14/181/IIH/241/3/406).
16. Lord Douglas of Kirtleside, Marshal of the Royal Air Force, *Years of Command* (Collins, 1963).
17. *Bombing Developments,* DAD, dated 11 May, 1933. (National Archives, Kew, London, AIR 116/3473 – X/L04406)X/L04406).
18. The need for heavy bombs for dive-bombing had been seen to be an essential requirement to make naval dive-bombing efficient against larger warships early on. However, even with 'B' bombs, it should always be realised that dive-bombers would rarely, if ever, *sink* a battleship, and certainly not a modern one. A combination of torpedo- and dive-bombing was essential. A great deal of nonsense has been written on this score, for example one account states that the dive-bombers

of 1939 were 'designed to crack open a battleship'. Casey, Louis S., *Naval Aircraft 1914-39*, (Phoebus, 1977).

19. Minutes from the *12th Meeting of Advisory Committee on Aircraft for the Fleet Air Arm*, dated 15 November 1934. (National Archives, Kew, London, AIR2/607/359533/34).
20. Partridge, Major R.T. DSO, RM, to the Author, 28 March and 12 April 1977.
21. Monk, Captain G.B.K., RM, to the Author, 30 March 1977.
22. Griffiths, Captain G.B.K., RM, to the Author, 30 March 1977.
23. Harrington, Captain T.W. DSC, RN to the Author, 29 June 1977.

CHAPTER THREE

'Something terrible had happened'

Earlier experimentation in Germany was given new impetus with the coming to power of Adolf Hitler, and all restraints were abandoned after a while. Although there was no overwhelming school of thought in favour of the dive-bomber, there had been steady progress, and some, like Ernst Udet, had taken note of American developments, while yet others, less vocal but equally convinced, had been steadily working away at dive-bomber projects of their own. It was soon clear that this method of bombing had a large role to play in the new *Luftwaffe*. By 1936 a secret British report was stating that, 'The He 51 form the equipment of No. 132 (Richthofen) *Geschwader* (9 squadrons) and also as a temporary measure of No. 162 (*Immelmann*) and 165 (6 and 3 squadrons respectively) *Geschwader*, which are intended for Low Attack or Dive-bombing.'[1]

As well as fighters used in the role, other stop-gap types introduced included the Fieseler Fi 98 and the Henschel Hs 123, both biplanes. But in June 1936 trials were held at the Rechlin centre to determine which of four new designs would prove the best dive-bomber to build up Germany's growing striking forces. The main competitors were the Arado Ar 81, the Blohm and Voss Ha 137, the Heinkel He 118 and the Junkers Ju 87, and it was the latter that was finally chosen. Many people consider that the decision had been made before the competition; there was no doubt after it as Udet flew and crashed the He 118, the only real contender.*

Thus British Air Ministry Intelligence was somewhat wide of the mark when it submitted the following evaluation in 1936:

> Little is known of the tactics of the dive-bombers, which appear to follow normal practice. At present there are 12 squadrons equipped for this purpose but whether or not this method will be proceeded with depends largely upon the ability of the Germans to produce dive-bomber aircraft which fit their purpose. It is likely

---

* See my books *Stuka – Luftwaffe Ju 87 Dive-Bomber Units, Vols 1 & 2*, Classic, Shepperton, 2006.

that this form of attack will be confined to operations in support of land forces rather than as a means of attacking this country. This conjecture is based on the fact that the dive-bomber aircraft are unlikely to have the endurance for long-distance raids.[2] [How very smug that report sounds today. Just four years later and the Ju 87s were just 23 miles from the English coast.]

Testing under full combat conditions was undertaken with the advent of the Spanish Civil War, and by the eve of the Second World War the improved Ju 87B was equipping most operational units. Only once during this time did the dive-bomber concept receive any real set-back, and this was on the every eve of the invasion of Poland.

In a final exercise held prior to moving up to their war stations against the Poles, General Wolfram von Richthofen, who had initially been against the Junkers Ju 87 concept completely, but had none the less been appointed to lead them into battle as *Generalleutnant*, had laid on a demonstration for the benefit of assembled *Luftwaffe* leaders, including Sperrle and Loerzer. This was to take place at the Neuhammer training ground with a mass Stuka attack using smoke bombs. Three *Staffeln* were to take part, led by *Hauptmann* Sigel of I/StG 76, followed by I/StG 2. Both the *Grazer* and *Immelmann* units were to attack in sequence.

One of the pilots flying that day was Friedrich Lang, and he described to me the resulting tragedy, as he saw it, thus:

> On this occasion apart from the *Grazer Gruppe* of *Hauptmann* Sigel, I/StG 2, *Immelmann* also took part, in which I was flying as left *Kettenflieger* with *Hauptmann* Hitschold. We flew from Cottbus and the weather was cloudless and our view was very good. Between Cottbus and Neuhammer the ground fog started and our group recognised it. The white fog cloud with a slightly woolly appearance was in beautiful sunshine right to the eastern horizon. In front of us, two to three kilometres to the right, was another *Gruppe* at a height of around 3,000 metres.
>
> On account of the ground fog I expected the *Verbandführung* to call the flight off. When I looked round again I saw, to my horror, huge dark columns of smoke pouring up from the target area. I knew straight away that something terrible had happened. We circled over the spot and then flew back to Cottbus. The news of the death of so many of our comrades did not take long to reach us there.[3]

The ill-fated Stukas had been instructed to approach the target from about 12,000 feet, dive through a cloud-layer, reported to have been identified between 2,500 and 6,000 feet, although Lang has doubts that this information was ever transmitted, and release their bombs at 1,000 feet. The official version is that the doomed *Gruppe* of StG 76 failed to realise that ground mist was what they were diving into and not the higher cloud layer. Consequently the whole formation tore straight into the earth at full speed, only a few aircraft from the second flight realising the error in time and pulling up, but many of these failed to clear the surrounding trees. In seconds the testing ground was littered with the exploding debris of thirteen Stukas as they hurtled to their destruction.

The immediate aftermath of this disaster is remembered by Lang as follows:

> About half an hour after our touchdown we had orders to repeat the exercise in low flight – the fog had lifted to about 140 metres. We received this order from General Richthofen himself, who, with Manstein, stood on the *Feldhernhügel*. At the time we thought it was callous and mad. In retrospect it is likely that Richthofen wanted to show his General what his *Sturzkampfflieger* were made of.

In Japan also, the dive-bomber was making great strides. With the adoption into service of its first dive-bomber, the Nakajima Type 94, the Japanese Navy soon began to flex its muscles. Although its re-lationship with Heinkel in Germany was to continue throughout the 1930s, it always adapted the German designs to fit its own special needs. Although dive-bombing did not form a very large part in the requirements of the Japanese Army Air Force, it too maintained a continued interest in new designs completely separate and apart from the Navy, which offers a good insight into inter-service relations in that, and other, nations.

The testing of the Type 94 developed a successor, the Type 96, which was similar to the original He 50A Japanese version, a two-seater biplane with a 550 lb bomb load, re-engined with the 600 hp Hikari engine and a top speed of 140 mph. With the outbreak of the Sino-Japanese incident in July 1937, the Japanese were also given the oppor-tunity of testing subsequent models under full war conditions, and the Aichi company came to the fore. A secret British report of the Japanese Navy's tactics in China gives us some insight into their methods at this period[4]:

> It is not possible to say whether the Japanese prefer the torpedo or the bomb as a weapon against ships. Pilots are trained to use both. Much attention has been given to dive-bombing practice, and the Naval Air Force has had considerable experience in China both of dive and level bombing against stationary targets.

Dive-bombing is carried out by light bombers and fighters and is particularly favoured when no AA resistance is expected. One of three methods may be adopted: single aircraft attacks, attacks by two aircraft, or attacks by flights in 'V' formation or in line astern. Against moving targets on land such as motor cars or mobile guns, two aircraft are normally employed; the first dives and opens machine-gun fire, causing the abandonment of the target; the second aircraft then makes a dive-bombing attack on the then stationary target. Dives are normally made at an angle of about 60 degrees and bombs are released at about 800 feet.

The importance the Japanese Navy attached to the dive-bomber is illustrated by the fact that some 428 Type 96 planes of this type were built, at a time when the US Navy's counterparts were only being ordered in batches of two dozen or two score and the Royal Navy still had no dedicated dive-bombers at all in service.

The first monoplane dive-bomber was the Aichi Type 99 (later to be codenamed 'Val' by the Western Allies), or D3A1, which bore some slight resemblance to the Ju 87 due to having a fixed undercarriage, but was developed quite independently by the Japanese on their own lines, although the wing form was partly influenced by the Heinkel He 70 *Blitz*.* An even more advanced aircraft was under design, the Yokosuka D4Y1 *Suisei* (Comet), later coded as 'Judy', which had a fully retractable undercarriage, internal weapons bay and a range of 800 nautical miles. The Army developed the twin-engined Kawasaki Type 99 (to be codenamed Lily), and the experimental Ki-66, which never finally saw combat service.

The third Axis partner was also pursuing experimentation into dive-bombers but with much less success. All aeronautical research was in the hands of the Italian Royal Air Force (*Regia Aeronautica*), and the Italian Navy had no say in the matter, and as the Italian air leaders were as totally committed to the high-level bombing concept as their compatriots in Great Britain and the USA, the dive-bomber type languished. It was not until the confrontation with Britain over the invasion of Abyssinia in 1935 that the need for a precision bomber to attack the Royal Navy in the Mediterranean became apparent.

As a result plans were put in hand for the rapid development of a dive-bomber by the Savoia company under Programme 'R', and the result was the twin-engined SM85 and SM86 projects. The first proto-type was flown in December 1936. The aircraft was a twin-engined monoplane with a cantilever wing and retractable landing gear featuring a very simple box-type fuselage with a marked upward sweep to nose and tail that earned it the title 'The Flying Banana'. Trials in April 1937 at the Furbara test centre were attended by Mussolini himself.

Thirty-two were subsequently built, to two modified designs, and although not a great success, they formed the first Italian dive-bomber unit, 96° *Gruppo Bombardmento a Tuffo* (BaT) in March 1940 with two *Squadriglia*, 236 and 237, with a total of nineteen aircraft. The solitary SM86 first flew in April 1939 at Vergiate, but received an equally luke-warm reception. It was hoped to combat-test this aircraft, and it joined 96° *Gruppo* in southern Italy on the eve of Italy's entry into the war in June 1940.

France also was experiencing the greatest difficulty in producing an efficient home-built dive-bomber despite her early experiments, mainly due to lack of funds. The GL-43OBI was tested throughout the mid-1930s, and a few experimental developments, the parasol-wing GL-342 and the GL-521 were built. The French Army blew hot and cold, and although the twin-engined Breguet 690 was later adapted as a dive-bomber prototype no real progress was made with it. It was left to the *Aéronavale* to continue on its own, and it was the little Loire-Nieuport LN-40, which first flew in June 1938, that provided a limited answer.

The LN-40 featured the same inverted-gull-wing configuration as the Stuka but it had a fully retractable undercarriage and was a single-seater. Initial trials led to orders for a Navy version, the LN-401, and an Army version, the LN-411, for the *Armée de l'Air* in 1938. Although several squadrons were formed by 1940, the Army handed over the planes it had to the Navy; these were not enough, and the French had to turn to America to resolve their dilemma, ordering large numbers of the Vought V156F variant of the Vindicator, and even some of the biplanes built by Curtiss, the SBC-4. Very few of these dive-bombers arrived in time to see combat, but a few fought with great distinction in the brief campaign of 1940.

Poland had followed the ground-attack policy following her war with the Soviet Union in 1919, but she could not ignore the dive-bomber and decided to design a basic airframe that could be adapted either as a two-seater fighter or as a dive-bomber. This was the genus of the P38 *Wilk*. An all-metal, cantilever monoplane with retractable undercarriage, it was underpowered, and slow development meant that, as it did not appear before the spring of 1939, it was never flown in battle.

Dive-bombers of various kinds, plus adaptations, served with most of the minor powers pre-war, notably in China and Spain. In 1934 the Central Government of China placed orders with Heinkel for twelve He 50As, re-powered as the He 66CH. A further batch of twelve, He 50bCH, followed after being used briefly by the fledgling *Luftwaffe*. All were assembled at Peking (now Beijing) in 1937, but only saw limited service against the Japanese.

Spain used the Hs 123 with some success, naming it the *Angelito*, so highly did they rate its flying qualities. Three Hawker Fury biplane fighters were also pressed into service as dive-bombers between 1936 and 1938.

Yet of all the smaller nations, it was Sweden that applied the most thought both to the development of a dive-bomber force of her own and in the true application of dive-bombing techniques, plus the development of an effective and efficient dive-bomber sight. Their detailed study resulted in the AGA sight, which aroused even the interest of the RAF. The Royal Swedish Air Force (*Flygvapnet*) had not been formed as a separate unit until 1926, and it was not until another decade that it became fully independent. At first, dive-bombing experiments were conducted with imported British Hawker Harts, the first trials being conducted by No. 4 Wing at Fröson in 1935. Licence-built Harts, designated as the B1 Light Bomber, further equipped units in the same year. The initial tests proved satisfactory. Lieutenant Carlgren reported that after intensive training he could maintain a diving angle of 80–85 degrees. In the summer of 1935 the F1 Light Bomber (Attack) Squadron was established at Västerat. The first tests were described by the Royal Swedish Aero Club in this manner:

> Our continued training for dive-bombing begins with the fundamental theoretical and practical training on the type of aeroplane to be used. It is the diving in vertical or near-vertical angles that puts both the pupils and the planes to he hardest tests. The dive-bombers are manned by one pilot bomb releaser in front and one observer-gunner in the backseat. Both men must be gradually accustomed to the special, distinctive sensations experienced in dive-bombing. Especially less agreeable are these for the observer-gunner in the backseat, who never knows beforehand what will happen in some near moment of when it will happen.[5]

In the summer of 1937 the first Swedish dive-bombing course was established under Lieutenant Ragnar Carlgren at Mälmslatt. Captain Carlgren described their introduction as follows:

> After learning to fly the B4s as pilots the pupils were placed in the backseat and had to pass through their first dives against the practice target with an instructor in the cockpit as pilot. After that, diving exercises followed for the pupils to teach them how to judge the correct diving angle, the selection of the correct aiming point connected to the intended moment of bomb release.

These courses were so successful that, in 1937, a special course was set up by No. 1 Wing at Västeras near Lake Mälaren, and a second wing, F6, joined F4. The B1s continued to be the main workhorse until 1940, when their Swedish-built replacements entered service, these being licence-built versions of the Northrop 8-A-1. These in turn were soon replaced by the first Swedish-designed dive-bombers, the SAAB-17, a low-wing monoplane, a two-seater powered by a 980 hp radial engine.

Dive-bombing in Sweden, as in other nations, meant utilising the element of surprise using cloud cover when available.

> The pilot must localise his target with the utmost rapidity and at once, like a thunderbolt from a clear sky, dive down onto it [read one contemporary account[6]] When starting the dive the flying speed is usually less than 200 km/h, but in the almost vertical plunge it accelerates quickly to about 400 km/h. Already the rise in velocity combined with the increased atmospheric pressure can be described in similar fashion to the dizziness experienced when falling or rushing rapidly downwards on ski or toboggan.
>
> The impression of the first dive-bombing attempt is that one is near to if not in the tangent zone of what the human organic system can endure. A freefall with such a speed would also possibly surpass this limit; the facts, however, become different when one is flying in an aeroplane and one also knows that a speed of 400 km/h is not at all the maximum speed of modern planes.

This account, written in 1940, goes on:

> The biggest physical strain appears, however, when the dive of the plane has to be changed to a rather steep rise. The blood of the crew is then forced down to the heels, the sight is more or less blackened out and both pilot and observer have to endure a certain dizziness. The second man has not much more to do in the dive than to accompany his pilot and try and hold himself firmly fixed, while the pilot has to keep his plane on exact course onto the target and attempt to correct his diving angle to 80 degrees in order to release the bombs in the right moment and then to draw the stick backward correctly ....[7]

*   *   *

Over in Germany, the *Luftwaffe's* dive-bomber units had, by the autumn of 1939, completely re-equipped with the Ju 87B1, giving them a total of 336 aircraft, of which some 288 were immediately serviceable for operations. At this juncture the B2 replaced the B1 on the production lines at the Weser works. There were many minor variants to this basic design, including Stukas specially modified to operate from Germany's planned future aircraft-carriers. These were stressed for catapult launching and fitted with arrestor hooks and were designated as the Ju 87C (*Cäsa*). A further refinement of this type, with folding wings and a jettisonable undercarriage for ditching at sea, became the

C-1. They were evaluated by the special carrier trials unit as the Ju 87-T (*Tragerflugzeug*, carrier-borne). Another development that paid handsome dividends was the Ju 87R (*Richard*), which, like the above marks, was introduced early in 1940 and was a long-range version for anti-shipping strikes featuring underwing fuel drop-tanks and extra radio equipment, while the R-2 was yet a further improvement on this type.

Training for Stuka crews was tough and detailed in order to produce first-class air groups for precision work. The first *Stukaschule* was set up at Kitzingen, and *Stukaschule 1*, and later *Stukaschule 2*, were established at Graz in Austria. As a temporary measure, there were also *Stukavorschulen* for preliminary Stuka training. All combat-ready units got *Ergänzungsstaffeln*, supplementary units mainly deployed at the home base in which new personnel for replacement crews were trained. But let a Ju 87 pilot who trained at this time tell in his own words of the Stuka training programme:

> Glancing at my own flight records for 1939, I see I was a trainee at *Stukaschule 1*, Kitzingen, from 4 July to 25 August. During this time Stuka training included aircraft familiarisation with the Hs 123 and the Ju 87A, formation flying, some fighter tactics and dive-bombing. I flew a total flying time of 54 hours 24 minutes, including 29 sorties with the Hs 123 and 51 with the Ju 87A.
>
> On 1 September 1939, I started to set up my own dive-bomber squadron at Kiel-Holtenau (2/StG 186T), in which I flew 112 sorties on various types of aircraft, mostly of course with the Ju 87B, with a total of 65 hours 19 minutes prior to my first combat mission (which was against the French airfield of Metz-Frescaty on 10 May 1940).
>
> Compared with modern pilots' training, this seems to be pretty poor, but with the equipment of those days we felt pretty well prepared for the tasks given to us. In the whole training period our Stuka Group lost only one crew through crashing during live bombing exercises. This would not work nowadays with modern equipment and flying techniques but I think you will agree it is interesting![8]

In the main the dive-bombers of Great Britain, the United States, Japan and France were *naval* weapons, and naturally their pre-war training concentrated on this aspect of their future employment to the exclusion of much else (although, in practice, Japanese Navy dive-bombers were at this period mainly employed against land targets in the China Incident). The exact reverse was the case with the bulk of the German dive-bombers, for, despite their achievements against shipping in Spanish ports, they were built and trained to act against land targets in support of the Army. How then did their subsequent sensational war record as ship-busters combine with their training methods? Again *Generaleutnant* Mahlke describes the stage for specialist units:

> In general terms, there was *no* dedicated procedure for dive-bombing any specific target during the pre-war training phase, except by experience: i.e. the smaller the target (and the quicker-moving) the nearer (deeper) you released your bombs. *The only specific training was against ship targets* (for as many crews as possible), due to the fact that it was difficult for an inexperienced pilot to estimate the altitude to release the bombs and pull up in time. This was especially so when the sea was smooth and visibility poor, giving no clear horizon.
>
> For this purpose a wooden target-cross was anchored near the shore for bombing exercises. At that time a normal Stuka pilot had *no* training to fly on instruments (or very little) since visibility was necessary to approach the target. The instrumentation of the Ju 87B was pretty basic. At the beginning of the war it had a magnetic compass and a turn-and-bank indicator only! (This was later much improved.) So it can be seen that to fly at a ship target with no clear horizon was no easy task for a novice.[9]

Helmut Mahlke and his contemporaries were forced to improvise and develop their own techniques in the hot-bed of combat, and we will describe these in their proper place.

Just prior to the war the existing formation of nine *Sturzkampfgeschwader* were authorised to be increased to twelve. This was in addition to *Tragerguppes* I and II/186; the first of these latter formed at Burg near Magdeburg, and the second was in the process of formation at Kiel. This was never completed and the naval units were later re-converted back to normal Stuka duties, though not before they had seen independent action.

Each *Geschwader* was divided in a Staff (*Stab*) flight and three or four *Gruppen*. Each *Gruppe* was divided into three *Staffeln* of nine (operational) and three (reserve) aircraft each, and the *Staffeln*, once airborne, into *Ketts* of three aircraft each.

The most advanced German twin-engined attack bomber on the outbreak of war in September 1939 was undoubtedly the Junkers Ju 88, dubbed the 'Wonder Bomber' by *Reichmarschall* Herman Goering. It was far in advance of its rivals in both Germany and abroad, and great things were expected from it. It did, indeed, prove itself the main workhorse of the *Luftwaffe*, proving itself to be adaptable in the extreme, and an enormous number of spin-off derivations came from the same basic airframe over the years. It was as a dive-bomber that it first made its mark, however, and this is the role at which it excelled, despite its size and weight.

Owing its origins to a 1935 requirement for a *Schnellbomber*, a hard-hitting medium bomber that could outpace any fighter then conceived, the first prototype twin-engined Ju 88 appeared in December that year. The usual pre-production batch of a modified design appeared for trials early in 1939, at which time the decision was taken to adapt it for dive-bombing.

Slatted dive-brakes were therefore fitted outboard of each of the engine nacelles. These brakes hinged below the front spar, which initially caused some problems in such a highly stressed design when they were extended. The first unit was taking delivery of these aircraft on the outbreak of war, and such was the demand that they included in their strength some of the test aircraft to bring their numbers up. This unit was the *Erprobungskommando 88*, and it was soon in action.

Meanwhile, back in America, the US Navy had accepted Ed Heinemann's XSBD-1 from the manufacturers, and in April they placed orders with the Douglas company for 144 SBDs, fifty-seven SBD-1s for the US Marine and eighty-seven SBD-2s for the US Navy. The latter mark differed from the former by the addition of an extra machine-gun in the rear cockpit and the fitting of armour plating for crew protection. In addition the Dauntless,[10] as it was later named, was fitted with self-sealing rubber-lined fuel tanks, and provision was made for two 65-gallon fuel tanks to increase range. It was the Marines who first took delivery of these new dive-bombers, and June 1940 saw the first entering squadron service with MAG-1 based at Quantico, Virginia.

Comparison of the training methods of the Dauntless pilots with those of the Skua in the Royal Navy, the Stuka in Germany and the B1 in Sweden reveals many similarities. Rear Admiral Paul A. Holmberg explained to me the situation prevailing at this time in the US Navy, as follows:

The SBD ('Slow But Deadly', or 'Sugar Baker Dog') was a monoplane with wing trailing-edge dive flaps (brakes) which limited the speed of the dive (vertically) to about 250 knots. The aircraft flying in this attitude was neutrally stable and controllable, allowing the pilot to adjust his flight path for wind variations and target ship motions. Much training and practice were necessary before a pilot became a proficient dive-bomber pilot (able to hit a fifty-foot bull's-eye repeatedly). The initial training taught the pilot how to fly in the vertical dive, and to become accustomed to a 'near zero' gravity force on the body, while accelerating to terminal speed in the dive and the 'six-times-gravity' force during the pull-out.

During my training there were some instance where pilots crashed because of their inability to determine (until too late) when to commence their pull-out. I observed that it was easy to

become engrossed in, and transfixed by, what one sees of the earth
or sea as they are approached in this manner. Those pilots whose
practice bombing scores were best were most often the ones who
were well co-ordinated physically (baseball players, golfers, etc.,
who could throw or strike balls with a bat). Dive-bombing then,
was mostly an art.

As for training in dive-bombing, during WWII I believe the
Navy syllabus called for fifty practice dives (ten flights to include
at least five dives per flight). Of course, the skill of the pilot influenced the pilot's degree of proficiency after this training. However, all during my operational flying the dive-bombers pilots took
advantage of every flight to get in a practice dive or two to retain
our proficiency.

There were no automatic pull-out devices used operationally
in the US Navy. I tested an experimental model installed in a
Dauntless at the Test Center, Patuxent River, in 1944. It worked all
right as I recall, but since the aviators in the fleet were not interested in having them in their dive-bombers they were not adopted
for operational use.[11]

The US Navy usually utilised the eighteen-plane squadron formation,
comprising three divisions of two three-plane sections. The normal
cruising altitude was 18,000 feet. The identification of the target was
followed by the unit commander placing his aircraft down-sun and
upwind, providing he had the time and opportunity to seek such ideal
conditions, whereupon the formation pushed over into their attack
dives from 15,000 feet, the peel-off commencing from the top of the
stack following the commander down in sequence with a small gap to
divide the defences between each aircraft.

The Dauntless unbraked could pick up speed to 425 mph, but the
brakes held this to a norm of about 276 mph in practice. The aircraft
was stressed to take up to 4 g, but was rarely called upon to do so in
practice. In war, however, caution often went by the board. The normal
angle of dive was 70 degrees, although the standard boast from USN
flyers was, 'When we say down, we mean *straight* down!' The wartime
Hollywood epics starring the likes of Errol Flynn and John Wayne just
wouldn't have it any other way of course!

Another pilot later described his own initiation into dive-bombing in
this manner:

Next came the phase of training which made a deeper impression
on me than anything I had ever experienced: dive-bombing. With
half-a-dozen practice bombs in the racks under our wings, we took
off and climbed half a mile in the air over a circular target marked

out on the ground. One at a time we peeled off from the formation and started down in vertical dives, eyes glued on the target through the telescope sights, engines roaring and wires screaming as the little thunder-birds neared terminal velocity. A quick jerk on the bomb-release toggle, then the steady, inexorable force of gravity pushing us down into the cockpit on the pull-out as we eased back to level flight. Then a glance backward to watch for the puff of white smoke from the exploding bomb, hoping to see it mushroom up inside of the target circle. This was dive-bombing, the greatest thrill in aviation.

In this work we used the F4B-2s, which were ideal for this training because of their low terminal velocity. This gave us more time to square away in the dive and steady down with the tele-scope sight on the target. Contrary to a lot of wild hangar-flying theories we had heard, there was nothing uncomfortable about a properly executed bombing dive. 'Going black' was unnecessary, and was the result of over-controlling or horsing back on the stick during the pull-out. Later on we were to practise dive-bombing at terminal velocity in modern planes hour after hour with no bad after-effects.[12]

While the Navy and Marines continued to practise hard and develop new aircraft and doctrine, the Army Air Corps continued, like the RAF and the *Regia Aeronautica*, to vacillate. No great work was done at all in this line, at least not until the fall of France in 1940, when there was a hasty re-think among all but the die-hards. It was to take this spur, plus huge orders placed by both France and Great Britain in 1939–40, to produce new aircraft for the job.

But in the States a new 'wonder' naval dive-bomber was being developed in response to the Navy's August 1938 specifications. Two designs predominated – the Curtiss SB2C Helldiver and the Brewster SB2A Buccaneer. Unfortunately both these designs promised the ulti-mate in engineering and refinements, with internal bomb-bays, in-creased speed and range, air-cooled radial engines of greater power and reliability, retractable landing-gear, de-icing equipment, armour protection – the list was endless and they ran into countless difficulties. The new dive-bombers had to fit the new *Essex*-class aircraft-carriers then building, two planes to a lift, and this imposed almost insur-mountable problems in coming up with a design compromise to meet this tight datum. Delay after delay occurred in both aircraft's pro-grammes, although Curtiss, with more experience, at least managed to get some early prototypes into the air.

It was perhaps, fortunate then that across the Pacific, the Japanese were having exactly the same problems with their new dive-bomber, the Judy. This sleek machine with an in-line engine first flew in December 1940, but was bedevilled with faults, and so the tried and combat-tested Aichi Val had to remain the front-line dive-bomber with the Imperial Navy until 1943–4.

In order to fill the gap the non-appearance of the Judy left, the Val had to be stretched, and this was done by fitting the Kinsei 54 engine and larger fuel tanks. A few modifications to the body and tail were also incorporated in the 'clean-up', and the new version began entering service as the Model 22 by the autumn of 1942, after some 470 Type 1s, the victors of Pearl Harbor, Port Darwin and the Indian Ocean raids, had been completed.

A further forward development, for a dive-bomber to replace both the Val and the Judy, was the powerful Aichi B7A *Ryusei* (Shooting Star), to be dubbed Grace by the Allies. Another very big bomber for a carrier plane, the Grace had a top speed of 352 mph and a bomb capacity of 1,760 lb, but was no more than a distant aspiration in 1941.

In France, the pitifully few squadrons of French Navy Vindicators and LN401/411s spent the first eight months of the war organising, taking delivery of a few more aircraft in penny packets, conducting deck trials whenever possible when the prior commitments and wanderings of France's solitary aircraft-carrier *Béarn* allowed, and carrying out routine training of the most elementary nature.

Forced to be land-based, their scope of employment was at this time limited in the extreme, but just adjusting to modern aircraft was time-consuming enough after the antiques they had been used to earlier, and for the first time in two decades the French aircrew's morale was excellent. Captain Mesny led the first operational unit, AB-1, on its first wartime patrols, which were mainly anti-submarine searches along the Channel coast and over the southern North Sea region. No action resulted, other than the unfortunate accidental bombing of a (then) neutral Dutch submarine in error!

In view of the destiny, fast approaching, of France, it is interesting to note that what limited dive-bombing training the French did undertake understandably failed to include land targets like tanks. It was to prove a fatal handicap when coupled with their slender numbers.

As war approached, then, most dive-bombers were in a state of transition, as were their crews, from biplanes to monoplanes, from light bombers to 'heavies'. Those pilots belonging to units of the German or Japanese forces who had been 'blooded' in Spain or China knew something of the potential of their machines. Others, serving with the Royal, United States or French navies, had faith and enthusiasm in the technique and their new mounts. Those serving with the embryo units of Italy or Sweden, mainly former fighter pilots, had little to go on but theory. The land-based air forces of every country save

Germany regarded dive-bombers as of little or no merit. Their eyes and imaginations were glued to the huge and expensive long-range bomber; they still dreamed of a war being won by strategic bombing of civilians alone, and army co-operation was very much a backwater, with dive-bombing itself even more so. The other services had little regard for it, either, as a battle-winning weapon. It could not carry a large enough bomb to hurt a modern battleship; it might damage a carrier, mess-up a cruiser and sink a destroyer, if it could hit such an elusive target, it was thought, but not much else, and these were considered secondary weapons anyway. The Army sometimes looked wistfully at opponents with strong aerial back-up but could not even begin to imagine the traumatic effect even just the threat of dive-bombing was going to have on raw, untried troops.

Had any them bothered to ask the dive-bomber pilots themselves, they might just have guessed in time.

We had a 'bomb-proof' shelter made of heavy timbers piled high with sandbags, where we could mark the drops with comparative safely, but the ordnance men were standing casually out in the open, retiring to the shelter only when it was obvious that the diving planes were headed in their general direction. The first time a plane dived I was standing about 10 feet from the shelter talking to another pilot who was observing the practice. I saw only the first part of the dive. For some mysterious reason I suddenly found myself crouching beneath the shelter, and I bumped heads with my friend on the way in. Neither of us remember starting for the shelter. The bomb struck over a hundred yards away, and the ordnance men gave us the merry ha-ha.

The next plane started its dive, and I resolved firmly not to move unless I was directly in the line of fire. My friend did likewise. Nevertheless we found ourselves back in the shelter several seconds before the bomb struck, even though it hit farther away than the first one. The plane swept by with a sinister, snarling roar that made the shelter vibrate, even though the pilot was more than a thousand feet overhead.

'Whew!' exclaimed the other pilot, 'No wonder they can't make ground-troops stand up and shoot at a plane in a dive-bombing or strafing attack! I would have sworn that baby was headed right for us.'[13]

Notes

1. *Report on the German Air Force 1936*, Air Ministry (National Archives, Kew, London, AIR 5/1137/04811).

2. *Air Intelligence Report*, dated 31 October 1936 (National Archives, Kew, London, AIR 5/1137/04811).

3. Lang, *Oberst* Friedrich, to the Author, 16 December 1976.

4. *Japanese Navy Air Force*, Air Ministry Intelligence Memorandum (National Archives, Kew, London, AIR 10/ 31647/04811).

5. KSAK (Royal Swedish Aero Club), *Svenskt Flyg och dess Män*, Stockholm, 1940.

6. *Flygvapnet*, Kindberg, Colonel Nils, *Notes on Hawker Hart aircraft bought and imported from Britain for Sweden and/or built in Sweden on licence*. A detailed Monograph prepared for the Author by *Flygvapnet*, in Author's files.

7. KSAK, *Svenskt Flyg och des Män*, op. cit.

8. Mahlke, *Generalleutnant* Helmut, to the Author, 20 March 1976, 12 December 1976 and 15 January 1977.

9. *Ibid.*

10. See my book *Douglas SBD Dauntless*, Crowood Press, Ramsbury, 1997, for the full story of this aircraft.

11. Holmberg, Rear Admiral Paul A., to the Author, 27 March 1977 and 5 June 1977.

12. Winston, Robert A., *Dive-bomber*, (Harrah, 1940).

13. *Ibid.*

CHAPTER FOUR

'We just pointed the nose downhill'

German forces opened the Second World War when they crossed into Polish territory at 0445 hours on 1 September 1939. In fact, for the dive-bomber, the war started some fifteen minutes earlier than this, and it was the Stuka that carried out the first combat mission of that conflict. The reason is not hard to find: the mission required accuracy and only the dive-bomber could provide it.

The *Luftwaffe* had 219 Stukas operationally available to take part in the first great offensive in the east; against the overwhelmingly superior strength of the French Army in the west Hitler gambled by leaving only a small covering force and virtually no aircraft. He staked everything on quickly crushing the Poles and then turning west before the Allies got into their stride. He had hoped for two weeks; the Allies gave him eight months!

Ju 87 forces available were mainly Ju 87B (*Bertha*) types, although the carrier group was equipped with converted models and a few of the new C-0 variants, a total of just twelve machines, and was itself attached to StG 2 for the assault phase. Operating with the *Luftflotte* 1 under Kesselring was StG 2, and with *Luftflotte* 2 were StG 77 and (ST) LG 2 under General Wolfram von Richthofen.

The very first mission was assigned to a *Kette*, 3/StG 1, commanded by Bruno Dilley. They had the task of attempting to destroy the special detonation points fixed to the twin bridges at Dirschau on the river Vistula where it crossed the Polish border to Tczew. These bridges were key points on the rail link that was to supply the twin thrusts of the German armies attacking east from Germany and south-west from East Prussia. The Poles had paid great attention to their early destruction in the event of war and the Germans were equally eager to preserve them.

The three young pilots had undergone intensive preparation in the days before the attack, carrying out a demanding programme of dives to achieve absolute pin-point accuracy against this minute target. Although German intelligence maps were very precise, it was obviously a difficult task to pick out these charges from the air at all.

45

The pilots took several train trips over the bridges to familiarise themselves with the area minutely, and they decided to go in at very low
level to ensure the greatest accuracy, despite the risks.

If they were successful, an armoured train would be in position to
cross the bridges and hold the bridgehead within hours; if they failed,
the advance might be delayed and the follow-up restricted. It seemed
as if fate was on the side of the Poles, for the morning of 1 September
dawned thick and misty, assisting the defender, but hardly dive-
bombing weather, as Neuhammer had so recently shown. The conditions handicapped the initial *Luftwaffe* effort all along the line and
thus allowed the Poles to escape being surprised on the ground when
the air strikes finally went in against their airfields later in the day.

Dilley's *Kette* were only eight minutes' flying time from their target
and took off exactly as planned at 0426 hours, flying very low to the
ground through banks of fog and mist, until they reached the Vistula,
whereupon they turned north and followed it to the bridges. Right on
the button, at 0435 hours, the three Stukas zeroed in on their targets
and, at a height of only 30 feet, released the first bombs of the war.
Their accuracy was extremely good and most of the detonation wires
leading to the bridges were cut. A follow-up attack by Do17s merely
razed the town, but despite Dilley's achievement, made without loss,
the resolute defenders managed to carry out sufficient repairs to enable
both bridges to be subsequently blown, although not efficiently enough
to stop one of them being taken later and made serviceable by German
engineers.

It was much later than planned when the main Stuka strike went in
against the Polish air force and they found that the Poles had managed
to evade them. For example a Stuka attack against Rokowice found
aircraft sitting on the runway and destroyed twenty of them or more,
but these were found later to be obsolete or unserviceable aircraft, the
fighters having already dispersed to secret bases and remaining un-
touched.

That not all the Stuka attacks went according to plan that fateful day
is well known. Just what it was like to fly a Stuka mission on the first
day of the Second World War was told to the author by Friedrich Lang
thus:

> The I/StG 2 was allocated various targets this day. Only 1 and 2
> *Staffeln* of the *Gruppenstab* were supposed to attack the hangars of
> Krakaner (Krakow) airfield. I flew in the *Kette* of *Staffelkapitain
> Hauptman* Hitschhold. Over the upper Silesian industrial areas
> towards the target area, heavy masses of cloud reached up to our
> height of 5,000 metres and even higher. We flew with oxygen
> masks on through a rough and overcast sky. Small icicles, fine as

needles, formed in our cabins. We could not see the ground for some time. It was all very gloomy.

3 *Staffel* left the main group to attack their target near the border. Estimating by the time we had been in the air we should have been just outside Krakow but we were not certain. Major Dinort therefore decided to dive down and pick up our orientation again that way. After an exciting nose-dive we came out of the clouds at a height of about 500 metres in a dale with a small river wandering through it.

All was dizzy and you felt you were whirling round, until we heard the voice of the commander through the R/T, 'Stop the attack. Disperse to the west.' Major Dinort took the lead in his barely controllable plane; we all fell behind him in an orderly manner. The small river led us out of the dark, cloudy valley and we were free.

We were still somewhere on the north face of the Beskide and we still had the bombs on our aircraft. We dropped them in a straight level flight from about 400 metres onto a Polish airfield that came unexpectedly into our field of vision. All we could see was a pole with a red and white striped windsock and a small wooden hanger. That was all.[1]

This proved to be one of the secret Polish bases that pure chance had led the Stukas to. They were able to see the Polish fighters scrambling to take off at 0520 when the bombs started falling and the CO of III/2 *Dyon*, Captain Mieczyslaw Medwecki, was shot down and killed during the subsequent engagement. What happened is told by Lang.

Shortly after our attack there was a surprise assault from two PZL-II fighters, one of them coming out of a left turn from below to straight ahead of me, starting shooting from some distance away directly at me. My left wing and the rear of my fuselage were soon full of holes and in seconds the fighter had vanished. We flew closer together and we still did not know where we were.

In the meantime we realised that only the *Gruppenstab* and part of 1 *Staffel* were still together and that the commander was also missing. The countryside below us was getting more active and alive. Hitschold flew towards a railway station and we could then read the name of it, quite clearly, and from that we then established our location. Twenty minutes later we landed at our airfield near Nieder-Ellguth, west of the 'Annabegres'. Dinort had got lost and landed at Brunn (Bruno) as he was running out of fuel. The rest of the aircraft of 1 *Staffel* under the command of *Oberst* Neubert, and 2 *Staffel*, under the command of Mertz, had carried out, after all, the planned attacks on the hangars at Krakow airfield.

Neubert had not noticed when our planes had suddenly fallen out of the clouds, and he carried on at a height of about 5,000–6,000 metres towards the east. When the clouds finally ceased and the sun at last came through he was alone with his *Kette* and the 2 *Staffel*. At Tarnow, 80 km east of Krakow, he regained his bearings and attacked the target some time after the scheduled time, approaching, with surprise, from the east. Neubert managed to shoot down a PZL-II fighter that crossed in front of him during the attack.

The left wing of my Ju 87 had to be replaced and so I could not take part in the next few missions.

There was little doubt about the eventual outcome of the Polish campaign. Right from the word go the modern methods and equipment of the Germans, coupled with their greater efficiency and expertise, foredoomed the very brave and gallant resistance put up by the Polish troops, with their outmoded equipment and methods. Utilising the unique power of the dive-bomber as their 'flying artillery', the Germans, even though their methods were still experimental, were able to smash every attempted concentration before it even got organised.

Dilley's second mission with I/StG 1 was an example of how the Stukas were learning on their feet, so to speak. They attacked the radio stations of Warsaw, at Babice and Lacy, in an attempt to black out the central broadcasting network, but they found that to score an actual direct hit on such a target was extremely difficult, even for a Ju 87. Near-misses looked spectacular enough, but the bomb blast was ineffective against the flexible masts, which merely recoiled, still in operational condition.

Helmut Mahlke explains the co-ordination of the Stuka units at this period, when it was still at a primitive stage:[2]

Of course, for targeting in close-support attacks very near or immediately in front of our own troops in order to break enemy resistance, the main problem was to make it *effective*. The means to solve this problem were pretty poor at the beginning of the war, but steadily improved. First of all the aircraft staff co-operating with the army in a battle were located as close together as possible at all times. Before a ground operation was begun, all Stukas available flew a massed attack, each unit against a specific target in a small area where the breakthrough was planned. Choice of target was sometimes based on photo reconnaissance with *exact* timing, so that ground troops could actually launch their assault directly the last aircraft turned for home. This aspect of planning and timing was rather simple.

The basic set-up from which everything later developed was this. The first thing needed was for the new airstrip, as we moved forward, to be connected telephonically with the superior staff, which used to be for Stuka Wings or Groups, an Air Division or Air Corps staff, or a 'forward control post' of such staff. The targeting procedures were different for other missions, depending of course on the nature of the target. Fixed points, for instance bridges, railroads and so on, were ordered on the basis of map grids only, which made them sometimes difficult to find and attack. Other fixed targets were sometimes photographed from the air first, but such targets seldom had pictures available for crews to study, especially when far ahead of the front line, like airfields, harbours and such.

Primitive it may now appear by later *Luftwaffe* standards, which I will describe as they developed, but against the Poles in 1939 these tactics proved deadly.

In the same way that the German dive-bomber tactics against land targets developed in the light of combat experience, so too did their application against warship targets. It was an aspect of their work that was to very quickly reach a devastating maturity, but, as with ground attacks, the lessons were first gained at the expense of the hapless Poles. The first dive-bomber attack against warships was by the eleven operational aircraft of 4/186 which attacked Hela naval base on the morning of 1 September through heavy flak, and these were followed during the day by other units from I and II/StG 2 and IV (Stuka)/LG 1, all of which were used in the north that day at one time or another. It was the Stukas of the latter formation, commanded by *Hauptmann* Kögl, which scored the first victory by sinking the torpedo-boat *Mazur* at 1400 hours in the naval harbour of Okswie.

Although AA defences were fierce, the Ju 87s pressed home their assaults, losing one aircraft (*Oberst* Czuprina) destroyed and others damaged by flak. The minelayer *Gryf* was caught in dry-dock and hit by a bomb, which started fires in her ready-use ammunition and oil tanks. She burned for two days before sinking.

These dive-bomber attacks continued all week. On the 2nd, IV/LG1 sank the *Gdynie* and *Gdansk* in the Gulf of Danzig, and on the 3rd, 4/186 made an assault during which Karl-Hermann 'Charly' Lion and *Oberleutnant* Rummel scored direct hits amidships and forward on the destroyer *Wicher*, which put her down, and the minesweeper *Mewa* was also sunk at Hela. On 6 September, it was the turn of the gunboat *General Haller* to be sunk, while her sister ship, lying alongside her,

Kommandant Pilsudki, was damaged and subsequently scuttled on 1 October. The minesweepers *Czapla* and *Jaskolka* were finished off on 14 September. What was left of the Polish submarine force fled to England or internment, while the small warships were captured by the Germans, who used several of them for themselves during the war. During the attacks on Hela as described, a Ju 87C-0 returned to base without its wheels and main undercarriage members. A photograph was reproduced which allegedly showed this aircraft on its way back to its home airfield. The story put out was that this aircraft had been dived too low in making attacks on Polish warships and had hit the water at the end of its dive, snapping off both wheels. Notwithstanding, the aircraft had been pulled up safely and returned to base despite the damage.

In fact it transpired that the aircraft had been slightly damaged by flak during its attack, and the pilot, anticipating a splash-down in Hela Bay, had fired the explosive bolts built in for just that purpose to jettison the main undercarriage members for an emergency water landing. But, after doing so, the aircraft was brought under control and got back to base, where it made a belly landing.

The doctored photo, however, was used to lend weight to a publicity campaign upholding the structural integrity of the Ju 87, but it was, in fact, faked. It was my old friend Hanfried Schliephake who confirmed this by producing for me the original photo, used before it had been 'doctored' by Goebbels' ministry, and which I had been fooled by. Case proved. The true fact, that the Stuka returned minus its wheels, was verified; it was how they had been lost that was rigged. However, Friedrich Lang stated firmly, and in perfectly good faith, that:

> This is no propaganda picture. I *saw* this plane at the Oronsko airfield, south-west of Radom, in September 1939, arriving and landing. On belly landing the dust of the stubble field flew up high.[3]

It should not be assumed from this lie that the Germans needed to fake such evidence, for the Stuka was acknowledged by friend and foe alike to be a strong and sturdy little aircraft. Again, Friedrich Lang describes some typical incidents involving his own unit:

> The body of the Ju 87 was very tough. It was not rare that branches of trees were on the wings after too low target shooting in peacetime. In February 1942, one of the Ju 87s brought home a 1½ metre and 20 cm thick beam. It was during an attack on a wooden bridge over the Msta (north of Ilmen Lake). It was thrown up by a bomb from the aircraft in front of it and was embedded in the wing of the following aircraft.

Further evidence of this ruggedness is shown by the severe flak damage Stukas survived after operations over Warsaw. In his memoirs General Kesselring paid glowing tribute after inspecting Stukas at this time. He though it a miracle that some of them had got back at all '... so riddled were they with holes – halves of wings were ripped off, bottom planes were torn away, and fuselages disembowelled with their control organs hanging by the thinnest threads ....'[4]

There was no doubt at all that the Ju 87 was a major factor in the outcome of the victorious campaign in Poland. Again and again it was dive-bombing which tipped the scales, smashing Polish counter-attacks before they could become serious, disrupting supply lines, thus hindering the movement of troops, supplies and vehicles to the fronts, and smashing concentrations of fighting units at key points in the battles.

Richthofen had two *Gruppen* of StG 77 commanded by Colonel Gunter Schwarzkopf, based initially at Neudorf, west of Oppeln. Schwarzkopf was an early exponent of dive-bombing in Germany, and this had earned him the title 'Father of the Stukas'. He had been *Kommodore* of StG 165, which later became StG 77. Under Colonel Baier, two more *Gruppen* lay at Nieder-Ellgut. Half of these were thrown in against Polish airfields at Katowitz and Wadowice. I/StG 76, led by *Hauptmann* Walter Sigel, struck at Wielun, and units of StG 77 hit Lublinitz on the first day's operation. After these initial strikes the dive-bombers were switched to army-support operations in the field. By 8 September, Stukas were flying missions against the outskirts of Warsaw itself from advanced airstrips at Tschenstochau and Kruszyna. The newly formed II/StG 51 had moved up from Germany to join the others in this final phase, and 140 Ju 87s went time after time into the cauldron. By 26 and 27 September they were pounding the last garrison holding out at the fortress of Modlin, some 318 tons of bombs descending upon its hapless defenders in two days, and their surrender followed on the 28th.

The dive-bombers theory had received a remarkable vindication on its first full-scale war operation. Hitler had hoped to turn west im-mediately and smash France once the Poles caved in, but the Army declared itself unready, and the winter weather closed in. The second stage of the German conquest of Europe had therefore to wait until the spring. 'Hitler has missed the bus', crowed Chamberlain, but before he found out just how wrong he was, an unexpected campaign in Norway the following April again brought out the unique qualities of the dive-bomber, this time operating on *both* sides of the conflict, into sharp focus, just prior to its greatest triumph.

*   *   *

Although the Western Front stagnated throughout the winter of 1939–40, and the pilots and crews of the dive-bombers on both sides had little to do but practise their art, carry out routine patrols and practise again, the signs were present early on that this lull would not outlast the spring. All eyes were turned to the Franco-German border, where hardly a man had moved for six months, when the Germans, with their usual combination of ruthless efficiency, daring force and speed and risk taking, suddenly moved forces in the neutral countries of Norway and Denmark.

In the case of the latter nation, the take-over was swift as far as the major ports and towns were concerned, and considerable boldness was shown by the Germans in moving against a target with a long coastline, open and inviting to counter-attack and interception from the Royal Navy, which had an overwhelming superiority over the German Navy. In this case boldness paid off convincingly, although the inevitable fight back was not long in coming. It was during this brief campaign that the power of the dive-bomber to influence events at sea was first demonstrated, a foretaste of things to come.

One of the most brilliant counter-blows was made by the Fleet Air Arm against a German naval squadron, which had captured Bergen. One of the warships of this force, the German light cruiser *Königsberg*, had been slightly damaged by Norwegian coastal guns during the initial landings on 8 April, but the main reason she did not leave was her unreliable engines. The Germans were trying desperately to get her away to safety and back to the Fatherland while there was still time. Bombing attacks by RAF medium bombers were totally unsuccessful, and so Nos 800 and 803 Squadrons of the FAA, stationed ashore at HMS *Sparrowhawk*, the naval airstrip at Hatston in the Orkney Islands, were briefed to make an attack at their extreme operational range. The mission was planned for 10 April, and the twin risks of running out of fuel and of encountering heavy fighter opposition were accepted.

Another problem was lack of up-to-date training in these two squadrons, one of the pilots recalling: 'My log-book tells me that I did only two sessions of practice bombing, totalling two hours twenty minutes, before setting out from Hatston for Bergen with the rest of 803 Squadron.'[5]

On 10 April 1940, at 0515 hours, all sixteen available Skuas, fully laden with fuel, took off from Hatston into the half-light and formed up as pre-arranged in two groups before setting off across the North Sea. No. 800 Squadron was led by Captain R.T. Partridge, Royal Marines, and No. 803 Squadron, by Captain E.D. McIver, Royal Navy. As they winged their way eastwards, one of the Skuas, piloted by Lieutenant Taylour, lost touch with the main party, but, nothing daunted, he navigated his way successfully on his own and was the last aircraft in over the target. Captain Griffiths later described the methods of approach and attack used by the FAA Skua at this time:

> The usual approach was above the clouds, by flights of three in vics, then we moved to fly in echelon to port or starboard, each flight commander, on reaching the point of 'flick-over', climbed up, rolled over and was on the dive path to the target, with flaps down. The height of the commencement of the attack varied according to the cloud, but, once on the path, it did not matter what height you started.[6]

The Skuas approached Bergen harbour from the south-east, and after a brief pause to scan where the two cruisers were last reported, they identified 'a cruiser of the *Köln* class' at her berth alongside the outer arm of the Mole. At 0720, the sections formed line astern to begin the final phase of the approach dive to clear the cloud layer at 8,000 feet. Below it, visibility proved excellent, at least 20 miles. The German defences, moreover, were caught flat-footed as the long line of Skuas barrelled in towards them out of the sun.

Most of the aircraft released their bombs at 2,000 feet from the final dive point of 5,500 feet and the majority went in at a 60-degree angle of dive, but there were, of course, variations to this norm. High dive-bombing was the term most pilots used in their reports; several indeed released at 2,500 feet, and two, Rooper and Harris, at 3,000 feet. Conversely, two others, Hanson and Spurway, pressed in to around 1,500 feet before release. Even more coolly, Church, having made his vertical dive down to the target, did not release, owing to bad positioning. Not satisfied, he pulled up, went around and made a second attack from stern-to-bow in a shallow run at 40 degrees and dropped his 500 lb bomb from 200 feet, clawing away through AA fire up to 3,000 feet and receiving considerable tracer from a new wide-awake flak ship which followed his withdrawal. This highly audacious attack was rewarded, for the Skua escaped with nothing more serious than 'one large hole in the mainplane, close to fuselage'.

Again, the angle of dive varied; 60 degrees was the norm, but several aircraft went in at 70 degrees and some at 50 degrees. The final run was bow-to-stern along the full length of the target, and the majority of bombs hit the ship aft. Aim at the stationary vessel was relatively simple, and for this the electronic gunsight was used:

> In Skuas we had the gunsight throwing an illuminated ring-and-bead onto the frontal armoured glass. It too was used for bomb aiming. The 500-pounder in the centre of the fuselage had lugs on each side and an ejector arm carried the bomb clear of the airscrew.[7]

This was one pilot's description, while another was more casual about the whole process:

> As far as I am concerned we just pointed the nose downhill and hoped for the best. We were much more concerned about the length of the flight, which was only just within the Skuas' endurance.[8]

Major A.E. Marsh RM, who also flew Skuas, although not on this mission, was later to recall of the Skua: 'As a dive-bomber it was fairly good, although it had the endearing trait of trying to go over onto its back in a dive and also had the disadvantage of shedding its tail if not dived correctly.'[9]

Another pilot added how, 'As soon as the bomb was released we dived straight for the ship to give it the minimum view *of* us, and maximum closing speed *to* us, and then escaped at sea-level.'[10]

The complete surprise achieved in this attack is shown by the slowness of the German reaction – about half the aircraft had completed their dives before the first guns opened up – and by the accuracy of the bombing.

Only a single AA weapon of large calibre appeared to be manned aboard the *Königsberg*; most pilots reported this solitary gun aft firing shells at five-second intervals that were bursting around the dive-bombers. The light weapons opened fire later, both from the target ship herself and from nearby vessels, in particular from one ship, described, presumably because of the weight of fire it was delivering, as a flak ship. Army AA units ashore were also noted, from a position about a mile south-west of the target ship, but no aircrew reported that these in any way affected their approach or aiming. They certainly did not affect the result.

As the bombs screamed down, the cruiser was enveloped in smoke and flames, which made aerial observation and confirmation difficult. Two hits were claimed amidships and one on the forecastle, in addition to at least one near-miss. The bombs that hit alongside on the mole, of which there were five, four of them very close, threw up dust and clouds of rubble which increased the difficulty of spotting.

The majority of pilots reported that they could not clearly estimate the damage, although a few seem to have had a better view. Riddler, for example, stated that his bomb missed the ship altogether and set fire to a building on the jetty. Spurway reported his bomb bursting internally, producing clouds of smoke and debris, while Russell reported that Harris's bomb was a hit on the cruiser's forecastle, which caused a large black hole from which white smoke and flames extruded.

'Three direct hits were achieved while a fourth burst alongside just under the water, blowing a large hole in her side, and she turned on her side to sink',[11] wrote one historian. To which Major Marsh added the opinion that, 'It is almost certainly the bomb dropped by McIver which struck amidships between the two funnels which was the lethal one which sank the ship.'[12]

Most of the other bombs were very close indeed: in fact the DNAD report estimates that the mean error in bombing in this attack 'was approximately 50 yards', which compared 'very favourably' with the 1939 practices which averaged 70 yards. It goes on: 'Considering that these aircraft had had little, if any, recent practice, and were under fire, it was a most creditable achievement.'[13] With which opinion we can most certainly agree.

Fortunately, also, we have a graphic eye-witness viewpoint of this attack from a neutral source with which to verify these accounts. This was a statement by Captain W.E. Wollaston, the master of the American freighter *Flying Fish*, who observed the attack first-hand after the Germans had boarded his vessel and placed an armed guard on his wireless-room.

> One bomb struck the *Köln* [sic] [he stated later in an interview in New York] squarely amidships, between the funnels. We saw clouds of smoke and at 9.00 am there was an explosion. The cruiser started sinking by the head. Flames were leaping 100 feet in the air as she sank deeper and deeper. Her stern went up in the air, showing her propeller, and 50 minutes later she capsized and sank as columns of smoke rose above her.

Petty Officer Gardner, the last pilot over the target from the main attack, reported that the target appeared to have been hit from the volume of smoke, but *Königserg* did not finally roll over until much later, as Captain Wollaston's account confirms.

Due to the surprise achieved, the British casualties were light. Only one aircraft failed to return. This was the Skua of Red Leader, Lieutenant Smeeton. All his section was complete when the force re-formed, and he appeared to be OK. He led his section into a cloud where his two wingmen lost touch with him. His aircraft was not seen by them again, but another aircrew reported seeing a splash in the sea about this time, about 40 miles to the west of Bergen.

Only two other aircraft of the force were hit by light automatic shells, which caused holes in the mainplanes, but the Skuas absorbed these without difficulty and both had no trouble in returning safely to base.

All the aircraft reassembled as planned, with the exception of Taylour, and all save Red Leader followed the planned route home. Taylour and Cunningham continued to carry out their solo mission with remarkable aplomb, and they also returned safely to Hatston. Light winds aided them and no aircraft had to refuel at Sumburgh, although the commander of No. 800 Squadron recalled, 'I think the Skua's official endurance was 4 hours 20 minutes, but I note from my log-book that during the attack on the *Königsberg* I was airborne for 4 hours 30 minutes.'[14]

The swift destruction of the cruiser made a deep impression on friend and foe alike, but the lessons taken to heart depended on the answers each was looking for.

First and foremost it proved, beyond any doubt, that, no matter what the trials and tests and graphs and figures trotted out by the RAF, the dive-bomber was far more accurate, and ten times more deadly, against warships than the standard twin-engined bomber. The stark contrast between the results of this, the *first* Skua operation *as a dive-bomber*, and the many complete and continuing failures of the Wellington and Hampden missions by Bomber Command, was plain for all to see.

Secondly, the attack succeeded only because both the requisites of dive-bomber attack (or indeed *any* bomber attack) had been met. Surprise was complete and the defences were weak, or, in the case of fighters, non-existent. Also, the bomb delivered onto the target was of sufficient size to do the job.

These points can be elaborated upon. Surprise was always important. The Battle of Britain would quite possibly have gone the other way but for radar and the vital part it played in eliminating this essential factor. Conversely at Midway the Japanese lacked this vital element and paid the full price for that omission. The fact that the attack was dive-bombing gave it the extra time factor to make it successful in that the AA defences were given no time to recover from the initial surprise as they would have been against level bombing, nor could they predict their targets so well. The DNAD, in his report, summed up the effect this had:

> Apart from the bombing results themselves, the relative lack of effect of the AA fire on the aircraft, including the two hits sustained, is encouraging. The Germans are clearly by no means past masters in this field.

This is important, for critics were to maintain later that one of the main arguments against the dive-bomber was the effectiveness of German flak compared with British AA defences. Here we see the opposite being demonstrated by dive-bombing.

Lack of fighter defence was, of course, vital to all attacks, dive-bombing no more and no less than other forms. For instance, would the Lancaster of No. 617 Squadron have been able to dispatch the stationary hulk of the *Tirpitz* four years on, 'Tallboys' or not, had the defending German fighters not proved equally impotent? The RAF had already provided the answer to that question when their Wellington bombers were cut to pieces over Wilhelmshaven in 1939, achieving nothing.

The correct target for the weapon carried is an equally crucial calculation. The 500 lb bombs carried by most dive-bombers at this early stage of the war were proved to be adequate to sink ships of light cruiser size downward (smaller vessels had already been sunk), but the lesson drawn by most observers is shallow and false. *Some* warships of this size were vulnerable to bombing, and especially so to dive-bombing, but not *all* warships. A modern battleship of the time, for example, could never have been totally destroyed by such means, nor indeed by 1,000 lb bombs on their own, especially if under way at sea. To sink capital ships required bombs so vast that, in 1940, they were undreamt of. To sink capital ships it was still the torpedo-bomber alone that could deliver the killer punch. Dive-bombers could provide additional weight and wear down the defences, but by themselves they could not yet deliver the knock-out blow. Dive-bombers were, of course, to show that armour could make all the difference to that most vulnerable of all warships, the aircraft-carrier. With deck armour they were to survive, but without it they fell victims with pathetic ease.

The DNAD summed up the operation, considering it to have been a model attack in every way and one that had reaped the reward it deserved. He felt that the principal lesson to be learned from the Skua sinking of the *Königsberg* was that:

> If Fleet aircraft are employed for the type of function for which they were designed, under careful planning and skilful leadership, they can achieve the results which have not been achieved by other aircraft when the prerequisites were lacking; and that these results can be most effective.[15]

Unfortunately, the next major attack that the Skuas undertook found none of these vital factors operative, for they were squandered by being sent in against a target they could not possible have hurt, without surprise, against fully alerted AA defence and against fighter aircraft, already airborne, of the most modern type, and with no fighter escort of their own. It is not surprising, then, that the results were somewhat different from their sensational debut. Never, since the Charge of the Light Brigade, have so many of the basics for an attack been totally ignored by those who ordered it to be carried out.

It would seem, in retrospect, that the Germans learnt more from the *Königsberg* attack than did the British. Whereas the few remaining Skua dive-bombers were largely wasted pretending to be fighter aircraft, the

Germans, with the largest dive-bomber force in the world poised and waiting, looked forward to taking on the Royal Navy with a renewed confidence.

None the less, the Blackburn Skua and its brave young aircrews will always have a unique and honourable place in the history of dive-bombing, indeed in any fair bombing survey, for being the first to sink a major warship in time of war by bombs alone.

Notes

1. Lang, *Oberst* Friedrich, to the Author, op. cit.
2. Mahlke, *Generalleutnant* Helmut, to the Author, op. cit.
3. Lang, *Oberst* Friedrich, to the Author, op. cit.
4. Kesselring, Field Marshal, *Memoirs* (William Kimber, 1956).
5. Harris, Major L.A., OBE, DSC, RM, to the Author, 31 March 1977.
6. Griffiths, Captain G.B.K., RM, to the Author, 3 April 1977.
7. Monk, Lieutenant-Commander H.A., DSC, RN, to the Author, op. cit.
8. Harris, Major L.A., OBE, DSC, RM, to the Author, *op. cit.*
9. Marsh, Major Alan E., RM, in the *Globe & Laurel*, Vol. LXXXIII, No. 6, November/December 1974.
10. Griffiths, Captain G.B.K., RM, to the Author, op cit.
11. Perret, A.J., 'Sku'd Prisoners for Breakfast', article in *The Globe & Laurel*, Vol. LXXXIII, No. 5, September/October 1974.
12. Marsh, Major Alan E., RM, op. cit.
13. *Notes* by Director Naval Air Division on *Report*, dated 25 April 1940 (National Archives, Kew, London, AIR 199/478/L04326).
14. *Daily Telegraph*, issue dated 4 May 1940.
15. Partridge, Major R.T., DSO, RM, to the Author, op. cit.
16. Notes by DNAD, op. cit.

CHAPTER FIVE

'Most courageously pressed home'

Germany took a calculated gamble in invading Norway, but although her own small Navy suffered crippling casualties, her troops and aircraft quickly established themselves ashore, and this, coupled with the sluggishness of the Allied riposte, enabled her to consolidate quickly. Only one *Stukagruppe* was assigned to this invasion; I/StG 1 operations started with a sortie from Holtenau near Kiel, under the command of *Hauptmann* Paul-Werner Hozzel. They attacked the Norwegian fortresses of Oskarborg and Akershus, which guarded the entrance to Oslo Fiord. Twenty-two Ju 87s made the attack, and although they scored the usual large number of direct hits, the defences, carved in places from solid rock, withstood the bombardment well. It was to take heavier bombs than those carried at this period of the war to penetrate such defence works, although the blast and shock kept the defending troops' heads down. The mission complete, the Ju 87Bs of I/StG 1 moved into Fornebu airfield near Oslo itself to commence close-support operations, and this move was completed by the evening of 9 April.

Against the stumbling Allied columns in the snow-girt battlefields around Namsos, Aandalsnes and finally Narvik, the Stukas operated with their usual efficiency: the little wooden houses of the Norwegian towns proved highly combustible when used as shelter by the poorly equipped British riflemen. The German Army pushed steadily north on the coastal roads until only Narvik held out against them, after its German garrison had finally been ejected after a long delay. In order to improve their striking range against such distant targets, the first long-range Ju 87Ds, the *Dora*, were brought in during May to reinforce the I/StG 1. With their two 66-gallon drop-tanks they had a radius of action of 400 miles compared with the 156-odd miles of the *Bertha*, and they soon proved invaluable.

The greatest impact made by the dive-bomber at sea during this campaign was its efficiency against small warships. The Royal Navy Skuas had shown the way, and I/StG 1, with such eager young aces as Hozzel, Gerhard Grenzel, Martin Möbus and Elmer Schaefer, all of whom were awarded the Knight's Cross for the actions against Allied shipping during this period, gladly took up the running.

I/StG 1 took part in the attacks which resulted in serious damage to the heavy cruiser *Suffolk* after she had ineffectually bombarded the Stuka base at Sola airfield on 18 April, but their greatest achievements were against lighter units of the British and French fleets. Owing to a lack of sufficient shore-based AA weapons the Army relied heavily on the Royal Navy to provide such protection at their ports of disembarkation and supply. Usually located at the heads of steep, narrow fiords, far from the sea and offering little room to the ships for evasive zig-zagging, the anti-aircraft cruisers, destroyers and AA sloops of the Navy fought daily duels with the Ju 87s. Losses soon mounted alarmingly as a result.

As an example of one such attack, the Stukas sank two large Allied destroyers during the evacuation of Namsos on 3 May 1940; these were the British *Gurkha* (1,870 tons) and the French *Bison* (2,435 tons). Hozzel himself sank the latter vessel with a steep diving attack down to a dangerously low level. One of his attacks, thought to be against the *Suffolk*, was later described thus:

> After his dive attack, while climbing again through about 3,000 feet, he perceived a massive explosion which pushed him hard against his canopy. For a moment he thought that he was finished. When he returned to base the crews of two Heinkel 111s of another unit reported a confirmation of his success, and since those crews were mainly ex-naval men Hozzel felt sure that the ship was larger than a destroyer and had four turrets.[1]

When the large destroyer *Bison* was sunk, and she was certainly larger than a normal destroyer, she was sunk outright by a single direct hit. Two days later the large Polish troop transport *Chrobry* was sunk when hit amidships by the Stukas with a 550 lb bomb that started large fires that eventually gutted her. On the 30th, the AA sloop *Bittern* was hit by a Stuka bomb that tore her entire stern section off after detonating her depth charges, and she, too, had to be sunk. Her sister ship, *Black Swan*, was also hit in a similar manner and had a lucky escape, for the bomb passed through her decks aft and between her propeller shafts, without exploding! By the end of this campaign there was no doubt about the effectiveness of the Stukas when deployed against the smaller warships, at least in the *Luftwaffe*'s estimation.

The final dive-bomber attack of the Norwegian campaign, conversely, showed up clearly and cruelly, the limitations of the dive-bomber. Just as the Skuas and Stukas had proved what they *could* achieve if directed at the right kind of target, lightly protected warships or merchant ships, so this final action showed the dive-bombers' limitations against large, heavily armoured capital ships, in this case the German battle-cruiser *Scharnhorst*.

After an earlier sortie, when she and her sister ship *Gneisenau* had sunk the aircraft-carrier *Glorious*, the *Scharnhorst* had been forced to seek shelter at Trondheim Roads anchorage, and plans were made by the C-in-C Home Fleet to attack her with a dive-bomber force launched from the *Ark Royal*, which was operating with the fleet off the Norwegian coast. Revenge for *Glorious* seemingly overrode common sense on this occasion, for the nearby airfield of Vaernes held the pick of German fighter forces in Norway. A pre-emptive strike by RAF Beauforts achieved nothing at all, likewise the promised RAF fighter support failed to turn up on time and the Skuas had to go in alone and unescorted. If anything, the contribution of the RAF merely ensured that the German fighters were brought up early, stirring the hornets' nest, so that the Skuas found Me 109s and Me 110s in the air and waiting for them as they arrived over the target. The German flak defences and shipboard AA gunners were likewise ready and waiting in good time to be effective. In fact, the RAF intervention cost the Fleet Air Arm its most effective asset, surprise. Under such circumstances the DNAD later considered that the Skua attack had a right to expect only one hit and a 25 per cent chance of a second, with 30 per cent casualties from flak and up to a further 30 per cent from fighters. His figures proved only too accurate.

Although the task force arrived at its flying-off position undetected, it was decided to mount a standing air patrol of three-Skuas sections over the ships between 2230 on the 12th and 0550 on the 13th, which left the final striking force with a total strength of fifteen dive-bombers, the maximum that could be accommodated on her after flight-deck for a single launch. These were six Skuas from No. 800 Squadron and nine from No. 803 Squadron.

On 13 June, therefore, the fifteen dive-bombers flew off the *Ark Royal*, each armed with a single 500 lb semi-armour-piercing (SAP) bomb on the swing crutch below her belly, destination Trondheim Roads and the *Scharnhorst*. No. 803 Squadron led the way, commanded by Lieutenant-Commander J. Casson RN, with No. 800 Squadron following, led by Captain 'Birdy' Partridge RM. Flying at 11,000 feet, they made their landfall north of the Halten Lighthouse at 0123 hours. The two squadrons then had to fly up the fiord for a further ten minutes, then turned south and approached the target zone at 10,000 feet, still at slow speed. Shortly before reaching the anchorage, No. 803 Squadron formed line astern, while No. 800 Squadron broke away to 11,500 feet to carry out a separate attack from a different direction. The weather was clear and fair over the assembled German fleet, *Scharnhorst*, heavy cruiser

Admiral Hipper, light cruiser *Nürnberg* and several big destroyers, and found that the German fighters and gunners were waiting for them.

Lieutenant Gibson described their experience as follows:[2]

> 803 carried out a shallow dive to 8,000 feet and made their approach while still north of the target, which was the *Scharnhorst* and *Admiral Hipper*. They were met by heavy anti-aircraft fire immediately. By the time I was in an attack position to run from north to south along the deck of the battle-cruiser, the anti-aircraft fire was exceeding fierce.

Lieutenant-Commander Casson led the squadron round to attack from south to north, bow to stern of the *Scharnhorst*, but as he was the last section to attack, Gibson considered it was not worthwhile to expose his section to the extra five minutes' gunfire this would entail, so his unit attacked from stern to bow instead, '... being in a perfect position to do so'. This was a wise decision, for there were only two survivors from the south-to-north run.

Gibson's section could not report a hit, but their bombs were seen to have fallen close, 'one being estimated at 15 feet from the stern'. All the survivors escaped from this death trap by flying through the ground mist. 'The exception was Sub-Lieutenant (A) G.W. Brokensha, who circled the area twice to see if he could help anyone.'

Many Me 109 fighters were seen to attack various Skuas, and four Me 110 twin-engined fighters were also present, though in general these held off. Gibson himself was subject to a 'poor-spirited attack by the Me 109s when in my dive'. One Me 110 was driven off by the Skua it attacked. From what Gibson's section was able to see, the Skuas that were attacked by the fighters were those that climbed after attacking instead of hugging the deck and the mist. 'As we had no height and negligible performance it would have been suicidal to have gone to their assistance.'

Gibson concluded that, in his opinion, 'The diversion created by the Beaufort bombers was a mistake. It appeared to take place a little too soon and destroyed any possibility of surprise.' He also noted, 'We did not see the Blenheim fighters until after we had *left* the coast. Four of our aircraft failed to return.'

No. 800 Squadron's attack was described by Lieutenant Spurway. They had approached Trondheim at 11,500 feet, quickly observing several warships at anchor off the town. On their approach they encountered intense anti-aircraft fire from both the warships and flak batteries ashore.

> The fire from the battle-cruiser and cruiser was very heavy and they appeared to be using many Bofors and Oerlikon, firing tracer

up to 8,000 feet and above. Each ship was using a separate colour of tracer and seemed to be firing by the hosepipe method.[3]

Both Skua units were therefore forced to take violent avoiding action, 'and the attack was somewhat confused'. Spurway followed Captain Partridge down onto the *Scharnhorst*. The splash from a near miss was observed close to the ship's quarter,

> ... and a vivid flash was observed by the pilot of 6K as he dived. It appeared to come from abaft the funnel on the starboard side. 6K's bomb was released at 3,000 feet and, on pulling away, the observer reported that he had seen a flash, possibly caused by 6K's bomb on the port side abaft the funnel.[4]

Spurway pulled up to 5,000 feet until clear of flak and then dived low over the land to the north as an Me 110 was spotted coming in on the starboard beam. It had help from an Me 109, which was observed some distance away. Both enemy fighters apparently failed to see the Skua against the dark background of the mountains, and joining up with 6Q, Spurway got safely away.

Other dive-bombers were seen to attack the *Admiral Hipper*, anchored to starboard of the *Scharnhorst*, but no hits were seen on her. The weather was hazy with a clear sky and the movements of the Skuas were hard for eyewitnesses to follow against the ground or the steely water. Two large fires were seen, from crashed Skuas, one near to Vaernes aerodrome and the other further west. 'No Blenheim or Beauforts were sighted.'

A large ball of flame was seen in the sky above the ships by Petty Officer Hart, another Skua hit by flak. Losses were grievous. Captain Partridge was seen to 'continue his dive very low and was not observed to pull out.' In total, four aircraft from No. 800 Squadron's six, and four of No. 803 Squadron's nine, failed to return. For this heavy casualty list it was believed that 'at least one and possibly two hits were obtained on the battle-cruiser *Scharnhorst*.'

Vice-Admiral Wells aboard the *Ark Royal*, who had dispatched the strike, stated that: 'There is no doubt that the attack was courageously pressed home by the striking force in the face of intense AA fire by the warships and the ground, and of enemy fighter opposition.'[5]

Admiral Sir Charles Forbes, C-in-C Home Fleet, was to agree. In fact, although two hits were claimed in good faith, only one direct hit was admitted to by the Germans and this bomb failed to explode. It was a tragically slight reward for so much bravery. The seven survivors had all landed back aboard the carrier by 0345, and the fleet returned to Scapa Flow in a thick fog, during which two of the escorting destroyers collided with each other and were badly damaged. It seemed to underline the futility of the whole mission.

Happily Captain Partridge survived the loss of his Skua, having survived and been picked up safely by a Norwegian fishing boat, badly burnt, but still alive. He was also to survive five years in a German POW camp, and he retired to live in Sussex after the war. I asked him his opinion on just why this attack failed when the *Konigsberg* assault had been such a triumph. He was positive in his reply:

> Surprise. The attack on the *Scharnhorst* at Trondheim was a very different kettle of fish and, in the view of those taking part, had little chance of success. We knew that the Germans had several fighter squadrons there. Trondheim lies 40–50 miles inland at the head of the fiord; it was June and there was no darkness in those latitudes to cover our approach; the weather was cloudless and visibility maximum, so no cover there either. We were told that fighter cover would be given to us by RAF Blenheims operating from North Scotland about 600–650 miles away; we thought that time synchronisation for forces operating so far apart was impossible and unfortunately we were right.[6]

*   *   *

The Royal Navy had learnt, as had the *Luftwaffe*, the hard way, that dive-bombing was effective if surprise, the right choice of target and determination were all combined in the right quantities. What had the RAF thought of it all?

On 5 May, a month prior to the *Scharnhorst* débâcle, a secret memorandum was sent by R.P. Willcock to Captain R.M. Ellis RN, of the Naval Air Division at the Admiralty. It commenced: 'The dive-bombing successes obtained in Norway by the Skuas and Junkers have raised in the minds of the Air Staff the suspicion that *perhaps the pre-war policy of neglecting the dive-bomber was not entirely sound**.'[7]

It was anticipated that they would be pressed to see what could be done to modify present bomber types, 'and probably the dive-bomber will be put forward as a future Air Staff requirement'. This would present a difficult problem, and before they became committed to a change in production, equipment and training, 'I would like to be assured of the good results which have been claimed for dive-bombing.' He therefore requested that the bearer of the letter (Squadron Leader A.E. Dark) be supplied with the necessary statistics. This was done.

Willcock summarised the findings of his query in a memorandum to the Assistant Chief of the Air Staff (Training) on 9 May, just one day before the Ju 87 dive-bombers smashed open the French defences on

---

* Author's italics.

the River Meuse. He wrote: '... as I anticipated, very little conclusive data are obtainable about the operations in Norway.' Further reports would be available when all the ships returned to their home ports. '... when this data is available it will be passed in the normal course of events to Dr Cunningham for his analysis.'

When this had also finally been complied with, little enthusiasm for dive-bombing manifested itself still at the Air Ministry. 'Although the Naval Air Division are enthusiastic about their own dive-bombing attacks, they have a poor opinion of the results obtained by the German Air Force.'[8]

He therefore concluded that:

> The above results only confirm what we have known for years – that dive-bombing gives greater accuracy than high-level bomb-ing. Low-level bombing, however, has been proved to be more accurate than dive-bombing [sic]. The question as to whether the dive-bomber is really a requirement for the RAF involves many factors ....'

To which there was a reply of some alacrity: 'There is undoubtedly a good deal of loose talk going on about German bombing results, and particularly about dive-bombing accuracy.' He went on to add that:

> The problem of making our existing bombers do steep dive-bombing is a formidable one, and is probably insoluble as a short-range project. I am therefore reluctant to embark on it until we have enough evidence to show that it will be worthwhile.[9]

The harsh truth was, of course, that the air marshals had been hope-lessly wrong and it was now too late to do much about it. But this was never officially admitted. As for further evidence, the *Luftwaffe* was just about to provide them with all the detailed evidence of the accuracy, power and effect of the dive-bomber anyone ought ever to require, and to prove by example, that the 'loose talk' was rather more than justified!

Whatever the RAF's opinion of the dive-bomber results up to that date, the French, at least, had got the message. On the outbreak of war their orders for American-built dive-bombers, which had been placed by their own Air Ministry, were combined in the Anglo-French Purchasing Commission shopping list. In April 1940 it had been approved to order for the French a further 192 dive-bombers, the Brewster Buccaneer. On the collapse of France shortly afterwards, this order was transferred to Britain, who thus became heir to American dive-bombers via the back door. The deal was going through even *before* the formation in the Britain of the Ministry of Aircraft Produc-tion, under the Canadian Press baron Lord Beaverbrook, and despite *official* RAF policy, which was still firmly against the type. The actual order was not, however, concluded until some months later, *after* the formation of the MAP, which led to complications, as we shall see.

* * *

As the echoes of the disastrous (for the Allies) operation were still reverberating around the fiords, the German offensive crashed forward into France and the Low Countries on 10 May 1940. Spearheading every tank assault were the Ju 87 dive-bombers. For the decisive battle in the West that now got under way, the *Stukagruppen* deployed no fewer than 324 Stukas, with StG 1, StG 2 and StG 77 operating under VIII *Fliegerkorps*, StG 3 and the Ju 88s of LG 1 operating with IV *Fliegerkorps* and II/StG 1 and IV(t) LG 1 operating with II *Fliegerkorps.* The first two commands worked in co-operation with Army Group B pushing into the neutral Netherlands and Belgium, before switching their attention to the main thrust through the Ardennes and across the Meuse at Dijon and Sedan, thrusting through the crumbling Allied armies and beginning the race to the sea. This was the real *Blitzkreig* in full cry.

The story of the Stuka's part in the Battle of France was a repeat, on a larger scale, of their debut in Poland, for while the Allies had learnt little from that campaign; the Germans had made many improvements in their technique and their application with all arms. Therefore, once the pin-point attacks of the dive-bombers had prised open the strong points along the front line and allowed the Panzers to stream through to the rear of the demoralised defenders, the Stuka's role became one of harassment, continually keeping the enemy on the run, preventing the build-up of defensive groups and smashing counter-attacks before they could commence. Helmut Mahlke explains:

> The missions in France were directed against targets beyond the line, which could be reached by our troops by the time the aircraft were over the target. These included enemy reserves marching, bridges or similar targets. With the head of our troops stopped by enemy resistance that they could not break with their own weapons, the forward troops reported to their command, and the specific target was relayed via air-division to the Stuka group or wing that would next be due over the area.
>
> Target description by telephone, based on maps, was used. This of course caused quite a lot of delay, which was not acceptable for a quick operation. Beginning in France, therefore, a special organisation was set up. A Stuka UHF wireless set was mounted in a tank of the Panzer force involved in the main battle. *Luftwaffe* UHF operators in these tanks participated in the main ground attacks,

as close as possible to the commander of the Panzer force. Where this system was in operation the Stuka unit was directed overhead and got exact targeting by wireless. In addition, the ground troops would shoot coloured flares near the target.

Beginning in France also, there was wireless connection (in addition to telephone) between Commanding Air Staffs and all of their subordinate flying groups and wings. There was also a liaison organisation – small groups of Air Force signal personnel, each attached to an Army Division as well as Corps or higher HQs. By this means our Air Force telephone net kept contact between all commands, thus abbreviating any delay in target location and mission strikes.[10]

*   *   *

The noises the Stuka produced when in a steep dive was found to be numbing on unseasoned troops not trained or experienced in being on the end of such an attack. Dive-bombing appeared to be a very personal form of assault, against which the infantrymen had little or no defence themselves, other than throwing themselves down flat or into the nearest ditch or hedgerow. So paralysing was even the sound of the Stukas approaching that whole divisions were tied down and mesmerised. This effect had already been seen in Spain and Poland, and in order to capitalise upon it, the natural scream and wail of a Ju 87 in a terminal power dive was enhanced by fitting a special wind-driven siren to the undercarriage legs of the Stukas. As Friedrich Lang recalled:

> We started the war without sirens in our Group in 1939. In April 1940 we were with the I/StG 2 'Immelmann' at Cologne-Ostheim airfield. There we had a home-made whistle and siren, but they did not work very well until the small, special-shaped wooden propeller was fitted to the *Federbeinverkleidung* on the *Falvwerk*. We did not get supplied by industry until later. They turned in the wind of the dive and created a noise that became louder with speed. The howling sound distracted and upset not only the enemy but also the crew! It became better when you could turn off the propeller by means of a *Seitzug*.[11]

The Stuka's aircrew called these sirens the 'Trombones of Jericho', and they certainly proved effective against the morale of the second-class French reservists who broke on the Meuse river front on those sun-drenched days of May 1940.

The first Ju 87 strikes were directed against airfields and front-line positions around the fortress of Liège in Belgium. The audacious capture of the strongpoint of Fort Eben Emael was achieved in the first twenty-four hours by a special shock-group trained for the task. All the efforts to dislodge this tiny force were frustrated by precision attacks conducted by the Stukas of StG 2, which carried out repeated bombings of the fortified positions along the Maas river. Likewise, at Moerdijk, the Stukas hit defence works and flak positions guarding the important viaducts over the Diep river, which were then taken and held by paratroops. These attacks continued throughout 11 and 12 May, and then the bulk of the dive-bombers were suddenly switched south to support the 19th and 21st Army Corps' bold thrust against Sedan.

The fall of France was accomplished by the breakthrough of the Panzer armies along the river Meuse, and in this the Ju 87 played a vital role. This is confirmed by the accounts of both the German and French soldiers on the spot. General Heinz Guderian was to write how the French artillery was more or less paralysed by the 'ever present threat of the Stukas'.[12] The French General, Ruby, told how the defending gunners 'stopped firing and went to ground, the infantry cowered in the trenches, dazed by the crash of the bombs and the shriek of the dive-bombers.'[13]

The damage done to the defenders' morale was shattering: Goutard wrote of how survivors were convinced there were no defending French fighters and that 'they were abandoned to the Stuka attack, and that this contributed more than anything else to the demoralisation of our troops.'[14] Another French soldier confirms this opinion: 'I believe this can be explained by the complete state of numbness caused by the Stuka attacks, and by the difficulties of identifying French planes at medium distance.'[15]

Goutard gives the reason why the Stukas were effective, despite strong French fighter sweeps over the front. He reasoned that this was because the Stuka units were controlled by one source only at a time and not strung out all over the front line, as were the Allied fighters. Therefore the German achievement was caused in the air, as on the land, by concentration of force at the vital spot, the *Schwerpunkt!*

> On 13 May the Germans put 700 planes in the air over Sedan, 200 of which were Stukas. But on the next day the *Schwerpunkt* was elsewhere, and there was not a single German aircraft in that sector, the air defence of which was left to the flak.[16]

The Ju 87s of StG 2 and StG 77 flew a total of 200 sorties on 13 May, commencing at 0600 hours, against the Sedan defences, while up the river at Houx and Dinart it was StG 1 which provided the punch that opened up the second bridgehead to Hoth's 15th *Panzerkorps*. By the end of the day the German tanks were over, and racing through hordes of fleeing French soldiers who abandoned their guns and threw away their rifles, milling around aimlessly and helplessly. The thin French shield shattered, the Germans found there was nothing behind it, and the race to the Channel commenced.

Compared with the hordes of Ju 87s pile-driving their way across northern France, the Allies had only their ineffectual medium bombers with which to hit back, and their long-held theory that low-level attack was more effective than dive-bombing crumbled and crashed as fast as the Allied armies. The long-cherished illusion of the Fairey Battle vanished in a day with their futile attacks against the Meuse bridges, when whole squadrons were wiped out without achieving so much as a single hit. No one questions the bravery of the young British aircrew, it was their *method* that was fatally flawed. The French light bombers suffered a similar fate. For example, their Breguet 69s made an attack in Belgium on 12 May, and of eleven bombers of GBS O/54, seven were shot down, two crash-landed and only two survived intact. In belated realisation, a form of semi-dive-bombing was adopted, utilising an angle of 45 degrees. This improved both accuracy and the ghastly loss-ratio, but it was by then too late; far too many aircraft and crews had gone.

The tiny handful of French dive-bombers available could not turn the tide on their own, although they tried most gallantly to do so. Of the fifty-two Vought V-156Fs, twelve were wiped out on the first day in a single attack on Boulogne-Alprech airfield. The main hangar was demolished by direct hits with the unflown aircraft of AB-3 still inside. The surviving pilots went to Lanveoc-Pulmic to get replacements, but not until 23 May did they rejoin the fight, far too late to affect the issue. The Chance Voughts of AB-1 were therefore rushed up from Hyères to Alprech to take their place, even though their training was incomplete.

On 15 May the *Aéronavale* dive-bombers of AB-2, nine strong, attacked a German artillery column on Walcheren Island, near Yerseke, with their LN401s without loss. On the 16th Captain Mesny with nine Voughts of AB-1 and Captain Lorenzi with nine Loires of AB-2 again headed for Walcheren Island, to smash the railways and canal locks and impede the German advance. Again, they were successful and no aircraft were lost, thanks to a strong fighter escort.

On the 17th these gallant pinprick attacks continued; ten Voughts and eight Loires hit the same targets, and further sorties were mounted by three Loires at 2230 and by two Voughts who dive-bombed German tanks soon after this at Flessingue, losing one of their number in that day's operations. This comparative immunity was not to last, however.

In a desperate attempt to stem the flood of German armour across the River Oise, all available French Navy dive-bombers were called in on 20 May. Captain Mesny could count on eleven Voughts of AB-1, plus one Loire of AB-2 and two of AB-4 that had survived earlier disaster intact. The promised fighter cover of RAF Hurricanes failed to show up when the two formations rendezvoused over Berck at 0930 hours that morning and set course for the target. The faster Voughts soon drew ahead as they flew towards the bridges, and very soon AB-1 was jumped by twelve Me 109s, while still some 20 miles short of their target.

In the battle which followed, five Voughts were destroyed in as many minutes, the others became dispersed and made ineffectual attacks in the face of fierce flak, before returning to their base at Boulogne-Alprech. While the V-156s were being destroyed, the flight of three LNs managed to slip through undetected (their similarity to the Ju 87, both having inverted-gull-wing configurations, may have helped them in this). They therefore achieved complete surprise. The German gunners failed to open fire until the French dive-bombers had already commenced their final attack dives. One Loire fell to the gunners but the other pair held on, and Petty Officer Hautin scored a direct hit with a 330 lb bomb, which destroyed the bridge. It was a magnificent effort; both surviving Loires returned heavily damaged, while a sixth Vought crashed on reaching her base. The dive-bombing attack on the Origny-Ste-Benoite bridge, however, virtually marked the end of the French dive-bombers' effective intervention in the war.

By contrast to this drop in the ocean, the Ju 87s seemed to be everywhere, British Air Intelligence reporting on 17 May that:

> Another dive-bomber unit has been identified as operating in the Liège area, and dive-bombers are being employed south-west of Luxembourg. Frequent requests for dive-bomber support are being made by land forces to attack fortresses in the Liège and Mézières districts, and it is now estimated that about sixty per cent of the dive-bomber force is being employed.[17]

As the pace hotted up, these Ju 87 units were moving their bases almost daily in an attempt to keep up with the pell-mell rush of the Panzers. Their short range made it essential that captured French airfields were quickly made operational as soon as they could be occupied. From 15 May onward, the Stuka units were constantly in action in this manner.

With the bulk of the Allied armies being gradually squeezed into the perimeter of Dunkirk, and with hastily organised evacuations by sea getting under way, the garrisons dug in on the Channel coast had to hold on as long as possible to help. Evicting them by land assault promised to slow up the German advance, and so the Ju 87s were called upon to help the Army do the job, especially at Boulogne and Calais.

StG 2 was involved in these attacks, and on 25 May it mounted heavy raids on Boulogne, which finally fell that same morning. At Calais, the British were still fighting hard, and StG 1 therefore devoted its entire strength to crushing this resistance and aiding the 10th Panzer Division. Inevitably the British and French destroyers operating off the coast by lending their support to the defenders by bombarding German tanks and troop columns ashore came in for their share of the dive-bombers' attentions, and soon the tale of Norway began to be repeated closer to home. One of the Stukas' first naval victims was the old destroyer *Wessex*, which was carrying out shore bombardments off Calais on 24 May. At 1645 hours, in company with two other destroyers, she moved in close to re-commence her gunnery duel, and as she did so, a formation of twenty-one dive-bombers was sighted and identified as Stukas. These aircraft immediately split up and attacked the three destroyers very effectively.

The Polish ship, *Burza*, was hit forward by a bomb and retired towards Dover in a damaged condition. The *Vimiera* sustained damage from near misses and splinters, which reduced her speed, but the *Wessex* took the brunt of the attack. As the Stukas screamed down, *Wessex* increased speed to 28 knots and zig-zagged. She opened a barrage fire with all her guns (4-inch barrage with maximum elevation of 30 degrees, pom-pom and two single Lewis guns). She thus managed to avoid the first two aircraft's attacks, although their bombs fell practically alongside the ship. The third Stuka made no mistake, as the ship's report graphically makes clear:

... enemy plane registered three hits between the funnels. The bombs penetrated the two boiler rooms and exploded, killing all personnel. Both boiler rooms were wrecked, the ship's sides and bottom sustaining severe damage, the foremost engine-room bulkhead was damaged, causing leakage into the Engine Room beyond the possibility of shoring-up.

Damage which also caused flooding occurred up to the fore shell room and magazine. All boats, deck fittings and foremost funnel disappeared and the after funnel fell aft. Foremast broke at height just above upper bridge and the after side of the bridge sustained damage. Flooding took place in compartments mentioned and the ship commenced to settle down forward.

No fires occurred but for the first few minutes bridges were enveloped in steam which made it temporarily impossible to see what was happening. 4-inch guns 'A', 'X' and 'Y' continued firing for the first few minutes after the *Wessex* was hit, but when it was observed that several Spitfire fighters had arrived and were attacking the enemy bombers, fire was ceased.[18]

Thus the old *Wessex*, a veteran from the First World War, met her end. She was not to be the last destroyer to become a dive-bomber victim in the days and weeks ahead.

Ashore, at dawn on 26 May, General Guderian prepared for his final assault on Calais. In conjunction with this, von Richthofen ordered every available Stuka into the fray. The first attack was mounted by StG 77 at 0930 hours that morning, and was followed up by StG 2. For an hour, wave after wave of Ju 87s pounded the defenders and reduced the old town to rubble. A vivid description of this dive-bombing was given by one of the British defenders, the late Airey Neave DSP MP.

The 60th, lying without cover in the streets, had little protection from the Stukas. No one who experienced the attack on the morning of the 26th is very likely to forget it. A hundred aircraft attacked the Citadel and the old town in waves. They dived in threes, with a prolonged scream, dropping one high explosive and three or four incendiary bombs.[19]

The hits made turned the Calais-Nord district into a sea of flames, and then the German assault troops followed up. Calais fell at 1645 that afternoon and the Germans took 20,000 prisoners.

Notes

1. Mahlke, *Generalleutnant*, to the Author, op. cit.
2. *Report*, dated 13 June 1940 (National Archives, Kew, London, ADM 199/480X, No. 11, (CAF) 3572).
3. *Report*, dated 18 June 1940 (National Archives, Kew, London, ADM 199/480X/ L04326).
4. *Ibid.*
5. *Report*, dated 27 June 1940 (National Archives, Kew, London, ADM 199/1118/ HF.1350).
6. Partridge, Major R.T., to the Author, op. cit.
7. Memorandum, dated 5 May 1940 (National Archives, Kew, London, AIR/2/3076).
8. *Dive-bombing – Review of Policy*, dated 9 May 1940 (National Archives, Kew, London, AIR 2/3176, S4583).
9. Memorandum, dated 12 May 1940 (National Archives, Kew, London, AIR2/3176, S.4583).
10. Mahlke, *Generalleutant*, to the Author, op. cit.
11. Lang, *Oberst*, to the Author, op. cit.
12. Guderian, General Heinz, *Panzer Leader* (Michael Joseph, 1958).
13. Ruby, Général Edmond, *Sedan; terre d'epreuve* (Flammarion).
14. Goutard, Général A., *The Battle of France* (Muller, 1958).
15. d'Astier de la Vigerie, Général, *Le Ciel n'etait pas vide* (Julliard).
16. Seive, Général, *L'Aviation d'Assault dans la Campagne de 1940* (Berger-Levrault).
17. *Summary of Air Intelligence, No. 302* (National Archives, Kew, London, AIR 22/9/ 04811).
18. *Loss Report of HMS* Wessex, dated 19 June 1940 (National Archives, Kew, London, AIR 2/4221/04811).
19. Neave, Airey, *The Flames of Calais; A Soldier's Battle* (Hodder & Stoughton, 1972).

CHAPTER SIX

'And dived almost vertically'

While the Stukas were harrying warships, pounding bastions into defeat and swarming over the evacuation fleet off Dunkirk, the British were forced to adopt dive-bombing methods despite themselves, only to find that they had few aircraft capable of performing in this role. Such as they were, they were pressed into service, but, as with the French, they were pitifully few, mainly Fleet Air Arm aircraft, and far too late to affect the final crash. Typical of the scratch forces that were thrown in the cauldron at this frenetic period were the old biplane Fairey Swordfishes of No. 812 Squadron.

On 26 May, eleven of these antiques were sent off on an offensive sortie against a reported concentration of Panzers in the Gravelines region. Each of the aircraft carried a mixed bomb load of 250 lb general-purpose (GP) bombs for their task. On arrival over the target area they were unable to find the reported German tank force and were forced to hunt for whatever suitable targets presented themselves; with the countryside swarming with advancing German columns, this was not too difficult.

They all carried out individual dive-bombing attacks against targets of opportunity, every one of the Swordfish dropping its bombs, a total of sixty-six 250-pounders, and they claimed to have made five direct hits on the road and to have destroyed three German tanks for the loss of one of their number from AA fire.

Even more desperate were the belated attempts by the RAF to enter the dive-bomber lists at this time. On 23 May, six Westland Lysander spotter aircraft were sent in to dive-bomb a German artillery battery south-west of Calais, but they were unable to observe the results of their attack. On 26 May even more antiquated equipment was thrown in as an act of desperation. Six Hawker Hector biplanes of No. 613 Squadron, which should have been in museums, were dispatched to dive-bomb a battery, probably the same one, south-west of Calais. These old veterans were commanded by Squadron Leader A.F.

Anderson. The actual plane he piloted on this mission was the same old crate he had flown at the Hendon Air Display in 1937!

Some of the aircrew had come straight from training school and had 'never flown in a Hector, fired a gun or dropped a bomb' before that day, but here they were, the RAF's only answer to the dive-bomber shortage. No results could be seen from their attack on the 26th, but they doggedly returned the next day, six Hectors and nine Swordfish which dive-bombed targets around Calais, while some Lysanders dropped supplies to the garrison, most of which fell into German hands, of course. Three of these old aircraft failed to return from this suicidal mission.

Off the Dunkirk beaches it was a different story for the Ju 87s. Up to 26 May, the Stukas had been fully committed at Calais, Amiens and Lille, and so the ships had a relatively easy time. On the 27th, however, this all changed, for it was then that VIII *Fliegerkorps* began to direct its full attention to the great mass of shipping assembled off the beaches and in the harbour itself.

First attacks by StG 2 sank the French troopship *Côte d'Azur* before the weather closed down *Luftwaffe* sorties until the 29th. On their return, the dive-bombers initially concentrated their attacks on the harbour itself, and caught many vessels inside, busy loading troops. At 1600, a heavy dive-bombing attack swamped the defences, sinking the paddle steamers *Fenella* and *Crested Eagle*, the trawlers *Polly Johnson* and *Calvi*, the minesweeper *Gracie Fields* and, more importantly, the destroyer *Grenade*, all of which sank with heavy loss of life among the soldiers packed aboard their hulls. Many other ships were hit and badly damaged in this attack.

The next day, 30 May, was another one of tragedy as the Stukas returned to complete their work. They bombed and sank the destroyer *Keith* in a series of attacks, described by the master of the tug *Cervia*, W.H. Simmons, in his report thus:

> A British destroyer outside of us began to fire at the enemy planes and bombs began to fall near her as she steamed about. At full speed with her helm hard to port, nine bombs fell in a line in the water, along her starboard side, and they exploded under water, heeling the destroyer over on her beam ends, but she was righted again and a sloop joined in the gunfire, also the shore batteries.

One of these near-misses jammed the *Keith*'s rudder, forcing her to turn in small circles at high speed, and then a second attack broke over her and a Stuka planted a bomb right down her after funnel and also achieved further near-misses. Her commander, Captain E.L. Berthon, brought her to a halt with a 20-degree list. Then yet a third wave of Ju 87s tore down upon her, scoring yet a further direct hit below her bridge, and she sank immediately. She was joined on the seabed by the destroyer *Basilisk* and the French destroyer *Foudroyant*, while many others were damaged. Ashore, the soldiers watched in impotence as their naval rescuers were pulverised before their eyes.

We also watched another raid directed against the shipping lying off the beaches, and this time the results were far more serious. One destroyer was hit amidships by a dive-bomber; the bomb must have penetrated into the ammunition magazine as there was a terrific explosion, followed by a column of smoke which mushroomed over the ship. As the smoke cleared, the destroyer had entirely disappeared.[1]

Captain Harrington recalled:

During the fall of France, our Skuas were operating from the RAF base at Detling, then under Coastal Command control. Hectic days indeed, living under canvas in glorious weather and fed like fighting cocks by a local caterer. He really did his stuff for the 'boys' and did not stint us in any way, despite the Admiralty's modest monetary contribution for our victualling.

Our main role was to cut any bridges the army wanted 'done', any enemy installation or invasion barges (which were found from our other role of taking part in a daily reconnaissance of the local French, Belgian and Dutch channel ports) and finally to provide fighter cover for any special convoys off the Kent or Essex coast. I will not digress on the reconnaissance or convoy roles, other than to say that in naval aircraft with sea camouflage, we seemed to form a legitimate prey for both the German and the British defences as well as a worthwhile target for both the Royal and German Air Forces. It was quite a novel experience fighting your way out of this country, weaving and dodging on the enemy side, and then forcing a passage back to your own airfield, However, this taught us another vital lesson.

Because our Skuas were not fast, even without bombs, we soon latched on to one or two fundamentals which have since formed basic requirements for naval attack aircraft. The first of these was that if aircraft were to successfully penetrate well-defended targets, for whatever purpose, then the first requirement to be achieved was surprise – almost Rule One of any warlike operation. This meant, wherever possible, a low-level approach, below the enemy warning system. This technique we developed, and our losses off the French and, later, Norwegian coasts were significantly less than those of our Air Force Blenheim and the like friends. This method provided for another vital element, namely, one of identification – was it the target, and was the target a real, worthwhile target? In a ship sense, was it theirs or one of ours that nobody knew was here?

The other lessons we learned were on the weapon-delivery side. On one hand if you had only traditional bombs, then you were committed to the classical 'dive' approach. In short, you had to arrive over the target at the right height for a 65–75-degree dive, release the bomb with the right sort of penetration speed (a function of height), then recover from the dive and make your way out like a 'half-tide' rock. With limited range of weapons and their associated limited fusing arrangements, you were always facing fairly critical limitations; compromising between a really highly productive run with the chance of target destruction and the maximum chance of getting home and hopefully being available for further strikes. In a carrier your replenishment of aircraft and crew takes time. The final lesson we learned, apart from the need for an aircraft with a really high performance, was that the aircraft should have a really effective, balanced and flexible in-air braking system.

The Skua dive-brakes were really in the wrong position, and they had the effect of pushing you forward and over your target. In other words, if you wanted to achieve a 70-degree dive, you had to start your dive at least at +80 degrees and aim somewhat short of your target, so that as the speed built up you finished with your final release-point at the correct point of aim and at the right height, etc. Correcting this floating-forward effect also had another dividend for us, as the flak had a great problem in tracking you correctly and anticipating this ever-increasing forward 'float'. It was comforting to see the stuff passing under your aircraft, which was good news for you and very bad news for anyone foolish enough to try and follow you down. I had first-hand experience of this: in one attack on Bergen harbour we entered cloud just before we had to start our dive; consequently, when I pushed over and emerged from the cloud, I found myself directly behind, but under, my chum ahead of me. I finished up with one side of my windshield and sliding hood missing, but luckily I had my seat down and head on one side fixing some fuse setting, as I was having trouble with the electrics.

The other additive and innovative trick we used on shore targets in France and Norway was to create a morale-lowering effect on the ground defences by getting our observers or air gunners to throw out of the rear cockpits a load of empty 'grog' bottles just as we went into our dives. This created a formidable whistle and became the precursor of the 'Whistling Bomb'. We listened to the

German broadcast of our attack on the Cap Gris-Nez fortifications (the first one ever made) and they stated that the British were using whistling bombs![2]

Not surprisingly, after its experience in France at the hands of the Ju 87, the British Army began to make increasing demands for a dive-bomber of our own with which to play the same game. The Air Ministry remained as adamant as ever that it did not want such a plane. The newly appointed Minister of Aircraft Production, Lord Beaverbrook, supported the Army's pleas, despite vehement opposition from the RAF, and, besides taking over the French orders for the American-built Brewster Bermuda (renamed the Buccaneer by the British), also ordered the new Vultee Vengeance in large numbers, but both were still in the prototype stage at this time and could not expect to be supplied for some time. Repeated further demands by the generals, wondering how to repel an imminent German invasion, were continually turned down by the RAF. As Beaverbrook stated to Air Minister Sinclair later on:

We ordered [dive-bombers] in the USA, as you know, because prior to July 1940, no one at the Air Ministry had included dive-bombers in their requisitions, nor had anyone even ordered a prototype. So we had none on home stocks and the quickest way of getting them was in the USA.[3]

A second order for a further 200 Vengeance dive-bombers was placed on 3 July. A.J.P. Taylor describes this in the following manner:

In July 1940 he [Beaverbrook] placed a large order for dive-bombers in Canada and the United States. Eden, then Secretary for War, was enthusiastic. The Air Ministry protested and refused to supply or train pilots.[4]

At a meeting to discuss the requirements of the Army for a close-support dive-bomber, the Air Ministry, as ever, had influenced the last say. 'While a steep dive-bomber was not essential, the aircraft should have as steep an angle of dive as possible, without prejudice to other essential requirements.'

This gave the RAF the 'out' they needed and ensured that the plane would not be a true dive-bomber at all, as they had all-along argued against. The Air Chiefs, mesmerised by the vision of German cities in flames, were not talking about a close-support dive-bomber at all, really, but merely the allocation of the existing medium bombers of the Blenheim type to the close-support role, despite the example of the Battle.

Meantime, they conducted a series of bizarre experiments in 'high dive-bombing' with No. 3 Group at Berriers Heath. The method they employed was '... to do a modified stall turn at approximately 1 mile from the target and to aim a 6 o'clock on the target in a dive of 30 degrees to 40 degrees, the bomb being released by the pilot on judgement as the nose is eased up over the target.'[5]

They were not enthusiastic. 'My own experience of high dive-bombing is that it is largely a matter of individualism; some pilots are naturally good at it, others will never be any good, however much training and practice they have.'[6]

While the British, desperately trying to make bricks without straw, turned to the United States for salvation, Italy, her own dive-bomber programme in ruins following the abject failure of their own Savoia designs, turned in a similar fashion to the Germans for a solution. On 22 July the Chief of the Air Staff, Pricolo, sent *Generale* Urbani and Colonel Teucci to have talks with Goering on arranging for the Italian purchase of Junkers Ju 87s and the training of Italian pilots in their use. Fifteen Italian fighter pilots were sent to start familiarisation flying with the Stuka at Graz in Ostmark [Austria]; a further fifteen followed in August, and a total of fifty were to complete the conversion course by the end of September 1940.

The training was carried out at *Stukaschule* 2 at Graz-Thalerhof on Hs 123s and Ju 87As. One of the first group of fifteen Italian pilots to undergo this course was Antonio Cumbat.

I had never flown any type of bomber prior to this course, being at that time a fighter (*Assalto*) pilot, and in 1939 I had trained on the API, the Breda 64-, Breda 65- and Breda 88-type machines.

As far as I can remember, we carried out no special training against moving targets at Graz; indeed my group only in fact completed fifteen hours' flying out of the twenty-five hours that had been programmed by the Germans for us, due to the need to form the squadron quickly. As we were the first fifteen pilots there was nobody in Italy to check what level of training we had reached on this course. Certainly the training we received was far below the German standard of the time.

During my whole training course, for example, I never saw a single model of either a British warship or aircraft to help in target recognition.

Flying the Ju 87 was therefore, in combat later, very much up to the Italian pilots and squadron commanders to improvise according to their own experience, which resulted in slightly different techniques to the German ones, although the basic flying units' methods were identical.[7]

The first batch of Stukas sold to Italy were of the Ju 87B-2 and R types, similar to the 'tropicalised' versions employed by the German units later in the Mediterranean area. They were fitted with sand filters and desert survival equipment and the like, for use by the *Gruppi Tuffatori*. Despite rumours and even books stating the contrary, *no* Ju 87s were ever built in Italy under licence; all were purchased outright.

On 15 August 1940, the first Italian Stukas lifted off from Graz for Italian use, B-2s and R-2s, arriving in Sicily on 21 August to set up the new dive-bomber unit at Comiso airfield there. The commander of this units, 96° *Gruppo*, was Captain Ercolani, and it comprised two *Squadriglia*, Nos 236 and 237, under Lieutenants Malvezzi and Santinoni.

Italy was not the only one of its allies that Germany equipped with the Ju 87. The Hungarian air arm, the *Magyar Kiralyi Legierö*, formed the nucleus of its first dive-bomber group, *I Onallo Zuhanobomazö Osztaly*, with two squadrons at the same period, equipped with Ju 87B-2s, although it was not until another two years later that it became fully operational, having in the meantime re-equipped with Ju 87-D8s.

Similarly, the Rumanian air force formed a dive-bomber group, *Grupul 6 Picaj*, also with B-2s. It consisted of three 9-aircraft squadrons and was ready for operations in 1941, in time for the invasion of the Soviet Union. Bulgaria also took small batches of Ju 87B-2s and later *Doras*, for her small air force.

Meanwhile, back on the Channel coast, the German Stuka units were reorganising and massing in order to prepare for the first stages of the invasion of Britain. StG 1 at Angers/St Pol, StG 2 at St Malo/St Omer, St Tron and Lannion, StG 77 at Caen, I/StG 3 at Dinand/Pleurtuit and IV (Stuka) LG1 at Tramecourt. But before the Battle of Britain got under way, British seaborne supplies and defences were to be tested, and the newly appointed *Kanalkampfführer*, Johannes Fink, was given the task of closing the English Channel, commencing this task on 2 July.

*   *   *

The closing of the Channel, the brief *Kanalkampf*, has since been dismissed by one American historian as being of 'not much importance', but this view reflects more the limited thinking of an air-force-type mind with no broader spectrum than immediate results. The long-term effects that a more sustained campaign could have had on the British economy at this critical juncture of our history are more truly reflected in the much more enlightened commentary of the official British Naval Historian, Captain Stephen Roskill:

> The seriousness of the enemy lay in the fact that, at their peak, one ship in three in these convoys had been damaged or sunk. Such unattractive odds could, if continued, make it impossible to man the ships.[8]

Had the English Channel been effectively barred to shipping, and the Thames itself been similarly closed with intensified minelaying and destroyer operations, then Britain's most important city, her capital, centre of commerce and government and by far the largest port, London itself, would have come to a complete stop, with serious effects on the economy of the nation as a whole and grave repercussions for the largest concentration of population and main centre of every facet of the nation's life: all were ultimately dependent on these supplies, and freight traffic by rail simply could not cope with a similar volume of traffic.

By their very accuracy, and the extent of their sinkings, the Stukas *did*, in fact, achieve this aim before their campaign was called off and the dive-bombers switched to different targets for the first stage of the German pre-invasion attacks on the RAF's airfields and radar stations. They forced the British to move the destroyer flotilla based at Dover elsewhere, out of the immediate area of the planned German landings, thus adding several vital hours' steaming to their anti-invasion inter-diction task. This is not to be lightly dismissed, for, had the rest of the *Luftwaffe* prevailed over the RAF, it was upon the destroyers, first and foremost, that the ultimate protection against invasion would have rested and Churchill's stated aim of 'drowning most of them at sea' would have relied.

Again, although it is true, as *Generalmajor* Dietrich Peltz stated later, that even in perfect weather conditions the dive-bombers would not have been able to prevent the Royal Navy from getting at least part of its forces through to strike at the invasion convoys,[9] there is equally little doubt that the destroyer casualties in any such encounter would have been severe, and that, in such an event, although the German invasion ships might have been smashed or turned back, the effect of such heavy destroyer losses on the outcome of the Battle of the Atlantic would have been catastrophic and Britain's end thereby achieved by starvation, if not occupation.

The destroyers based in the 'hottest' place were those of the 4th Flotilla at Dover. Of the nine destroyers which had formed its full complement in May, two had already fallen victims to the Ju 87s at Dunkirk, the flotilla leader *Keith* and the *Basilisk*. Their places were taken by the *Codrington* and the old *Walpole*, and so the flotilla was back at full strength by June, but by the end of July only one ship of those nine was left intact!

First to feel the effect of the Stuka's accuracy were the *Boadicea* and *Bulldog*. On 10 June, they had been sent across to the French coast to silence a troublesome artillery battery. They steamed straight into a hornets' nest. Their experience demonstrated that the Admiralty had learnt little or nothing from the lessons of Norway and Dunkirk on the vulnerability of destroyers to dive-bombing, as their subsequent battle reports show.

The two destroyers were working close inshore, in position 49°53'N, 00°28'E, steering on course 237° at a speed of 18 knots. The weather was cloudy with blue sky and some haze.[10] *Boadicea* led her sister by about half a mile and they were just about to commence their shore bombardment when the former ship sighted 'nine Junkers aircraft, type 87' approaching from landward behind clouds.

> When first sighted they were almost immediately overhead, crossing from port to starboard. The formation split by a form of corkscrew movement and the attack was made by a flight of three, singly, in quick succession by dive-bombing. The centre aeroplane of the flight of three attacking amidships, the two wing aeroplanes for'ard and the after ends of the ship.[11]

From *Bulldog* warning was received even later than this, for, after the first three Stukas had commenced their dives upon *Boadicea*, 'a formation of six aircraft was sighted almost directly overhead. One of the aircraft appeared to fire a signal, which was probably a dispersal [*sic*] signal.' The Ju 87s immediately went into their attack dives.

> Black crosses were easily discernible on the underside wing surfaces of the aircraft. Both ships immediately opened fire. At the same time another formation of three aircraft was sighted steering on an opposite course to the first formation. These planes broke formation and dived, six planes attacking *Bulldog* and three *Boadicea*.

Both ships increased speed to 28 knots, but the planes were already upon them. The effectiveness of their anti-aircraft fire is apparent from their comments. *Bulldog*'s CO stated that: '4.7 barrage was not possible due to the angle of sight. 3-inch HA opened fire with short barrage, number of rounds fired, seven. Pom-poms fired 50 rounds.' *Boadicea* got off fifteen ineffectual rounds from her 4.7-inch guns using a barrage fuse 'to intimidate the aircraft'. In this she failed. Her single pom-pom managed to get off 45 rounds of 2-pounder shells, equally without effect.

Both ships were hit three times each in this attack. *Boadicea* had fifteen bombs aimed at her; she survived solely due to the fact that it was three of the small 110 lb bombs that actually struck her and not the main 550 lb. Even so, one of these smaller missiles penetrated her upper deck and severed her main exhaust pipe, and, on passing out through her thin hull on the port side, just above the waterline, the bomb burst. One other bomb failed to explode and was recovered and sent to HMS *Vernon*, the Navy mine and explosive school at

Portsmouth, for examination. *Bulldog* counted twelve bombs, of which, again, three hit, these going through into the engine room and after boiler room, causing considerable damage. Crippled, both ships limped back to base. The captain of the *Bulldog* summed up his experience of dive-bombing thus: 'A successful attack carried out at lightning speed, previous information probably having been given from the coast.'

If fast-moving, agile destroyers, with heavy gun armaments (albeit having only 40-degree elevation) could be hit so easily, what then of the fate of the slow, virtually unarmed little steamers and coasters that each day panted their way up and down the English Channel with the coal, munitions and other life-blood of London in their grimy holds? Denied even the opportunity to hit back, or the speed with which to dodge, it took men with the special courage and fortitude that British merchant seamen were renowned for in those distant days, to continue their prosaic duties in the circumstance which developed from June through to November 1940 in that narrow stretch of water. One of the first mercantile losses in this battle was the SS *Aeneas*, and we can gain a first-hand picture of what a Stuka attack was like from the receiving end from the interview given by her master, Captain David Evans, after the event.

The *Aeneas* was part of the ill-fated convoy OA168, a coastal convoy of larger vessels which had entered the Channel on its way out and which had been located by *Luftwaffe* patrols off Portland. StG 2 deployed its whole strength against this important convoy, and the results created a furore between Churchill, the Admiralty and the Air Ministry, which had unilaterally declared that 'the duty of Fighter Command was the defence of the United Kingdom, not shipping protection'. The results were significant. In total, the Ju 87s scored hits that sank four large merchant ships (16,000 tons) and badly damaged nine others (40,000 tons). They also sank one of the Navy's principal anti-aircraft ships, the *Foylebank*, which, although powerfully armed against air attack with four twin 4-inch, two quadruple pom-poms and four of the brand-new Oerlikon 20 mm cannon, was hit and sunk in Portland Harbour. The whole attack only cost StG 2 one aircraft.

> We were bound from London to Glasgow with a general cargo of 5,000 tons [said Captain Evans afterwards]. We were armed with a 4.7-inch, a 12-pounder and a Lewis gun. The number of the crew, including myself, was 109 and we also had aboard the Vice-Commodore of the convoy, Captain Roberts, three naval ratings and one Lewis gunner.

Already damaged in one attack, the *Aeneas* was steaming at 7 knots at 1630 when the Stukas arrived again, unheralded.

The attack came from right overhead. The plane seemed to start at about 3,000 feet and dived almost vertically, and from photographs shown to me I think I can almost certainly identify the machine as a Junkers Ju 87. The first bomb dropped ahead of the port side and made a hole about 6 inches in diameter amidships, but it dropped back into the sea. The explosion shook the vessel considerably and set her on fire.

The second bomb fell abaft the funnel. She took a list of about 25 degrees to starboard. He dropped another bomb about 100 yards away on the starboard beam.

Yet a third attack followed, resulting only a near miss, but the damage had already been done.

I could see that now they were definitely intending to get us, so I immediately put all confidential books in a weighted bag and threw it overboard. There were several wounded on deck: I gave the order for the boats to be got ready and we put the wounded in the starboard boats. While getting the port boats ready the plane made another attack but the bombs missed us.

I was not at all worried about the ship capsizing, although she kept going over, but the Vice-Commodore said we must abandon ship. The steam pipe had burst, and, although I realised we could not do anything, I did not like leaving the vessel. They were all in the boats and kept calling for me to leave, but I said I was going to have another try to find the missing men. I again went all over the ship, listening mainly for groans, but I could hear nothing at all and I felt satisfied that there could not possibly be anyone left alive. I then left the ship.

Our escort, the [destroyer] *Witherington*, convoyed the ships a little while before coming back for us, and as the small boat we were in was damaged by the last attack, he picked us up first. After getting aboard the *Witherington*, we saw a man on the *Aeneas* waving his arms. It turned out to be the steward. The *Witherington* sent over a boat to bring him back. The crew had another look round the *Aeneas* but could find no one else. We returned to Plymouth that night. I did not see my ship sink.[12]

All told, three crew members were killed in the bombing and nine injured, while eighteen more were drowned when she sank. Thus passed one ship victim. It was to be a story that was to be repeated many times over the next few weeks in these waters. The other ships lost from this particular convoy were the *Britsum*, *Dallas City*, *Deucalion* and *Kolga*. The ripples of anger at this action were more widespread. The Navy stopped at once all routeing of Atlantic convoys through the

Channel; only local coasting convoys remained active for the time being. Premier Churchill, outraged that such a massacre could take place under the very noses of this much-vaunted Air Force, insisted that Dowding provide six-plane escorts for future convoys. The Stuka pilots were happy to have got in their first blow so effectively.

In order to draw further RAF fighter aircraft into battle, yet more Stuka sorties were mounted in the days that followed, but Dowding refused the bait. Targets afloat were sparse for the dive-bombers on the 7th, so they attacked static gun positions on the Isle of Wight. On the 9th the Stukas sank the coaster *Kenneth Hawksfield* off Sandwich, Kent. A larger effort was mounted on the 10th, in which the twin-engined Ju 88s also participated for raids on Falmouth and Swansea. But on the 11th it was the turn of the Ju 87s once more.

Strong Stuka attacks were mounted by StG 2 and StG 77 against Portland on this day, and a convoy was again hard hit at 0700 that morning, despite interception attempts by RAF fighters. The German dive-bomber pilots were still learning at this stage of the war, and Helmut Mahlke described to me the state of the art as it was at this point:

> We always tried to dive right against the head-wind, taking the wind-drift after bomb-release into account by two or three or less degrees in our sight (*Reflex-Vizier*). This brought out another problem for us. We never knew the exact wind direction over the sea in our delivery altitude. When the wind direction fluctuated at the various altitudes (the normal conditions met at sea), the aircraft heading against the wind had to turn slightly during the dive against the (turning) wind. Before release of bombs you had to keep the aircraft definitely on the sight line – otherwise the bomb would fail – following the tangents of your turn.
>
> This was our situation on 11 July about noon, when we attacked a ship off the English coast. Just short of our delivery altitude the wind came from quite another direction; we had to turn into the target and delivered our attack while so doing, all our bombs thereby missing their targets. We were rather discouraged by this, but we set to work out new tactics to ensure that this did not happen again.[13]

Their only victim was the patrol ship *Warrior II*, which was sunk.

Just what new anti-ship measures the Stuka pilots adopted are again spelt out by Helmut Mahlke, thus:

> We found a solution, at least against merchant vessels, or warships with poor AA armaments, which was used by our III/StG 1 from that time on.

Disregarding the wind direction, we attacked in a steep dive (70 degrees to 90 degrees) far behind the ship, heading along the ship's course. At about 1,500 feet altitude, we pulled up to 40–45 degrees, taking the ship's stern into our sight. Strafing with our two fixed wing machine-guns any of the ship's AA guns to intimidate the gunners and make them take cover, we followed through. Pulling out further, and still shooting along the ship's deck, we continued until the forward AA position and a further pull-up was necessitated due to the ship's mast. When the first of our machine-gun bullets were observed to be hitting the water in front of the ship's bow, we pulled the bomb-release switch, thus being definitely sure that the bombs would strike the ship just behind the bridge, in a position where they would not bounce off the deck, but be held by the superstructure and penetrate the ship's vitals.

Released at such a low altitude, the ignition of our bombs had to be delayed 2–4 seconds after impact. That is why numbers two and three aircraft of each *Kette* had to follow-up very close to number 1, which they succeeded in doing without exception. The bomb load per aircraft for such attacks was one 500 kg plus four 50 kg demolition bombs. There was very little chance for a merchant ship of any size attacked with this Stuka tactic. Most of them were broken in half by the explosion and sank immediately. Stuka crews, especially number 3 crews, had to have good nerves, because the bomb of number 1 could explode immediately beneath them. But we soon realised that our estimates had been correct and wreckage from the exploding ships would not reach them due to wind resistance.

Thus prepared, the Ju 87s returned to the assault on the coastal convoys, and ship losses now began to mount alarmingly. On the 13th, StG 1 hit a convoy off Dover, and next day IV (Stuka) LG 1 caught another off Eastbourne, sinking the *Betswood* and *Bovey Tracey*. On the 18th, Stuka sorties found that the Channel was clear of targets; the only ships that ventured out on its almost-empty waters that day were the anti-submarine patrol drifters and trawlers, and these were heavily punished that day.

On the 19th came a major attack on Dover harbour itself, and next day the Stukas found the coastal convoy codenamed 'Bossum' 10 miles off the same port. II/StG 1, led by *Hauptmann* Anton Keil, who had earlier distinguished himself with III/StG 51 during the French campaign, was intercepted by RAF eight-gun fighters, which, in turn, were driven off by the German fighter escorts. The Ju 87s then hit and sank the collier *Pulborough I* and damaged several others. They also inflicted further casualties upon the 4th Destroyer Flotilla: the *Beagle* was near-missed and damaged by bomb splinters, while the *Brazen* was more heavily hit and badly damaged, finally sinking in two halves the next morning. This left five!

Dover was hit again on the 20th, but the climax came five days later when Convoy CW8 attempted to run the gauntlet. Twenty-one coasters were sighted off Deal, Kent, that afternoon. StG 3 and StG 1 were unleashed by Fink, together with thirty Ju 88s of KG 4 against this concentration of vessels. The carnage was widespread. Five ships were sunk outright, *Ajax, Coquetdale, Empire Crusader, Henry Moon* and *Summity*, and another six badly damaged. E-boats sank three more that following night. Half the convoy had been wiped out at a cost of only two Ju 87s. Next day two of the 4th Flotilla destroyers were attacked, and *Brilliant* took two direct hits aft, which, fortunately for her, failed to explode, even though they pierced her quarterdeck. Another destroyer, *Boreas*, was also hit twice in her bridge structure, which was demolished, and she had fifty men killed and wounded, a third of her complement. These two destroyers steered back to the haven of Dover out of the fight for quite a while. And then there were three!

The remain trio of the flotilla based at Dover did not long survive their sisters. Two massive Stuka strikes were made on that port on 27 July, but a new form of attack, by Me 110s fitted to carry bombs and attacking under the radar at near sea-level, caught the defences off guard. The flotilla leader *Codrington* was near-missed by one of the latter, and the water-hammer effect as she was moored alongside her depot ship, the *Sandhurst*, broke her back. She was later beached but never repaired. The *Walpole*, also secured alongside, was also heavily hit, damaged and had to be towed away to Chatham for repairs. And then there was one!

During the same day the Stukas also savaged convoy 'Bacon', which I/StG 77 found off Swanage. On the 29th, yet another mass Stuka strike mounted by six *Staffeln* from IV (Stuka) LG1 and II/StG 1, four dozen Ju 87s in total, again reinforced by the Me 110 bombers, completed the rout, sinking the patrol ship *Gulzar* and another destroyer, *Delight*, off Portland, with one direct hit and one near-miss.

At this latest blow the Admiralty had to forbid the use of destroyers at all in the narrowest part of the Channel during daylight hours. This was no mean achievement by the German dive-bombers, after only a few days' action. Their very success, indeed, tended to deprive them of further targets for a while, and there was a short lull in activity for several days while both parties regrouped. Respite for the ships came with the opening *Adlertag*, with the Stukas being switched from the tactical role for which they had been designed to a strategic role, for which they were not equipped. Thus the Ju 87s were grossly misused, and, thrown in against top-class fighter opposition with radar warning of their approach, it is little wonder that their hitherto relative immunity received a heavy blow.

Notes

1. Bryant, Arthur, *The turn of the Tide 1939–43*, based on the Diaries of Viscount Alanbrook, KG, OM (Collins, 1957).
2. Harrington, Captain T.W., DSC, RN, to the Author, 29 June and 29 July 1977.
3. Letter from Beaverbrook to Sinclair, dated 28 May 1942 (National Archives, Kew, London, AIR 19/233).
4. Taylor, A.J.P., *Beaverbrook* (Hamish Hamilton, 1872). See also Memo, DO (41) – 10, dated 2.9.41 'But, although it may be true that dive-bombers were ordered at the request of the Secretary of State for War, it does not follow that the Air Ministry opposed that order. My impression is that it was decided to take note of Lord Beaverbrook's letter and that no reply was sent – for the Air Ministry did not want the dive-bomber.'
5. Memorandum from Wing Commander (Ops), dated 6 August 1949 (National Archives, Kew, London, AIR 14/672/IIH/241/3/3).
6. *Ibid.*
7. Cumbat, *Generale* B.A. Antonio, to the Author, 9 May 1977.
8. Roskill, Captain S.W., *The War at Sea, Vol. 1* (HMSO, London, 1954).
9. Price, Alfred, *Could Sealion have Succeeded?* Article in *The Battle of Britain* (New English Library, 1977).
10. The fact that conditions were cloudy may have led the ships to imagine that dive-bombing could not be carried out, it being put about by the Air Ministry pundits that an essential requirement for this type of attack was '... almost cloud-free skies up to 8,000 feet'. Unfortunately, the Stuka pilots apparently had not read the RAF memo. On the attack itself see – *Secret Report of damage in action to HMS Bulldog*, dated 11 June 1949 (National Archives, Kew, London, AIR 2/4221).
11. *Ibid.*
12. *Confidential Report of an Interview with Captain David L. Evans, Master of SS Aeneas*, dated 5 July 1940, Shipping Casualties Section – Trade Division, Admiralty (National Archives, Kew, London, AIR2/4221).
13. Mahlke, *Generalleutnant*, to the Author, op. cit.

CHAPTER SEVEN

'Severe and brilliantly executed'

After suffering high losses in the opening stages of the Battle of Britain, the Stukas were rested and re-grouped in readiness for their tactical role, which was expected to follow for them shortly, with the planned invasion. Accordingly, the Ju 87s were moved north to the Pas-de-Calais area behind the 16th Army, and discussions began with the commanders of the leading infantry and tank units which were to carry out the landings, on how best to co-ordinate the dive-bombers once the troops got ashore on *Der Tag*.

For Operation Sealion, it was decided that the Stukas should concentrate their efforts in supporting the Army around Dover, Folkestone and Sandgate, two complete *Geschwader* being allocated for this. At the same meeting, held on 13 September, a specially equipped *Staffel* was decided upon whose mission was to destroy the suspected nests of heavy gun batteries located at Dungeness. Two further *Gruppen* were allocated for the support of VII Corps, while I/StG 3 was to be held in Brittany in reserve for opportune use should the troops ashore need to call for further assistance.

RAF fighters would obviously prove the most formidable hazard, but the British anti-aircraft guns were held in contempt by the much more lavishly equipped Germans, and it had already been shown that, despite expressed opinions to the contrary, anti-aircraft fire had little effect in stopping a determined dive-bomber, once it was committed to its final dive. Anyway, the scale of Britain's AA defences at this period of the war was little more than pathetic. Helmut Mahlke recalls a case in point that had taken place earlier, during the Battle of Britain:

On 16 August III/StG 1 attacked, with two squadrons of seven and nine aircraft respectively, the air base of Lee-on-Solent, and with the other squadron of eight Stukas, led by *Oberleutnant* Skambraks, the radar station at Ventnor. We suffered zero losses in these attacks and we felt that this was due to our decision to return, after dropping our bombs, at the lowest possible level across the Isle of Wight, and that this had surprised the AA defence. In fact, the

88

only flak we encountered at all came from a small vessel north of the Isle of Wight, and this was promptly stopped by one of our Ju 87s, the pilot of which had forgotten to unlock his bomb-release during the main attack![1]

The new dispositions of the Stuka *Gruppen* had not gone unnoticed by the British Army commanders charged with defending their homeland from the expected invasion, with precious little resources. They did not, therefore, join in the premature rejoicing and the RAF's euphoria at the sudden 'demise' of the dive-bomber that was claimed after a few days' air fighting. These men were realists, looked beyond the ridiculous newspaper figures and Churchill's wild claims in Parliament, and they had no illusions as to the dive-bomber's ability to affect the issue should the German Army establish itself ashore.

Thus General Brooke recorded in his diary on 7 September: 'All reports look like invasion getting nearer. Ships collecting, dive-bombers being concentrated, parachutists captured ....'[2]

Meanwhile, behind the scenes a bitter argument was raging over the RAF's interpretation of the Army's close-support aircraft requirement. General Ironside recorded his almost daily struggles to convince the Air Ministry that his request for such an aircraft was both justified by recent events and urgent. The Air Ministry conceded neither point. Moore-Brabazon, with the support of Hore Belisha, urged the Air Ministry to design, and produce in quantity, large numbers of small attack dive-bombers to work with the ground forces, pressed out of steel, powered with the Gypsy engine and mass-produced in Canadian factories, but this was given very short shrift by the RAF hierarchy.

The Vice-Chief of the Air Staff (VCAS) later wrote to the Secretary of State and the CAS, giving the official RAF distaste for any such attempt to produce a British dive-bomber 'via the back door'. He wrote: 'We must take a strong line and refuse to allow the time of the Air Staff to be frittered away in the writing of carefully argued Staff papers on this project.'[3] He went on: 'If the close-support question is raised by the Army, I think we must go straight to the Prime Minister on the question of the fundamental strategical principle.'

In other words, never mind the impending invasion, everything must be subordinated to the heavy bomber which would win the war unaided; that same old line again. Others did not agree; one of them was Beaverbrook, who, his biographer records:

... had no faith that independent, or, as it was called, strategical bombing, could win the war by itself. This faith was uncritically held at the Air Ministry, and it provided the underlying reason for the ceaseless carping which flowed from the Air Marshals.[4]

But Churchill himself, at this period, was bedazzled by the vision of German cities reduced to ruins, and whatever dive-bomber policy remained would have depended totally on the promises of the American companies to deliver the goods soon. The first USA-built dive-bombers were still not expected until January 1941 at the earliest. It was, perhaps, doubly fortunate, then, that, with the failure of the *Luftwaffe's* strategic offensive in the summer and autumn of 1940, its hitherto faultless tactical methods were not put to the test against the British. Luckily for the British, *Seeloewe* turned out to be a dead duck.

With the abandonment of the invasion of England and with the much more palatable final reckoning with his nominal ally, but hated ideological foe, the Soviet Union, already replacing it as the main priority in Hitler's mind, the Stukas' future employment lay in the south and the east of mainland Europe. But the crank-wing shape of the Ju 87 had not yet totally vanished from the skies over southern Britain in 1940. With the new policy of blockade replacing invasion, it was decided to use the opportunity to update the anti-shipping data they had compiled, by launching a series of selective dive-bombing attacks in the Thames area, before the Stukas finally moved off to the new combat zones in the spring. Helmut Mahlke's III/StG 1, having a large number of former naval personnel on its strength and a good record behind it in this form of warfare, was selected as one of the main vehicles for these experiments in early November 1940.

Their targets were the much larger ships of convoys *en route* to and from the London Docks, for the wide Thames Estuary was well within the range of both the Stukas and their fighter escorts. Attacks of this nature took place on 1, 8 and 11 November, and were quite successful. No Ju 87 was lost in any of these first three attacks, and they scored damaging hits on seven merchant ships, *Letchworth, Catford, Fireglow, Ewell, Colonel Crompton, Corduff* and *Corsea*. Before they finally left for warmer climes, one more such attack was launched. The dive-bombers on this occasion were intercepted by RAF fighters in some strength, and wild claims of enormous losses were made in the Press and touted about for many years later by historians. Helmut Mahlke, who was there, recalls what really took place:

> We were escorted by two fighter wings on each of these missions, and these were the biggest air battles I had experienced during the entire war, and we were pleased, and surprised, at our low casualty rate. As you know, some of the German Stuka groups had much heavier losses during the Battle of Britain.
>
> We thought at the time that our immunity was due to our (individual) solution to the main problem of all such dive-bomber operations, which we found worked very well. The problem was,

how to abbreviate the phase of maximum vulnerability of the dive-bomber after the dive and attack, until the formation could re-group once more, for mutual fire-support.

In the Battle of Britain phase the Stukas flew as single aircraft in a more or less large area where it was impossible for our fighters to protect all of them individually. Therefore our standard orders for our pilots were to close up to the group commander and squadron leaders as quickly as possible. But this order was more easily given than carried out, as you can imagine.

If and when the targets were spread over a broad area, as with the elongated convoys in the Thames, the group approached in close formation, well protected by our own fighter escort. We then split into small formations of three aircraft for attacks on the biggest ships of these long convoys. This made for a long haul to rejoin the section leaders and to make out who was who. With junior pilots, the tendency was for them to assume the commander was well ahead and use their maximum power to close, making it impossible to get all our aircraft together again.

We had given much thought to this problem, without any practical solution. Finally, we got the message from HQ that formation leaders should no longer fly in front of their groups (due to heavy leader losses) but direct the formation from a position in the middle of it. This gave us the key for the solution of our problem. We knew this order could not be carried out by Stuka formations, because we had to keep radio silence (save in an emergency) in order not to draw enemy fighters onto our formation earlier than was unavoidable. This meant that, for Stukas, the leader *had* to be in front to keep control. But, to make certain all pilots knew where to find their group commanders, especially in the reassembly period, we gave the order in our group to paint both the legs of the landing-gear of these commanders yellow, which could be picked out at long range. Squadron commanders painted just one landing-leg yellow.

Our orders then read that whoever overtook an aircraft with yellow-coloured gear during the reassembly period would be punished, and this worked very well.

It was also during these missions that we adopted the scheme whereby I, as *Gruppe* commander, flew at very slow speed in serpentine lines, like a snake, the other aircraft coming up to me so quickly that they had to slow down in case they overshot. Then all went home at the lowest level in what we called *Sauhaufen* formation, which meant in gaggle or close mass, but not in any set order other than bunched tight together at very slow speed.

When an enemy fighter approached, he would normally head onto one of the last or outer aircraft of this mass. The Stuka pilot involved would then change his position at maximum power to bring himself into the middle or front of the group, ensuring that, should the fighter follow him in, then he would have to face the maximum defensive fire from all the group. Although the Ju 87 had only two fixed machine-guns and one swivel gun, the fighters, we found, did not like to have large numbers of these close astern of their own aircraft, and, in almost every case, they broke off and made another approach. This helped a lot.

Then came the final mission, on 14 November.

'The last mission in this area', recalled Mahlke, 'was bound to become a fiasco because of the kind of mission order we were given.'

When the Ju 87s arrived over the Thames they duly found the sea empty of ships, but the skies full of RAF fighters. 'Our escorting fighters were with us and saw us all the time, but since there were no ship targets we received the order from *them* to attack an alternative target, the wireless station at Dover.'

This order, however, was not to the liking of the German fighters themselves, which prudently stayed well outside the flak zone of the Dover defences, and thus left the Stukas to fend for themselves.

That is why they were not on hand when the RAF fighters attacked us instead of the British AA guns. I think there were quite a lot of RAF fighters in the sky in this battle; at any rate, our Stukas were greatly outnumbered (I had nineteen Stukas on this mission, the average for all these November attacks being between eighteen and twenty-one Stukas per mission). However, *we did not lose more than two Ju 87s* in the area of Dover, and the crew of one of these, *Oberleutnant* Blumers was the pilot, were rescued and made POWs. Most of my aircraft were, however, damaged, but all managed to get home.

Some two or three of these had to make forced landings in France near the coast. All the others succeeded in landing on our home airfield, despite a hell of a lot of hits (the maximum on one Stuka that day was eighty-two holes). Only one Ju 87 returned without a single hit, *Oberleutnant* Schairer, who managed to outmanoeuvre many fighter attacks.

All our aircraft, except the two shot down over Dover, were combat-ready again in a few days.

Mahlke added that:

I think this incident is evidence of the good quality of the Ju 87 to take punishment, as well as evidence of poor leadership of our higher authorities. They knew a lot about fighter tactics and fighter missions, but less, or far too little, about Stuka operations. I think this was the first time a Stuka unit had been given its operational orders by a fighter commander, and it was a failure, for this CO was court-martialled the next day.[5]

Back in Britain the Royal Navy's No. 801 Squadron also spent the winter in action, dive-bombing whatever targets presented themselves, but still operating under the uncomprehending orders of RAF Coastal Command over the Channel, and then transferring north to Hatston or the aircraft-carrier *Furious*, for strikes against targets in Norway. Like the German Stuka pilots, they soon found that their new bosses had little or no understanding of dive-bomber missions and work, as Captain Harrington recalled:

Whilst on the subject of dive-bombing techniques I have two incidents, which illustrate some of these points. At RAF St Evel, while waiting to have a go at the famous 'Salmon' and 'Gluck' pair of battle-cruisers, then holed up in Brest harbour, we were briefed to go in and attack them using 500 lb SAP bombs (one per aircraft and maximum load). The conditions were very cloudy (cumulus) and it looked as though we should be lucky if we could even *see* them from above 7,000 to 10,000 feet.

It was pointed out that we needed to make a dive attack from a minimum height of 15,000 feet, with a dive angle of at least 70 degrees, and release these weapons at 7,000 feet. This was in order to achieve the right terminal velocity with this bomb in order to penetrate the targets' protective armour. [*Scharnhorst* and *Gneisenau* had a maximum of 3-inch deck armour, with 4-inch-thick sloping armour over magazines.] An emotive hush greeted this technical dissertation! The RAF group captain was, for some reason, furious, and seemed to think it was a lot of technical nonsense – anyway our minimum figures were confirmed by Plymouth Naval Operations.

Our CO, Ian Sarel, and a few of the old hands, volunteered to have a go in the hope that there might be some holes in the clouds, but this was turned down.

The opposite end of this story was an occasion when there was an invasion scare and panic, and we were told by the local RAF command to carry out low-level attacks on a group of enemy transports, alleged to be making for the UK coast. The orders were to carry a 250 lb GP [general-purpose] bomb with an instantaneous fuse and attack at 100 feet! It would not take even a half-headed guy long to work out that such a trip would be a one-way one. When we suggested delayed fuses would be better, and thus avoid destroying ourselves as well as the enemy, much surprise was registered![6]

This fuzziness was reflected throughout the RAF. One of the more bizarre experiments it carried out at this time was the evaluation of dive-bombing trials with heavy bombers. Flying Officer I.G.O. Fenton's report details the first experiment, in which a Wellington was used to ascertain dive-bombing accuracy in such an aircraft with a bomb release height of 8,000 feet. He carried out a few practice runs himself and then tried to instruct a fresh pilot; Sergeant Pilot Milstead of the Reserve Training Flight was the candidate.

In six trials, hampered by poor weather, results varied wildly, Milstead's first attacks having an average error of 350 yards; his third (on 10 November 1940), in which he dived from 5,000 to 3,000 feet, scored one hit in the first stick and three direct hits in the second. Fenton's best average was 31 yards on his second attempt (29 October). Both crews reported no ill effects due to diving, and Milstead felt confident he could improve his results with more practice. The trials continued with both Wellingtons and Hampdens.[7]

At the same time, the Royal Aircraft Establishment at South Farnborough made a detailed report on the methods employed by the German dive-bombers (Ju 87s and Ju 88s) compared with those *proposed* for a British system.[8] In the main, not surprisingly, the German system was found to be superior. As a result, a meeting was held in Room 5002 of Thames House South to discuss further the development of the German method of dive-bombing with automatic pull-out and automatic bomb-release. This meeting took place on 14 December 1940, its purpose being given as, '... the trial of the German method in lieu of the system now in development at RAE which is based on the gyroscope, with a view to its eventual adoption, if it should prove satisfactory in any aircraft in which dive-bombing will be an operational requirement.'[9]

One would have thought that, in German hands, the German system would have been proved satisfactory enough during the previous twelve months to please any critic!

The work involved the provision of a contacting altimeter, some modification to the standard bomb-release control box, aerodynamic work in relation to the chosen aircraft, including possible wind-tunnel tests, design of the servo motor for operation of the trimming tab, installation of the whole in an aircraft and flight and bombing trials.

The method 'demands an aeroplane which can dive at approximately a constant speed at an angle in the region of from 40 degrees to 70 degrees from the horizontal'. After some discussion, the aircraft chosen to pioneer the British answer to the Ju 88 was ... the Fairey

Albacore! 'As dive-bombing is one of its operational duties, the Fleet Air Arm would be able to take immediate advantage of the method.' The Skua was not chosen, despite being a more advanced monoplane specially designed and built for the job, because 'it will soon be used for training purposes only'. The Chesapeake (the British name for the Vought Vindicator, or 156F), another dedicated monoplane dive-bomber inherited from French orders, was similarly rejected in favour of this wire-and-struts biplane. When somebody at the Air Ministry expressed incredulity at the choice of this obsolescent biplane of anti-quated design and limited performance for such a vital trial, it was stated in defence of the decision that the Albacore was 'of the same vintage as the Wellington, and therefore quite suitable'.[10]

All this did not bring any workable dive-bombers onto the strength of the RAF, of course, but it was probably not meant to. On 9 December 1940, the Air Minister (Sinclair) wrote to Beaverbrook with a further request, having somewhat changed his tune:

Invasion next Spring. The Army have been relying on me to re-equip their Lysander Squadrons with Brewsters [Bermuda] and Vultees [Vengeance]. We understood from your Ministry that these would begin to come in February. Now we hear that there is a delay in production and that they will not be here until May.

He went on:

It occurs to me that it is not impossible that these firms will be supplying the United States Army with the same types of aircraft. Do you think you could persuade the United States Government to let us have any machines of these types of which they may be taking delivery in January, February, March and April ....[11]

However, it was on the shop floor of these brand-new American factories that the delays were occurring, with huge expansion plans and orders and untrained operatives and incompetent management, all unable to cope with the demand. There would be no Brewsters or Vultees for *anyone*, for years yet. Meanwhile, the orders just kept piling up. Between September 1940 and June 1941 a further 1,850 dive-bombers were asked for.

*   *   *

While the British strove vainly in every direction to make up for two decades of blindness and neglect of dive-bombers, the Germans were busy shifting their highly efficient Stuka units to where they could do the most good, to bolster their failing and floundering Italian ally in the Mediterranean by driving out the Royal Navy.

One of the principal instruments of *Il Duce's* discomfiture and humiliation had been the aircraft-carrier HMS *Illustrious*, fitted with an armoured deck that was claimed to be capable of withstanding 500 lb bombs. She had launched her torpedo-bombers which had scored such a startling success against the Italian battle-fleet at the base of Taranto earlier, and was now roaming the eastern and central Mediterranean at will with Admiral Andrew Cunningham's battleships, penning the Italian fleet firmly to its harbours and immune from the attentions of the *Regia Aeronautica's* altitude pattern bombing. Not surprisingly, then, this one vessel became the number-one target for the Stukas of *Fliegerkorps* X under *General der Flieger* Geisler, the anti-shipping expert, *Oberst* Harlinghausen, his chief of staff, and the rest of the crack team, when they set up shop in Sicily toward the end of 1490. The Sicilian airfields of Catania and Comiso soon reverberated to the roar of Jumo engines as I/StG 1 and II/StG 2, under Major Enneccerus and *Hauptmann* Hozzel respectively, began an intensive training programme, dive-bombing a floating mock-up of the carrier moored off the coast.

Harlinghausen was convinced that, with his Stuka crews worked up to a fine pitch, they would achieve the four direct hits considered essential from all estimates to actually *sink* a carrier. On 10 January 1941, they got their chance. The Mediterranean Fleet was active again in the central basin, and entered the Sicilian Narrows to cover a convoy operation. They had no fear of the Italian Fleet or the high-flying SM79s of the Italian Air Force as they paraded off the Italian coast, for both had repeatedly shown themselves impotent. But it was known in Britain that the German dive-bombers were now in strength in Sicily, so why did they put their necks into the noose in this way?

Admiral Cunningham was a fearless officer, as his combat record amply demonstrated, but he was not foolhardy. The basic reason would seem to be that he had been convinced by his RAF advisers that the Stukas were a spent force after the Battle of Britain. They totally believed their own propaganda that many hundreds of Stukas had been destroyed, when the total was only fifty or so. Cunningham, being a professional sailor, would naturally enough accept another professional's opinion on such matters. Thus, when told by one senior RAF officer that Stukas were sitting ducks and that 'our fighter pilots weep for joy when they see them',[12] he would assume he was facing nothing he could not handle. He was not long in being disillusioned!

This classic dive-bombing attack has been described before, but here we will use the words of the men themselves on the receiving end from their official reports, words that therefore need no embellishment.[13] Using the lure of a torpedo-bomber feint by two SM79s to tempt the fleet's fighter cover down to sea level out of the way, the ships were left wide open to dive-bombing and dependent solely upon their own anti-aircraft guns. The two battleships, *Valiant* and *Warspite*, were heavily equipped in this respect and were able to throw up an imposing barrage. But to prevent them from so aiding *Illustrious*, a preliminary attack by a small force of Ju 87s was directed against them to engage the full attention of their host of guns. The bulk of the Stukas then went *en masse* for the *Illustrious*, dropping 1,000 lb armour-piercing bombs after a preliminary wave of 550 lb weapons had smothered the ship's own anti-aircraft defences. Each phase of the attack worked perfectly; only her unexpectedly tough armoured deck proved to be her salvation.

The two torpedo-bombers were first sighted visually at 1222 hours, coming in low, and were duly met by a barrage. They dropped their torpedoes at a range of 2,500 yards from the *Illustrious*, off her starboard beam, but these missiles were easily avoided. The SM79s were then chased away by the standing air patrol, but outdistanced the Fairey Fulmars. The *Illustrious* then came round to regain her station astern of *Warspite* at 1228 hours, and speed was increased to 18 knots. Meanwhile the fleet's radar had picked up a large group of aircraft at a range of 28 miles, approaching from the north. The Fighter Direction Officer immediately recalled the four Fulmars and made preparations to fly off four more at once. The carrier had to turn into the wind in order to do this at 1234 hours, but one minute later the Stukas were sighted visually: 'A large loose formation, estimated at 30–40, was sighted on the port bow flying at about 12,000 feet.'

At 1236 hours, long-range barrage fire was opened by the 4.5-inch gun batteries aboard the carrier, even though the Fulmars were powering down the flight deck to get airborne at the time; the last fighter clawed into the air at 1237, and the fleet altered course and adopted loose formation to prepare for air attack.

The oncoming aircraft consisted of two formations of Ju 87s with German markings, the report was to state. Fulmars that got close enough later reported that they were camouflaged black and grey mottling above, half black and half white below. As soon as the anti-aircraft fire became threatening, the formation split into two groups, one half of which worked round astern of the fleet, while the other half began their attacks.

It was difficult to count the numbers exactly, but the first formation consisted of fifteen and the second of twenty to thirty aircraft. They were in a very loose and flexible formation, constantly changing their relative positions, and split when engaged by long-range fire. It is estimated that the dive was started at about 12,000 feet and checked at 6,000 feet to 8,000 feet, before going into the aiming dive. Bomb release varied from about 1,500 feet in the first wave to 800 feet in later ones. Most aircraft continued to dive after releasing their bombs and flattened out low over the water, having crossed the flight deck. At least one aircraft machine-gunned the ship.

The attacks on *Illustrious* appeared to come in three main waves, in each of which two sub-flights of three carried out synchronised attacks from different bearings, the majority coming from astern and fine on each quarter. At any one moment there were about six aircraft in their dives requiring to be fired on. Time was hard to judge but each wave probably lasted for about one minute, the pause between waves being about thirty seconds. The average angle of dive was about 60 degrees although a few aircraft seemed to dive at about eight degrees. Each aircraft dropped one bomb – estimated size 1,000 lb. From inspection of the damage it is probable that the earlier bombs were fitted with direct action fuses with the intention of wiping out exposed personnel, while the later ones were armour piercing.

The Ju 87s scored no fewer than six direct hits and three near-misses in less than seven minutes in this attack, an outstanding achievement.

1. Hit on loading platform of P1 pom-pom, passing through and striking the ship's armoured side without exploding.
2. Went through the flight deck right forward on the port side, through the recreation space before exploding. It tore two large holes in the ship's side, starting fires and flooding the paint store and anchor gear store.
3. Burst on S2 pom-pom, killing the crew and most of S1 alongside, just missing the bridge.
4. Hit directly on the after lift and burst on the port side of the after lift well, wrecking the lift.
5. Hit on the starboard forward corner of the lift well, was deflected and burst at the after end.
6. Pierced the flight deck and burst on the hangar deck in which it made a large hole and caused a violent explosion in the wardroom flat. This bomb blew up the foremost lift, bulged the hangar deck forward, and the combined effect of this and No. 4 hit wrecked the hangar fire screens and set fire to 'C' hangar. Many casualties were caused in the hangar and the wardroom flat. Fires were started in the cabin flats on the upper decks.

While 1 and 2 caused only slight damage, 3 also destroyed the flight deck travelling crane, whose jib fell across S1 pom-pom, jamming it. No. 4 hit, beside wrecking the after lift and the Fulmar going down on

it, cut all power to the after 4.5-inch guns and wiped out their ammunition supply parties. The ensuing fire rendered both groups of main
guns untenable and halved her defences at a stroke. Nos 5 and 6
hits added to the extensive damage, but luckily no bomb penetrated
through as far as her engine rooms or she would have been lost.

As it was, although very badly wounded, *Illustrious* survived. Her
report continued: 'When this severe and brilliantly executed dive-
bombing attack was over, the ship was on fire fore and aft, the flight
deck wrecked and I decided to make for Malta at once ....'

She went on to do this, despite the extreme difficulties and further
attacks, but it was an equally brilliant achievement by the ship's company. But for the Mediterranean Fleet, the arrival of the dive-bomber
ended its easy dominance of the central Mediterranean and boded ill
for future operations by the British, whether by land or sea, in that
area.

The first attack on the carrier was by far and away the most powerful
single blow struck by dive-bombers against warships up to that date,
but subsequent assaults mounted against her as she struggled back to
Malta were handicapped by the fact that the special heavy bombs
designed to finish her off, now that her defences were down, were not
immediately available.

The Fulmar fighters, which eventually caught up with the retiring
Stukas, managed to get in only a few firing passes. Yellow Section
leader reported how:

> I noted some of these Ju 87s making away to the northward.
> Engaged one of these and saw it swerve, drop out of formation
> and continue down in a left-hand turn into the sea.

Another Fleet Air Arm pilot stated:

> Almost immediately after crossing the coast encountered about
> seven Ju 87s making away to the northward, having dropped their
> bombs. Attacked the left-hand aircraft of the formation, two others
> dropped behind and came in on my tail. On completing the first
> attack turned to attack one of the two who had dropped back.
> Registered large number of hits on his fuselage which caused his
> rear gunner to cease firing. Did not notice other damage. He
> continued away to northward.

The summary of the six defending Fulmars on their engagement with
the Stukas threw up the following points on their actual combat
methods:

> A single Ju 87, when attacked, will pull up the nose in order to
> allow the rear gunner a good downward shot. If attacked in

formation, two of the formation drop astern and use their front guns on attacking aircraft. A Fulmar should have no difficulty in catching or out-manoeuvring a Ju 87 [*sic*]. Being of metal construction, a Ju 87 will not burn like an Italian aircraft. Ju 87s appear to be well protected from stern attacks. Every effort should be made to carry out beam and quarter attacks.

Two certain kills were claimed by the fighter defenders, while the ship's guns claimed another three. Thus:

About 20 feet of the wing of a Ju 87 fell on the after lift. Aircraft assumed to have crashed. A Ju 87 was seen to fall into the sea by the Chaplain and another crashed into the sea just astern of one Swordfish on A/S patrol.[14]

Apart from the hits made on *Illustrious*, the first wave had managed to penetrate the battleship's barrage to score another hit on *Warspite*, but the 550 lb bomb bounced off her massive armour and failed to detonate. *Valiant* was near-missed, but her batteries claimed to have destroyed one Ju 87 at close-range, shooting it to pieces as it levelled-off alongside.

Then, at 1604, *Valiant's* radar picked up another formation, and five minutes later they were sighted and engaged by a controlled barrage. This raid comprised fifteen Ju 87s escorted by five Me 110s.

This attack was neither so well synchronised, nor so determined as that at 1240. The first wave of about six aircraft attacked from astern and both quarters and were well engaged; fire was continuous in spite of the difficulty of seeing targets to port owing to the smoke and haze from the fire in the hangar. Only two bombs fell near the ship. Three aircraft carried out an attack from the starboard beam at least a minute after the first wave; the last aircraft pressed home his attack well and scored a near miss abreast the funnel. The remaining six aircraft were seen retiring to the north-east at a considerable height, and two attempted to attack through clouds on the port beam, but, on being engaged, made off without dropping their bombs. Nine bombs were dropped, one hit the after lift (the seventh hit in all) causing casualties among those tending wounded and putting out fires. There were two very near misses; one starboard side caused damage aft and killed a number of wounded and those tending them on the quarterdeck.

By 1808, *Illustrious* had reached the entrance to the swept channel into Malta harbour, having survived another high-level attack. It was sunset. At 1922, two SM79s tried a night torpedo attack, without any success, and the crippled carrier finally berthed at Parlatorio Wharf at 2215, but her ordeal was by no means over.

Robbed of their prey by nightfall, the Stukas returned to the hunt the next day. They probed to the east of Malta in case the carrier was attempting to reach Egypt under the cloak of the previous night's darkness. They satisfied themselves she was not. But what Major Enneccerus and his unit did find was the cruiser squadron that had escorted her into Malta, now themselves hurrying eastwards. This force consisted of the two 10,000-ton cruisers *Gloucester* and *Southampton*, escorted by two destroyers, *Defender* and *Diamond*. For some reason, these ships appeared to be under the impression that they were safe and beyond the range of the Stukas. Neither vessel was fitted with radar and so they had no warning when a Heinkel He 111 led Enneccerus and his twelve Ju 87Rs to them. The long-range *Richards* had been widely reported in action off Norway the previous year, and *Southampton* herself had been in action there at that time, which makes this unpreparedness all the more inexplicable. Whatever the reason for their complacence, the dozen Stukas dived down on them out of the sun, catching all the ships totally unawares, and split their attacks between the two cruisers. *Gloucester* was hit by a 1,100 lb bomb, which penetrated her director control tower and wrecked her bridge, killing nine and wounding fourteen. Again, the bomb itself failed to detonate, or the carnage would have been far worse.

Southampton was less fortunate. Two hits were registered on this ship, one of which smashed through into her wardroom, the other penetrating her petty officers' mess. Both confined spaces were crowded with off-duty personnel relaxing in what they were confident was a safe zone. The resulting casualties among these key crew members were terrible and far-reaching. The fires spread to the engine room and got further and further out of control. At 1605 hours she slid to a halt, heavily ablaze, and later had to be sunk. She was the largest warship yet to be sunk by air attack alone, and her loss caused quite a stir for she was a modern ship, well equipped with AA weapons and deliberately built with smaller 6-inch guns in order to devote more allowance to armour protection, in order to withstand hits from 8-inch shells from enemy heavy cruisers. The Ju 87s suffered no losses whatsoever in achieving this particular milestone of dive-bomber history.

Once the damaged *Illustrious* had been located still inside Malta dockyard carrying out emergency repair work, the Stukas returned to the fray in a determined effort to destroy her once and for all. They now had the advantage that she was a static target, but the disadvantage that she was well protected by the island's AA defence and shore-based fighters. Despite this, the Stukas all but succeeded in their aim, but her luck held to the end. In making their massive and sustained assault, the dive-bombers of *Fliegerkorps X* caused widespread devastation to the dockyard and the adjacent airfields, but they also met with stiff aerial opposition, and their own losses of irreplaceable, highly trained aircrews were grievous.

On 16 January, two attacks were made, at 1440 and 1610 respectively. They hit *Illustrious* for the eighth time. The bomb passed through the after end of the flight deck and burst on the quarterdeck. Remarkably, no damage was done to the vital steering gear, but this further blow so weakened the stern of the ship that yet further work had to be carried out, and this deferred her sailing yet again. Also, during these attacks, 'overs' hit and badly damaged ships in adjacent berths, including the Australian light cruiser *Perth* and the merchant ship *Essex*.

On the 18th, the dive-bombers switched target to Hal Far and Luqua airfields in an attempt to eliminate fighter opposition. Some considerable damage was done, but ten Stukas were claimed shot down in reply. By that same evening *Illustrious* was almost patched up sufficiently enough to start her dash for safety, but two further heavy Stuka raids took place on the 19th, at 1015 and 1310 hours. About seventy bombs fell close to the ship, there being many near-misses, but no hits were made and again the Ju 87s were badly mauled, nineteen being claimed destroyed this day. Nevertheless, the carrier was badly shaken by those near-misses and took on a list to port.

Hozzel's I/StG 1 was now employing the special heavy bombs on these missions, which, if they had hit fair and square, would have probably finished the job for good, but this bomb load made the Stuka more cumbersome in the air, and losses were so high that the *Stukagruppen* had to pause to recoup, and while they did so *Illustrious* was finally able to slip away. She sailed to Alexandria and thence via the Suez Canal and the Cape to an American naval dockyard, where she lay for over a year undergoing extensive repairs.

Hitler had personally ordered her destruction, and he also instructed the Stukas to close the Sicilian Channel to the Royal Navy, and this, while never fully accomplished, as with the English Channel the previous summer, later severely restricted British operations. Not for more than two years were big ships risked inside that area, and the Royal Navy specified special areas around Malta for the small ships to try and keep clear of it they could. Outside these appropriately termed danger zones were safer waters, thought to be beyond the extreme range of the Ju 87. The Navy termed these areas 'Stuka Sanctuaries', but they were *not* outside the range of the twin-engined Ju 88s!

Notes

1. Mahlke, *Generalleutnant*, to the Author, op. cit.
2. Bryant, Arthur, *The Turn of the Tide*, op. cit.
3. Churchill, Winston S., *The Second World War*, Vol. 2 (Cassell, 1948).

4. Taylor, Beaverbrook, op. cit.

5. Mahlke, *Generalleutnant*, to the Author, op. cit.

6. Harrington, Captain T.W., to the Author, op. cit.

7. *Memo*, AOC No.1 Group, dated 13 November 1940, 1G/2016/6/Amt (National Archives, Kew, London, AIR 14/181/IIH/241/3/406).

8. *Reports on dive-bombing*, RAE South Farnborough, dated October 1940 (National Archives, Kew, London, AIR 14/181/IIH/241/3/406 and AIR 2/3176/Inst/3005/AAH/93). See also *Notes on Dive-bombing and on the German Ju 88 Bombing Aircraft*, Air Ministry, dated February 1941 (National Archives, Kew, London AIR 14/181/IIH, 241/3/406).

9. *Memorandum*, dated 14 November 1940 (National Archives, Kew, London, AIR14/181/IIH/241/3/406).

10. *Ibid.*

11. *Memorandum*, Air Minister to MAP, dated 9 December 1940 (National Archives, Kew, London, AIR 19/233).

12. Tedder, Lord, *With Prejudice* (Cassell, 1966).

13. *Report of Air Attacks on H.M.S.* Illustrious *on 10th January 1941, during Operation MC4*, dated 26 January 1941 (National Archives, Kew, London, AIR 2/4221/ 0404/427/172. No.3320/0197).

14. *Ibid.*

CHAPTER EIGHT

'This type accelerated very rapidly'

I t remained the German dive-bomber which continued to dominate events in the Mediterranean theatre throughout the rest of 1941, in the North African desert campaign, the overrunning of the Balkans, Greece and Yugoslavia, the airborne conquest of the island of Crete and against the Royal Navy during many hard-fought convoy battles. In addition to supporting the Italian Navy at sea, the Ju 87s and Ju 88s were able to assist the small German mobile armoured force sent to Libya, Rommel's *Afrika Korps*, during its battles against the British Eighth Army.

In the latter case, *Fliegerkorps Afrika* was set up, initially commanded by General Frohlich, and initially equipped with Ju 87s (*Trops*) of StG 2, about fifty of which were soon on hand. They quickly made their mark at sea as well as on land, with attacks on British and Commonwealth naval vessels operating off the North African coast and attempting to supply Malta. The destroyer *Dainty* was sunk by Ju 87s in Tobruk harbour on 24 February, while a rather larger victim was the old 15-inch-gunned monitor *Terror*, which was dive-bombed and sunk off the same port soon afterwards. Aid from the bombarding warships of the Royal Navy's Inshore Squadron was vital to the British Army, and in order to reinforce these first attacks against them, Mahlke's ship-busting III/StG 2 was also moved into the area. 'Since our group had originally been set up by the German Navy, we specialised in the Stuka attacks against ships at this time in the area Tobruk/Sollum, as well as other missions from our base at Derna, where we had two squadrons.'[1] III/StG 2 operated thus from 12 April to 8 May. One of their earliest missions took place on 18 April.

> The Army had asked for help, stating that a 'battleship' was shooting with very heavy guns at their positions. We duly flew off to the limit of our range and, just at the point-of-no-return, when I had to make my decision to turn back, I saw a rather big man-o'-war and attacked immediately. Owing to the severe haze, details of the ship could not be clearly made out until we were below

4,000 feet. The first flight hit the bow of the ship which went under the waves within seconds, when the second flight also attacked and hit her in the stern. The third and fourth flights returned with the bomb-loads intact, reporting that the ship was already under the water when they finished their dives. During our debriefing we had the problem of identification of our target. We knew, of course, it was not a battleship, but what kind was it? Finally, we decided to report it as a 'Warship, most probably Monitor or Coastal type' of about 8,000 tons.

Their victim was probably the old *Terror* built as long ago as 1916.

Both German and Italian Stuka units were now operating in the Western Desert to good effect, and the RAF was forced to issue an evaluation of their methods, which gives some insight into what the British *thought* their tactics were.[2]

In view of the reports that Italian pilots are being trained by German Instructors in dive-bombing and the following tactics are worthy of note. Aircraft usually approach the target at about 10,000 feet, steering an erratic course. On reaching a position approximately above the target, the aircraft operating individually, carry out a spiral dive at an inclination of 60 to 70 degrees. After making two or three turns, the aircraft straighten out at about 2,000 feet, releasing their bombs at approximately 1,500 feet. The aircraft then pull out of the dive and increase speed so as to be ahead of the bomb explosion.

Ju 87s attacking shipping in the Mediterranean have been endeavouring to evade attacks by Tomahawks by closing the throttle and using their air-brakes to make the fighter overshoot. The Ju 87 then does a stall turn towards the sea level, repeatedly, in order to avoid attacks from astern.

The first mission of the Italian dive-bombers mentioned took place on 2 September 1940, when they made an abortive search for a reported convoy near Malta. That convoy was actually located next day, and at 1425, five Ju 87s of 96° *Gruppo*, went into action against it with an escort of six Macchi 200 fighters. They claimed to have hit a cruiser, but in reality no hits were made. A second sortie with four Stukas made the same claim, and a third attack added yet another fictional cruiser, plus a carrier damaged, but, yet again, no hits at all were recorded on any ship of this convoy (Operation Hats).

On 5 September, five Italian-manned Ju 87s dive-bombed Malta, and further such sorties followed: on 17 September the *Gruppo* had its first losses when twelve of its aircraft attacked Mikabba airfield. They were intercepted by Hurricanes from No. 261 Squadron and lost Sergeant

Catani of 237 *Squadriglia*, who became a POW. On 11 November a second Italian dive-bomber unit, 97° *Gruppo*, was established at Comiso with 238 and 239 *Squadriglia*, first seeing action over Greece in attacks on Janina, Presba and Florina airfields on 5, 14 and 16 November. On 5 March 1941, a third Ju 87 outfit commissioned, 101° *Gruppo* with 208 and 209 *Squadriglia*, and began working on the Albanian front. In February 96° *Gruppo* transferred to Benghazi and then joined the Germans in raids on the Tobruk garrison.

During the brief Balkan campaign, Italian Stukas were joined by the *Luftwaffe*, with Hitler making the pertinent comment just before operations commenced that the British would not budge otherwise. 'Only when our dive-bombers and armoured corps appear will they get out of Greece as hastily as they have on every other occasion that we employed these means.'[3] These words proved themselves totally correct. Although the British commander, Wavell, was outwardly scornful of the dive-bomber, stating in a boastful report that, 'The effects of dive-bombers in Greece were on morale rather than material, and fighter defences would have prevented every success', he was soon begging permission from London to evacuate his troops out of Greece and away from them, exactly as the *Führer* had predicted.

His report listed some of the targets that Ju 87s had pulverised, '... ships in ports and at sea. Towns and villages, particularly at important road junctions, transport columns, railways, bridges, AA guns protecting aerodromes, headquarters, artillery, individual tanks or vehicles, troops and defences',[4] and he was thus completely confounded by his own rhetoric!

'Normally, not less than one squadron at a time was employed,' Wavell wrote regarding German Stuka methods and strengths during the Greek campaign, 'but numbers varied from a single machine or a few machines following one another in succession, usually on communications targets'. He added that, 'Dive-bombing is usually carried out on previously located targets after reconnaissance or in close cooperation with land operations. Enemy striking force obviously in close W/T communication with forward troops and own reconnaissance aircraft.'

The Greek Army, which had held out against the Italians all winter, was defeated within a few days, going the same way as the Yugoslavians, and the British beat a hasty retreat. There proved to be heavy loss of life to the complaisant Wavell's troops even once they had gained the 'safety' of the water, for the Ju 87s once more turned their attentions to the rescuing ships, sinking the merchantmen *Hellas*, *Pennland* and *Slamat* packed with troops, in addition to the troopship *Costa Rica*, and also sinking the escorting destroyers *Diamond* and *Wryneck*.

The story was repeated on the island of Crete, where, despite the fact that the British knew the exact details of the German plan, and vastly outnumbered the lightly armed paratroops, the difference was the Stuka. After the normal predatory softening up by the dive-bombers, the German airborne troops forced a landing at Maleme airfield, steadily enlarged this foothold and continued until, once more, the sea beckoned to the defenders. The whole Mediterranean Fleet was committed to rescuing the troops, and there followed a pitched battle with the Ju 87 dive-bombers, during which the Stukas emerged very much on top. The Royal Navy lost three cruisers and six destroyers sunk in this battle, with three battleships, the aircraft-carrier *Formidable* and numerous cruisers and destroyers all hit and damaged in varying degrees, as well as many merchant vessels. That appalling casualty list could have been even larger had not the Stukas been urgently required for the impending attack on the Soviet Union and had to be hastily pulled out and transferred north to Poland and Rumania in readiness.

Many of the troop casualties caused by the dive-bombers at Crete were brought about by a typical piece of Stuka improvisation, at which the *Luftwaffe* was good. In order to increase the killing power of their bombs against ground troops, which were not so effective in Greece because the rocky ground tended to vent their explosive force upward on detonation, the Stuka crews adopted a new fusing method to give their weapons a more lethal lateral spread against concentrations of soldiers. This device was later to be named the *Dinortstäbe*, after the commander of StG 2, which initiated the system during this campaign, as Friedrich Lang explained to me:

The *Dinortstäbe* were invented in the middle of May 1941 at the Molai airfield, where I/StG 2 was under *Kommodore Oberstleutnant* Dinort. They were supposed to detonate the bombs before they reached the ground and thus scatter their charge and explosives more effectively. The first trials were with 60 cm long willow sticks, which we screwed into the screw hole on the point of the 50 kg bombs. The trial area, marked with a white sheet, was a wheat field with some olive trees scattered in it. You could easily see the depth of the shallow crater, and the scatter effect around it, by the damage to the wheat.

The willow stick did not work out, as it broke off and did not detonate the bomb before impact. The next trial was done with even lengths of round metal rod. That, also, did not come up to expectations. The rod became embedded in the ground and the bomb detonated too late. We were successful with the third attempt. On the end of the metal rods we welded a metal disc 8 cm in diameter. The bomb now detonated at about 30 cm above the ground. The scatter effect was high, as expected. The rods were, at the beginning, made in our own workshop wagons, and first used when we attacked Crete. Later, they were made by industry under the name of *Zunderabstandstäbe*, or *Dinortstäbe*.[5]

As the final battered warships of the Royal Navy sailed away from Crete for the last time to Egypt, the Ju 87s of those units employed in the brief Balkan episode, I and III/StG 77 from Rumania, I and III/StG 2, I/StG 3 and the crack II (*Schlacht*) LG 2 from Bulgaria and II/StG 77 from Ostmark, prepared to shift base of operations, from the sun-drenched Greek islands up to the glowering Soviet border. But some remained behind: Mahlke's Ju 87s, for example, were still operating from the desert bases.

On 31 May, my group had a mission to attack ships south of Crete. We took off from Heraklion airfield at 0605 that morning, but all the British naval forces appeared to have withdrawn out of our range and we did not see any warships. Finally, at the extreme end of our range, we saw in the haze a big merchant ship. Dive attack! While diving through at about 4,000 feet I observed a Red Cross on top of the ship and I gave the order to all my aircraft: 'No bombs – hospital ship – level off', and we returned to base with all our bombs. I wondered at the time, and since, whether in fact this 'hospital ship' was not being used as a troop-carrier for the evacuation of Allied troops from Crete. However, she gave us no AA fire so she did not get any of our bombs. At least, I'm sure, her captain had a good drink when we disappeared without having bombed his ship![6]

After Crete, the remaining dive-bomber units left in the Mediterranean theatre were fully committed to supporting Rommel's thrust east to the Egyptian border that left Tobruk isolated and cut off. The supply and troop reinforcement of this garrison gave the depleted Mediterranean Fleet a further chore, and one of which the Stukas were able to take due advantage of. Heavy Stuka attacks were also kept up against Tobruk harbour itself by II/StG 2, I/StG 3 and the Italian 96° *Gruppo*.

During the period 11 April to 24 June 1941, no fewer than forty-six different Stuka attacks were mounted against the Tobruk defences. The number of dive-bombers in each sortie varied considerably, three to six on some dates, as many as forty to fifty on others, with a peak of sixty Ju 87s on 29 May and 2 June; in total 959 dive-bomber sorties, during which the defences claimed, rather optimistically as it transpired, to have destroyed no fewer than fifty-four attackers! The AA gunners were becoming seasoned at standing up to dive-bombing, according to British reports of this time, but, more importantly, the dive-bomber was now being taken seriously by the Army, and special training was now given so that even fresh, untried gunners stood a chance if they did not panic. The *theory*, at any rate, read well in Whitehall.

There is a crucial moment in a dive-bombing attack on a heavy gun site, when personnel must take cover or not at all. When the first dive-bomber is above them at 4,000 feet. A ferocious burst of fire at this moment from the guns will make him release his bomb prematurely, and make his successors pause in their attack [*sic*]. Complete silence at this moment, if the section goes to ground, allows every Stuka in the formation to pick his mark and come down to 500 feet. Then, and only then, will guns and command posts be damaged and men killed.[7]

The difference in attitude and effect was said to have been demon-strated by a comparison between two Stuka attacks. On 27 April, fifty Ju 87s attacked a heavy AA site, at least twelve aircraft attacking each gun. The sites were singled out and two were hit. In these cases it was found that:

1. The dive-bombers were engaged on their run-ins by one site only, and then ineffectively. On the other site the dive-bombers were not seen until the first bomb burst on the position.
2. The dive-bombers all came down out of the sun, one after the other, without bothering to attack from different directions.
3. After the first bomb had fallen, personnel took cover.
4. The dive-bombers were then able to put practically all their bombs on the position ....[8]

Against the ships supplying the Tobruk garrison, the dive-bombers proved no less effective. Among the many vessels sunk at this period was the armed boarding vessel *Chakla* on 29 April and the *Sidonis*. On 4 May, the hospital ship *Karpara* was hit. It made outraged headlines back home, but Helmut Mahlke, who flew this mission with his twelve Ju 87s, explained to me just why this came about:

The event started with a telephone call by the operations officer to me on the afternoon of 4 May: 'Reconnaissance reports a big ship of 10,000 BRT approaching Tobruk from the east. Take off im-mediately and sink her.' I asked, 'What sort of ship? A merchant ship?' I didn't believe that such a large vessel would be sent into Tobruk after our attacks on shipping there. It might therefore be a hospital ship under the Red Cross, which should not, therefore, be attacked. The operations officer checked with the recce-crew; I was present when he made the call. They had seen no Red Cross on the ship. I asked, 'Has the ship white colouring with a green stripe at sea level?' Affirmative. I replied that these were the signs of hospital ships, and that therefore the fighters overhead should be asked to confirm absolutely what kind of ship it was. The operations officer contacted them accordingly.

About twelve minutes later the inflight mission report came in from the fighter patrol. 'When we approached the ship we were fired on with AA'. I therefore said, 'If it was a genuine hospital ship it would not fire. If we get the order again, we go.' I got the order and we made the attack.

When we approached, the ship was alongside the quay at Tobruk. During the dive I got a hell of a lot of light and medium AA from this 'hospital' ship, beside the normal flak from the Tobruk defences, which were well known to us. Indeed, I had never seen before so many 'red mice' so near to my canopy. I was pretty sure that I would not get out of this concentrated flak this time and decided to release my bombs from 1,500 feet instead of 900 feet as originally planned. I did not see how it was possible for me to escape from this 'red tube of red mice' which seemed to enclose me. Nevertheless, I miraculously got out of it without taking a single hit.[9]

Ashore, the tempo was no less intense. The feelings of those who had to undergo the constant attentions of the dive-bombers are to be found reflected in a letter sent home by Lieutenant-Colonel Allan Apsley on 29 June 1941, and on file at the National Archives. Even that many years ago he was protesting against the constant inaccuracy of BBC reporting, something that has not changed in over sixty years.

I really must protest against the constant advertisement given to the RAF by the BBC. It is doing immense harm among the troops out here, where they are in a position to know that the claims are not true, because it makes them wonder whether other claims are equally exaggerated. Here, while I sit in the desert with an Me 110 circling overhead, the wireless broadcast of 0915 hours is telling us that the great feature of our recent operations here was that the RAF held complete mastery of the air by the simple procedure of preventing the enemy aircraft leaving the ground. *This is completely untrue.* In this regiment alone we had thirty casualties from air attack alone. It is true that, from time-to-time the RAF makes a sortie and bombs known enemy aerodromes. But Jerry does not rely on them alone. He scatters his aircraft all over the desert, which is full of natural landing grounds, and feeds and maintains them, if necessary, from the air. While our sorties are sporadic, Jerry is always in the air, watching every movement and attacking every target worthwhile with bombs and machine-gun fire – and his needle bullets go *through* our armour. His army co-operation is fine – whenever he wants air support, his front-line troops wireless 'Stuka' and give a map reference and it comes at once, whereas we have to apply through Brigade to Division, and from them through ALO [Air Liaison Officer] to RAF Command. When (and if) it comes, it is two hours late and the whole situation has changed and the bombs are dropped in open desert, or, as on more than one occasion, on our own troops.[10]

Small wonder then, that Kesselring was to record: 'The British dread of the Stukas equals our men's affection for them.'[11]

* * *

While the men in the Mediterranean Fleet and in the Eighth Army were undergoing the same kinds of ordeal at the hands of the German dive-bombers in the spring and summer of 1941 that their compatriots had undergone in Norway and France a year before, progress by the RAF in producing a British equivalent remained zero. The behind-the-scenes battle was being conducted on increasingly bitter lines; the RAF was tooling up for Hamburg and Dresden and had no inclination of being distracted one iota by lesser things like supporting and assisting the other two services.

Relations between the RAF and the MAP, never cordial, became ever more strained during this period, especially when it became obvious that even the American-built dive-bombers, on which the Army, at least, had set so much store, were not going to arrive for a considerable time. Churchill himself wrote to Beaverbrook on 15 December 1940:

The reason why there is this crabbing as at A, is of course the warfare which proceeds between AM and MAP. They regard you as a merciless critic, and even enemy. They resent having the MAP functions carved out of their show and I have no doubt they pour out their detraction by every channel open.[12]

All, no doubt, true, but hardly a satisfactory state of affairs for a nation fighting on its own for its very existence. The medium bomber high-diving experiments were the only slight, if unrealistic, concession being made to any dive-bomber concept by the RAF at this time, and were, of course, futile.

On 28 March 1941, a further report was submitted on these trials by the Air Vice-Marshal Commanding No. 5 Group. The tests were conducted with a Hampden bomber. The memorandum commenced without compromise:

The results obtained from the trials carried out have been disappointing. Line errors were small, but range errors showed no appreciable improvement on those from level bombing.[13]

It had been found that the angle of dive necessary for the pilot of a Hampden to hold the target in view resulted in such a rapid increase in speed that even small corrections in sighting were impossible and the recovery from the dive very difficult, especially in the event of the bombs not having been released. The report continued:

> Since the whole essence of this method of dive-bombing is for the pilot to aim and release the bombs, it is not therefore considered to be a practicable method in the Hampden. Continual practice will, no doubt, assist pilots in the development of their judgement, but the method is essentially one of 'trial and error', and there are few targets and fewer occasions of favourable weather conditions when these tactics can be carried out. In general, it is considered to be a method of bombing which will only be effective when adopted by individuals who have a natural judgement both for the actual bombing and of suitable opportunities in which to carry it out.[14]

A similar study came from Wing Commander A.E. Dark of the Bomber Development Unit at Boscombe Down. Trials were conducted here with both the Wellington 1c and Hampdens, by crews with considerable operational experience in these types. The first stage involved a large number of dives without bomb-release to determine suitable methods of entering and recovering from the dive. The second stage involved the release of the practice bombs diving between heights of 10,000 and 7,000 feet, the average height of bomb-release being 8,000 feet.

> With the Wellington, it was found best to approach the target so that it could be seen on the port side, almost stalling the aircraft, and then making a diving turn to the left. The average angle of dive was 50 degrees, but dives between 30 and 80 degrees were also tried. The average air speed at the moment of release was 140 mph, and 190 mph the speed of recovery from the dive. The method of attack used in the Hampden was the same as for the Wellington. It was found, however, that this type accelerated very rapidly so that the speed limitations were often exceeded before a recovery could be made.

This report concluded: 'High dive-bombing is not a practicable method for modern heavy bombers, and is unlikely to give an accuracy equal to that obtained in level bombing from the same heights.'[15]

No one should have been very much surprised to find that a Wellington was not as accurate a dive-bomber as a Stuka, and I doubt whether anyone was. The real point was not that, but where were the RAF's equivalents of the Stuka? The answer, apparently, even at this stage of the war, was the Westland Lysander! In another fatuous memorandum, the DNC stated:

> In view of the German experience and our own, it is clear (pending the introduction of faster two-seaters) Lysanders can operate satisfactorily where air superiority is maintained. It appears undesirable, therefore, to rush, regardless of other commitments, into a general re-equipment of Army Co-Operation Squadrons with Tomahawks for a brief period. A partial re-equipment, by way of insurance, seems preferable.[16]

The conclusion, that there was 'no rush' in modernising the RAF's Army Co-operation units, may not have exactly cheered Lieutenant-Colonel Apsley very much, had he known of it, lying in his dugout under Stuka attack in Libya.

In fact, the whole edifice of Army Co-Operation was creaking from years of indifference. A report from the same office showed that the total strength available to 'support' the Army consisted of 12½ Lysander squadrons (168 slow and obsolete spotter aircraft) and 1½ Tomahawk squadrons (twenty-two made-over Curtiss fighter planes), with a total of 164 pilots! Blitzkreig, RAF style, was *not* a very formidable force at the end of 1941.

For this parlous state of affairs the RAF later blamed Beaverbrook, or so his biographer maintained:

> In February 1941, Sinclair persuaded Margesson, who had become Secretary-of-State for War, to drop any further orders for dive-bombers. Complaints about lack of dive-bombers came from the armies fighting in North Africa. Beaverbrook was blamed for this deficiency. After he left office, he wished to tell the true story in his own defence. Churchill forbade it.[17]

If the new and untried dive-bombers from Vultee and Brewster were still not much more than blueprints on the designers' drawing-boards, then at least the Douglas SBD Dauntless, and its USAAC equivalent, the A-24 Banshee, was operational and under full production. The SBD was probably the most advanced dive-bomber actually flying anywhere in the world at that time, with the exception of the Junkers Ju 88. Better yet, it was readily available, and indeed was offered by the Americans as an immediate solution to Britain's appalling lack of such a vital weapon.

In a cypher telegram sent to the MAP from the BAC [British Air Commission, located in Washington buying suitable American aircraft] on 4 April 1941, this was fully spelt out:

> OPM [Overseas Purchasing Mission] have expressed considerable doubt as to the delivery of further orders of the Brewster dive-

bomber until the end of 1942. They are of the opinion that, at earliest, delivery will not begin until August 1942. Douglas capacity, however, is such that it would be possible for them to give delivery of 300 A24 dive-bombers between January and September 1942. The A24 is the Army equivalent of the Navy SBD-3A.

A brief description of the A24 followed. 'It will be seen that the performance of the A24 is considerably below that of the Brewster or Vultee dive-bombers and its defence is poor.' They concluded that: 'While we feel that in certain operational conditions this aircraft might be usable in the dive-bombing role, the Air Staff will probably agree that it will not be adequate for tactical reconnaissance ....'[18]

And so the chance of getting the Dauntless, the aircraft that almost single-handedly won the Pacific naval war in 1942, sooner, rather than some untried and untested aircraft years in the future, was passed up; indeed, a year later the RAF was in denial, claiming that no such offer had ever been made!

Just how much the Air Ministry viewpoint had been foisted on the Army by the new and compliant Army Minister is clear in replies given to Beaverbrook by Margesson soon afterwards:

> ... we have agreed with the Air Ministry that it is, at present, most undesirable to order bomber types, which are suitable for one particular purpose only, and which cannot be used for general operations. Dive-bombers would not be suitable for any oper-ations except those closely connected with the Army; and until that demand arises they would lock up valuable men and main-tenance effort without any useful operational results. Moreover, they would not contribute to the general RAF effort. It is for this reason that we have set our faces against any insistence on a dive-bomber type.[19]

One might have asked what other 'particular purpose' the huge and costly [in terms of money, production costs and manpower to fly] Short Stirling or Avro Manchester were, other than reducing Berlin to rubble? But, of course, everybody knew – none at all. It was the old 1930s argument trotted out again by the entrenched air marshals, reintroduced at a time when the need for accurate close air support, rather than 'general-purpose' machines (the Lysander!) had been proved beyond all doubt. All military aircraft were built for a *main* purpose, but it is hard to understand, other than in terms of total indoctrination, that this was a decisive or convincing argument. The discarded and discredited hordes of Battle aircraft had shown that that argument was sterile, and merely an excuse.

Following the humiliating reverses in Greece, Crete and Libya, on top of Norway and France the year before, there were rumblings in the Press (although not at the BBC) about the lack of dive-bombers in Britain's armoury to do to the Germans what they were so frequently doing to us. Having persuaded the War Office to drop its demand for dive-bombers proper, the Air Minister now declared his innocence in all this: it was not him [the Air Minister] to impose on the Army any particular type. The Army had not up to the present decided that the dive-bomber was a machine it wished to operate.[20]

This touched raw nerves in both Whitehall and Fleet Street. 'May Allah have mercy on our souls!' was Cassandra's despairing reaction in the *Daily Mirror* on Sinclair's' latest gaffe.[21] This unfortunate pronouncement aroused much anger, so much so that the Premier was forced to react. Cassandra's heavy irony roused Churchill to pen a typical 'Action This Day!' memorandum, demanding answers. In reply, the Air Ministry summoned up all its big guns to help draft a justification of their stand. Churchill had written to the CAS that:

> We cannot leave this matter in the very bald and helpless terms in which it was expressed. Although he meant to do the best he could, the statement in fact, reflects upon the War Office and the Air Ministry. As you know, I have always had grave doubts about whether the Air Ministry was right in banning dive-bombers.[22]

Slessor had already drafted a long and detailed attack on dive-bombers in readiness, and this was filched in preparing the Air Ministry reply to the Premier. Slessor had drafted this tirade some time before, and we shall return to it later. The CAS said bluntly that:

> In the view of the Air Staff, the dive-bomber is an efficient weapon only when: (a) it operates with a high degree of air superiority or without fighter opposition, and (b) it is not opposed by a heavy scale of light anti-aircraft defence at the target.

The riposte also claimed, after listing more important requirements and lack of cash, 'A dive-bomber, which of necessity would be inadequate for any of these roles, was a luxury which we could not afford.' That it was a luxury that had cost them Western Europe was not mentioned, and they could, of course, afford the Battles and target tugs made over from potentially high-class dive-bombers like the pre-war Hawker Henley. This was also omitted from the accounting to Churchill. CAS went on:

> ... it was agreed to order in quantity two existing American types, the Vengeance and the Bermuda. These will begin to arrive in the

Autumn and it is planed to re-equip ten Army Co-Operation
Squadrons with them.[23]

Beaverbrook drafted a curt refutation of some of the statements made,
once he got wind of them:

> Sir Wilfred Freeman has written a minute to the War Cabinet. He
> defends the policy of the Air Ministry and its hostility to program-
> mes of dive-bombers. He says that dive-bombers were, however,
> agreed to by the Air Staff in the autumn of 1940 'in spite of
> doubts'. In fact, the dive-bombers were ordered by the Ministry
> of Aircraft Production three months before the 'autumn', on the
> authority of Mr Anthony Eden, Secretary-of-State for War, and in
> opposition to the opinion of the Air Staff.[24]

*   *   *

Whatever the feuding and smokescreens in Whitehall, however, the
Axis dive-bombers continued to contribute meaningfully to the see-
saw struggle in the Western Desert, although much reduced in numbers due to the needs of the Eastern Front. They were also very effective indeed against the supply convoys that periodically tried to make
their way from either end of the Mediterranean to sustain Malta.

However, since June 1941, it was the Russian Army and Navy which
were now on the receiving end of most of the Ju 87's attentions.
Assembly of these units was done at great speed and under the highest
secrecy. Friedrich Lang described to me the route his unit took on this
long journey across Europe in late May 1941:

> The aircraft of I/StG 2 (*Immelmann*) flew from Rhodes via Herak-
> lion, Molai, Athens, Skopje, Belgrade to Kecskemet in Hungary.
> There we were greeted by the German *Stutzpunkkommandanter*,
> *Hauptmann* Arrigi (a former famous Austrian fighter-pilot from
> World War I). The next day we returned to our peacetime flying
> base at Cottbus via Breslau.[25]

On the eve of Operation Barbarossa the Stukas were in the line with the
eighty-seven dive-bombers of II and III/StG 1 and the eighty-three
dive-bombers of I and III/StG 2 as part of *Fliegerkorps VIII* supporting
Army Group Centre, while the 122 Ju 87s of I, II and III/StG 77 were
under *Fliegerkorps II*, with the forty-two aircraft of IV (Stuka) LG1 being
based at Kirkenes, Norway, under *Luftflotte 5*. The bulk of these dive-
bombers were still of the well-tried Bertha and Richard variants, but
under development was the Junkers Ju 87D (Dora), which was, in
essence, a cleaned-up Bertha with a redesigned cockpit and improved
armour protection for the aircrew. The defensive armament was also

modernised and the power-plant boosted to 1,400 hp. Bomb capacity was also improved, and after the usually initial teething troubles the Dora began to roll off the production lines at the Bremen-Lemwerder factory with 1,000 D-1s on order. Although the first D did not see action until January 1942, the renewed faith in the dive-bomber by the most successful proponent of close air support seen to date was obvious.

On the other side of the new battle front, the Soviet Air Force had concentrated much on ground-attack and light bombing aircraft, of which the most successful *Shturmovik* units were available in very large numbers. But, after the Spanish Civil War, in which the Soviets participated widely, some rethinking was done, and in 1939 the brilliant aircraft designer Vladmir Mikhailovitch Petlyakov had conceived a sleek, high-altitude, twin-engined fighter of great potency, the VI-100, which Stalin ordered he make over into an equally high-speed dive-bomber, and this was the Pe-2 *Peshka*.[26]

The specification was duly changed, not without difficulty, keeping the main features of the prototype, but fitting her with underwing dive-brakes of the slatted type and other necessary refinements. The resulting *Pikiruyuschii Bombardirovschchik* (PB) was an outstanding aircraft, the prototype of which first flew on 22 December 1939, with the test pilot P.M. Stefanovskii at the helm. Flight testing continued to June 1940, by which time it had proved itself a superb dive-bomber. It is notable that the Soviet Union, with little or no previous experience in dive-bomber design or operation, could come up with a first-rate aircraft of modern design and very high speed, the first time around, when the RAF was saying over and over again that these two qualities were totally incompatible with a dive-bomber.

The Pe-2 had a top speed of 335 mph, thus overcoming the limitations of all foreign dive-bomber types, for it could now outpace most fighter aircraft! It was a three-seater and was put into production as the Pe-2 in 1940. This aircraft had a range of 932 miles and could carry up to 2,200 lb of bombs. All-in-all it was a most impressive aircraft by any standard of the day. Unfortunately for the Soviets, although production had been under way for some time at the time of the German invasion, few of these dive-bombers had reached front-line service when the new enemy opened their attack all along the 1,000-mile front.

The *Luftwaffe* assault upon the Soviet Union was the most spectacular air offensive yet seen, for, despite many warnings, the Stuka units, supplemented by the medium bomber and fighter-bomber squadrons acting in a tactical role, found the great masses of Soviet aircraft lined up on their runways and wide open to destruction. The first day's total of destroyed Soviet aircraft was claimed to be an astonishing 1,600 machines, and all achieved for the loss of just thirty-five German aircraft. A week later and the tally had risen to an incredible 4,000 aircraft destroyed for the loss of just 150 *Luftwaffe* aircraft, a mere twelve of which had been Ju 87s.

Once more, the dive-bombers set to work in the well-tried and tested routine, taking as their targets the tanks, motor transport, bridges, fieldworks and AA sites of their dazed enemy. Yet again, the 'Flying Artillery' of the GAF provided the spearhead of the thrusting Panzer columns that quickly broke resistance and poured forward in huge enveloping movements that netted hundreds of thousands of Soviet troops in the wide maw.

StG 77 operated initially against defence positions along the Bug river, forcing the way for the 17th and 18th Panzers in their push toward Minsk and Smolensk. The powerful fortress of Brest-Litovsk was pounded by the StG 1 and fell on 30 June. Smolensk was surrounded on 27 July. The huge size of their new battlefield meant that the tactical support provided by the *Stukagruppen* was stretched to the limit, with the aircraft and ground crews (Blackmen) moving bases forward continuously, in order to keep up with the advances. For example, II and III/StG 1 operated from the line Vilna–Berezovaka on 25 June; on the 29th they were 150 miles on at Widzjuny–Moldechno–Baronowichi; a week later had a further 150 miles tucked behind them and they were operating on the Lepel–Dokudovo front. Next, another huge leap took them on to the line Surash–Demidov–Moscha–Schatalowka, just west of Smolensk on 21 July, having advanced their operating bases some 360 miles in one month.

Meanwhile, back in Britain the official line from Slessor was still being put forward by the Air Ministry to anyone who would listen: 'The aeroplane is *not* a battlefield weapon!'

Notes

1. Mahlke, *Generalleutnant* Helmut, to the Author, op. cit.
2. Notes on Air Tactics, Air Ministry Memorandum, 1941 (National Archives, Kew, London, AIR/23/5287).
3. Irving, David, *Hitler's War* (Hodder & Stoughton, 1977).
4. *Memorandum*, C-in-C Middle East to War Office, dated 12 May 1941, 0/63425 (National Archives, Kew, London, AIR /8/631).
5. Lang, *Oberst* Friedrich, to the Author, op. cit.
6. Mahlke, *Generalleutnant* Helmut, to the Author, op. cit.
7. *AA Defence Tobruk*, Appended 'D', I.G. Report No. 712 (National Archives, Kew, London, AIR/20/2970). Italics in original.
8. *Ibid.*
9. Mahlke, *Generalleutnant*, Helmut, to the Author, op. cit.
10. Apsley, Lt.-Col., Letter, dated 20 June 1941. (National Archives, Kew, London, AIR 8/631). Not just BBC mis-reporting has remained unchanged since 1941. Compare Lieutenant Apsley's complaint with the comment made by Major James Loden of No. 3 Para fighting the Teleban in Helmand, Afghanistan, in September 2006. In an

. The legendary Junkers Ju 87 Stuka which led the German assaults on Poland, Norway, the Low Countries, France, Yugoslavia, Greece, Crete, Malta, North Africa and Russia between 1939 and 1941, and was still in action in the final days of the war. *(P. K. Grosse)*

2. The lean and menacing outline of the Junkers Ju 87 D slipping down a Norwegian Fiord to hunt Allied shipping in 1940. The Dora was equipped with long-range fuel tanks which gave her the reach to hunt down the Royal Navy off the coasts of Norway, Malta and North Africa and she gained many scalps including damage to the heavy cruiser *Suffolk*, the aircraft carriers *Illustrious* and *Formidable* and sinking the cruisers *Southampton* and *Gloucester* as well as many smaller warships in the period 1940-41. *(Author's Collection)*

Sugar Baker Dog! The incomparable Douglas SBD Dauntless in flight. This air-to-air shot shows one of the earliest production models in 1940. The 'Barge' or 'Slow But Deadly' had an outstanding war record with the US Navy and US Marine Corps in the Pacific, winning the Battle of Midway almost by herself when she sank four Japanese aircraft carriers and a heavy cruiser. She served in all the major carrier-to-carrier battles, and from shore bases at Guadalcanal and in the liberation of the Philippines in 1944-45. But she also fought with the French Air Force and Navy in France against the Germans in the same period, hunted German convoys off Norway, had been at the invasion of Morocco and bombed a French battleship and continued to serve post-war against Communist forces in Indo-China. *(Photograph presented to the Author by Douglas Aircraft during a visit to the plant at Long Beach)*

4. The Blackburn company artist's dramatised pre-war impression of the Royal
   Navy's only true dive bomber, the Blackburn Skua in a dive over the aircraft
   carrier *Glorious*.   *(Author's Collection)*

5. What might have been! Artist's illustration of the Hawker Henley dive bomber in action against the Meuse bridges in May 1940. Instead of the straight and steady low-level flight up the river into massed German AA fire, the Henley would have dive bombed almost vertically with far greater accuracy, as proven by the Vengeance in Burma in 1943, and only be in the sights of the gunners for a few seconds each, thus avoiding the enormous lossses that the Fairey Battle's actually suffered that day. *(© John Dell, World Rights Reserved, reproduced courtesy of the artist.)*

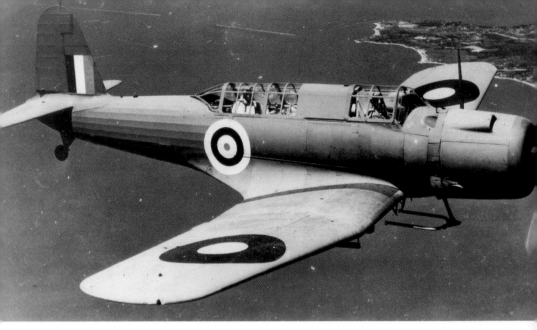

6. What never was! The Vought SB2U Vindicator served pre-war aboard carriers of the US fleets, and fought her only battle with the US Marine Corps aviators at Midway in June 1942. The French Government had earlier ordered an export batch as the V156F in 1939, and some of these fought in the crash of France in May and June 1940 before being wiped out. The few that survived were taken over by the British and trialled by the Royal Navy for a brief period, but as an anti-submarine aircraft for escort carriers! Not surprisingly, they proved unsuitable in the role and the squadron reverted to Fairey Swordfish biplanes, a typical inexplicable British decision that left them totally bereft of any dive bombers by mid-1941.

(RAF Museum, Hendon, London)

7. The Soviet dive bomber *par excellence*, the Petlyakov Pe-2 *Peshka*, an outstanding aircraft and as fast as most comtemporary fighter aircraft. This machine is seen undergoing maintenance at a forward airfield. Notice the glazed underside of the aircraft's nose for maximum visibility when attacking, the lowered pilot access hatch and the distinctive radio mast. *(Author's Collection via TASS, Moscow)*

8. Straight Down! The outstandingly accurate portrayal of USAAF North American
A-36 Apache dive bomber pilot attacking targets over Sicily in 1943. Nicknamed
Invader this dive bomber saw extensive combat service with two groups at the
invasions of Pantelleria, Sicily, Salerno and Anzio as well as in northern Burma
and China in 1943-44.

*(© Estate of Reynolds Brown, reproduced by courtesy of his widow, Mary Louise Brown
and her daughter Franz Brown)*

9. Bombs Away! Artist's impression of Soviet twin-engined Petlyakov Pe-2 dive bombers in action over Stalingrad in 1942. *(Author's Collection)*

Mass flight of US Marine Corps SBDs of
VMSB-241 seen over Samoa in 1942 prior to the
deployment in the Solomon Island campaign.
(Courtesy of Vic Wier)

11. Soviet Dive Bomber aces. Colonel
A. G. Federov conducted intensive
tests and trials with the Petlyakov
Pe-2 dive bomber, making
improvements to the 'Dipping
Wheel' tactic and increasing the
proper use of this highly
sophisticated aircraft in front-line
dive bombing on the Eastern Front.
(Author's Collection)

12. Soviet Dive Bomber aces. Artist's
impression of Major Ivan Polbin
briefing his Petlyakov Pe-2
aircrew prior to a mission.
Polbin was the Soviet Union's
outstanding dive bomber
exponent during World War II,
whose exploits and accuracy
became legendary. He was
finally killed in action on his
40th birthday leading the assault
on the German city of Breslau in
1945.
(Author's Collection)

13. The magnificent rebuilt Yokosuka D4Y Suisei (Comet), code-named Judy by the Allies, on display at the Yasukuni Shrine Museum in Central Tokyo.

4. A Vultee Vengeance dive bomber of the RAF over the mountains of Burma supporting Orde Wingate's Chindit operations behind enemy lines.

(© Kenneth Gray, World Rights Reserved, reproduced courtesy of the artist)

5. Aerial view of Royal Navy Grumman TBA Avenger bombers of No. 848 Squadron, Fleet Air Arm. The Avenger was an American built torpedo-bomber which was made available to the Royal Navy under Lend-Lease and used by them almost exclusively in the shallow dive-bomber role in the Far East between 1944-45 as they lacked any true dive bombers. *(Author's Collection)*

16. Royal Navy Grumman TBM Avenger bombers of No. 848 Squadron, Fleet Air Arm, making a dive-bombing attack on an enemy airfield in southern Japan in July 1945, as part of the 'softening-up' operations for the planned Operation Olympic, the invasion of the Japanese home islands. *(Author's Collection)*

17. The Bent Wing Bird! Royal Navy Chance-Vought Corsair fighter-bombers with
long range drop tanks in place, warm up on the decks of the aircraft carrier
Victorious prior to the dive bombing attack on Songei Gerong oil refinery in
Sumatra, January 1945. *(Commander Ronnie C. Hay, DSO, DSC, RN)*

18. A dive bomber that never fought. The Brewster SBA, known to the US Navy as
the Buccaneer and to the RAF as the Bermuda, this dive bomber was an advance
model ordered direct from the drawing board in the United States by the French
government in 1939. French orders were taken over by the British in the desperate
days of 1940, but, despite the expenditure of millions of dollars incompetent shop
floor management at the new plants failed to deliver the aircraft on time. The US
Navy only eventually used them as dive-bomber trainers, as seen here; the RAF
used them as target tugs!

(Jesse E. Hartman, Brewster Aeronautical Corporation via Donald B. Cooney)

19. 'The Beast'. A Curtiss SB2C-5 Helldiver of VB-80 'takes a cut' to land aboard the escort carrier *Wake Island* in the Pacific in 1945. The Helldiver had enormous production problems due to the US Navy's insistence that she be built so that two could fit on the lift of an *Essex*-class carrier, a design restriction that caused infinite problems and long delays, but she eventually served with great distinction in the Pacific 1943-45 dropping five times the weight of bombs of the SBD and helping sink the giant Japanese battleships *Yamato* and *Musashi*.
(Courtesy of Charles R. Shuford, US Navy)

20. 'Fist of the Fleet' SB2Cs on flight line at Ream Field, San Ysidro, California in October 1945. These dive bombers belong to Air Group 80.
(Courtesy of Charles R. Shuford)

21. A dive bomber that never was. The Douglas AB2D Destroyer, a bold new heavy dive bomber concept from the brain of Ed Heinemann, only a handful were ever produced. This is one of the few surviving examples photographed by the author.

22. French matelots of the *Aéronavale Flotille* 3F with their Curtiss SB2C Helldivers resting at the forward ground base of Bac Mai, near Hanoi, with mail from home between dive-bombing sorties against Communist Viet-Minh forces besieging Dien Bien Phu in French Indo-China, March 1954. *(A. Delin)*

23. Impressive line up of Douglas AD Skyraiders of the US Marine Corps Air Group (carrying tail code AK) pictured here at Osan Air Base, Korea in 1952. *(James V. Crow)*

24. Hands-on History (1). The author in June 2002 operating the restored power-operated turret as fitted to later marques of the Douglas Detroyer aircraft at Kevin Smith's Dauntless Aviation facility at Fredericksburg, Virginia.
(© Peter C. Smith, World Rights Reserved)

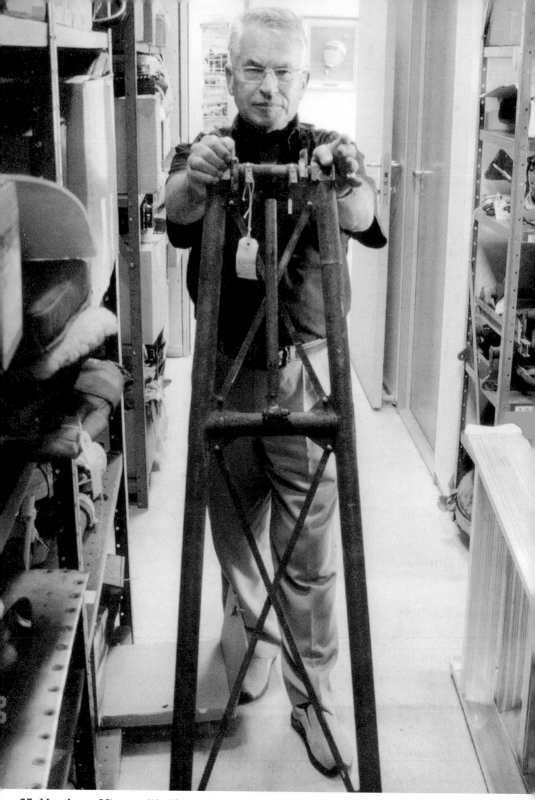

25. Hands-on History (2). The author in June 2006 with the swinging bomb crutch from a crashed Blackburn Skua, salvaged from its wreck site in Norway by Klas GjØlmesli and being rebuilt by the team under curator and founder Birger Lansen, at the Norsk Luffartsmuseum at Bodo, Norway. This is part of the Operation Skua project sponsored by Ølyvind Lamo.

26. Preserving the legend. One of the last Petlyakov Pe-2s, this machine belonged to the Polish Air Force post-war as part of the Warsaw Pact forces and is preserved near Warsaw. *(Author's Collection)*

27. The last dive bomber to see combat. This in a Douglas A-1E Skyraider (133862) coded 23-F-5. This aircraft fought in Vietnam with both the Republic of Vietnam Air Force and the USAF in what were the last of the true dive bomber missions. *(Author's Collection)*

28. Keeping them flying! A magnificent in-flight shot of a restored Douglas SBD Dauntless over Deanville, Quebec in 2001, showing her clean and elegant lines.

(© John P. Baert, Deanville, Quebec, courtesy of the aircraft's owner and pilot)

e-mail, later forwarded to Sir Richard Dannatt, Loden stated that the RAF was '... utterly, utterly useless' in supplying support for the troops on the ground there. Citing one incident from many, Loden wrote how one Harrier pilot 'couldn't identify the target, fired two phosphorus rockets that just missed our own compound so that we thought they were incoming RPGs [rocket-propelled grenades] and then strafed our perimeter, missing the enemy by 200 metres ....' Other Parachute Regiment officers, reflecting what officers were saying privately and at odds with the MoD's official statements, told one reporter that they much preferred to call in American A-10 Tank busters for air support when under fire because of what they saw as the RAF's ineffectiveness. The predictable public reaction to this criticism from the front line was typical, and focused entirely on defending the Air Force's bravery, but it was *not* the RAF pilots' *bravery* that was being questioned, either in 1941 or in 2006: it was their efficiency, tactics and equipment!

11. Kesselring, *Memoirs*, op. cit.
12. Churchill, Winston S., *The Second World War, op cit.* 'A' was Archibald (Sinclair), AM the Air Ministry and MAP Ministry of Aircraft Production.
13. Report of No. 5 Group – *High diving bombing trials*, dated 27 April 1941, BDU/S.403/1/Amt (National Archives, Kew, London, AIR/14/672/IIH/241/3/631).
14. *Ibid.*
15. Report Number 9, *High diving bombing trials*, BDU, Boscombe Down, dated 25 April 1941, BDU/S.403/1/Amt (National Archives, Kew, London, AIR 14/672/IIH/2451/3/382).
16. *Memorandum*, DMC Office, dated 14 May 1941 (National Archives, Kew, London, AIR 8/631).
17. Taylor, A.J.P., *Beaverbrook*, op. cit.
18. *Telegram*, from BAC to MAP, dated 4 April 1941, Briny 4274/4/4 (National Archives, Kew, London, AIR 19/233).
19. *Letter*, War Office to MAP, dated 11 March 1941. SG/H/1170. (National Archives, Kew, London, 19/233).
20. *Hansard*, 11 July 1942.
21. *Cassandra*, article in *Daily Mirror*, issue dated 12 July 1941. National Newspaper Library, Colindale, London.
22. *PM Personal Minute to CAS*, dated 14th July 1941 (National Archives, Kew, London, AIR 8/631).
23. *CAS Minute to PM*, dated 16 July 1941 (National Archive, Kew, London, AIR 8/631).
24. *Memorandum* DO(41) 10 to War Cabinet Defence Committee (Operations), dated 2 September 1941 (National Archives, Kew, London, AIR 8/631).
25. Lang, *Oberst*, Friedrich, to the Author, op. cit.
26. For the full history of this aircraft see Peter C. Smith, *Petlyakov Pe-2 Peshka*, Crowood Press, Ramsbury, 2003.

CHAPTER NINE

'It needed a lot of experience (and courage)'

To understand something of the thinking behind the British viewpoint on dive-bombing, the long paper drawn up by Air Vice-Marshal Slessor, which formed much of the basis on which the Air Ministry based its reply to Churchill's querulous enquiry, has to be examined, for it became virtually the 'Holy Writ' of the RAF top brass throughout the war.

Slessor had written: 'I feel that it is essential to recognise, and to get the Army to recognise, certain basic principles ....' He admitted that, '... I have been considerably ragged after the Battle of France, and no doubt shall be again after Greece, for writing a book of which the main theme was "The Bomber is not a Battlefield Weapon".'[1] Despite Poland, Norway, France, Greece, Crete and North Africa, however, he remained unrepentant: 'I do not feel that my contention has in any way been invalidated by the events of the past year.' This seemed to show a dedication to a principle over a fact that, if admirable in some respects, was rather blinkered, not to say myopic!

He went on to specify the reasons for his attitude. These German victories were not, much as it may have surprised many people, including the Germans themselves, 'due to the dive-bomber as a type, or to its employment on the battlefield as a policy. It has been due, in my view, to three factors.' These he listed as complete air superiority and an overwhelming number of fighters, bombers in enormous numbers and their superior AA equipment compared with that of the armies they had defeated.

The first two points on which he based his claim have since been shown to be totally invalidated. In total numbers of aircraft the Allies were not outnumbered, any more than they were in tanks or armoured vehicles, quite the reverse in fact. It was the way they were used that counted, a use which the RAF was totally opposed to for its own aircraft. The German *Luftwaffe* close-support leader, von Richthofen, once declared that, 'The wishes of the Army are my orders!' Such a viewpoint was nothing less than pure and total heresy to the British air marshals.

Slessor elaborated his last point. Should the German invasion come, dive-bombers would not help the British defence, he claimed.

In invasion, every single bomber and every single fighter ought to be concentrated against the beaches and the shipping and, in my view, it would be fatal if we are to have bombers scooting about Kent trying to shoot up individual tanks. It is not the job of the Air Force to destroy tanks. That is the job of the anti-tank weapon on the ground ....

Such an argument, of course, totally ignored the factor of flexibility and speed of redeployment that an anti-tank aircraft brings to a battle-front, conditions the German Ju 87 thrived on.

Slessor concluded that, 'In other words, I do not believe in close support at all, except in very rare occasions when you have to throw everything in to avert a disaster or turn a retreat into a rout.' His steadfast opposition was shared absolutely by his fellow senior officers, and indeed it had been their article of faith for two decades and would continue for many more. The long-range strategic concept dominated RAF thinking totally.

One of the Fairey Battle pilots, a squadron leader who had been shot down over the River Maas in 1940, and later escaped to Britain, gave his viewpoint on the futility of close-support missions, although in his case he had been shot down trying to smash the bridges over which the Panzers were being supplied. 'I regard any pre-arranged allotment of bombers to the specific role of close support of land forces as a waste of effort', he stated baldly. He described vividly his own eyewitnessing of the massacre of the Battle aircraft in their straight and unswerving, low-level attempts to bomb-hit these vital bridges and so slow down the German advance. 'The crews of the Day Bomber Squadrons at that time were highly trained; their morale was first-class and no one in the Service had any idea of the stopping power of modern AA fire at low altitude; crews of the future cannot be so well trained ....'

His mistake, of course, due to the trauma and scale of that defeat as he watched his compatriots slaughtered in vain, was to equate exactly his own type of low-level attack, which gave the gunners ample time to home in, and the lumbering bombers, with the dive-bombers' methods of high approach out of range, followed by a steep dive, during which the aircraft was only in the gunners' sight for a few seconds before they had to switch to the next fleeting target. By utilising dive-bombing instead of the low, slow-and-level approach, the Germans had achieved, and were still achieving, the exact opposite results to the Battles. The Americans in the mid-1920s had already worked out this vital difference, but in 1941 the RAF could still not apparently differentiate between the two in terms of sheer effectiveness.

I hold the opinion that German dive-bombers would achieve poor results if our own land forces were equipped with AA defences on the same scale as the German army [in truth, the German flak guns were all part of the *Luftwaffe*, and *not* part of the German Army]. In fact I would say that the German dive-bombers would not achieve the results they have done if the tables were turned and they had to fly through German flak. The German advance into France and Belgium was not due to their dive-bombers but to our lack of proper AA defences in the field ....[2]

However much these opinions suited the Air Ministry and blinded the War Office, the plain facts were that, at the same time as they were being expounded to avoid the RAF having to build and train for dive-bombers, the German Stukas were achieving their greatest successes yet recorded, on a far vaster scale than in France, and, it should be noted, against an enemy, the Soviet Union, that was far more lavishly equipped with 'proper AA defences in the field' than any other army before, or since, probably. While the British theorised and agonised, the Germans by contrast got on with demonstrating just what the dive-bomber was capable of. Nor were they content with their past achievements, but constantly strove to perfect still further their Army Co-operation skills.

*   *   *

To maintain such a pace of advance as the Germans did in Russia, with all its attendant problems of supply and maintenance over vast distances, speaks volumes for the efficiency of their organisation. Not only was the pressure kept up day after day, week after week, but there was no marked falling-off in the accuracy or efficiency of the dive-bombing attacks delivered. Again and again it was the sight of the *Stukagruppen* peeling off over Soviet strongpoints and troop concentrations that turned a right situation on the ground into victory over always-superior numbers for the advancing *Wehrmacht*. The anti-aircraft fire received from the Soviet defenders was fierce, but fighter interference was initially ineffectual, and so Ju 87 losses were minimal at this time. In contrast with the prevailing RAF viewpoint of their vulnerability to flak defences, StG 77, for example, recorded that during the first six months of the Russian campaign they had destroyed an estimated 2,401 soft-skinned vehicles, 234 tanks, ninety-three gun batteries and twenty-one trains, all for the loss of only twenty-one of their aircrew!

The perfection of the Stuka/Panzer combination was now nearing its peak. This was achieved as much through the dedication with which they applied themselves as to improved weaponry. Helmut Mahlke described it to me thus:

In Russia we had a large number of UHF crews with the Army, travelling in the same vehicles as the Army troops were equipped with. They were a kind of forward air-controller group. As there were never enough for us to attach one to each Army division, they were moved into the main battle areas as needed and attached to the Army units fighting in the centre of the battle.

The personnel were normally signals men, with sometimes the addition of a Stuka pilot. In my experience of this, I found the most important part of these units was to get well up in the battle and be as close as possible to the Army commander at all times during the battle. For *Luftwaffe* personnel this was much more difficult than the learning of the UHF procedure of good target information to the flying crews. This is why signal officers learnt to handle this job even better than a pilot, who was just ordered to carry out such a task now and then. It needed a lot of experience (and courage) to do this task efficiently in a major battle.

We found that our Air Force telecommunications system was far superior to that of the Army. In Russia, the Army frequently had to make use of the Air Force telecommunications network in order to keep contact with their superior or subordinate commands. I think, too, that part of the reason for this was the basic essentialness of Air Force communications systems to be brief and precise in orders, to avoid giving any delay in target location and mission-orders.[3]

Despite the overwhelming victories thus achieved and the heavy casualties inflicted upon the Soviet armies, not everything went smoothly, of course. One nasty surprise for the Germans was the size and number of the Soviet tank force, which they had vastly underestimated on both counts before the war began. This was demonstrated early on, as was the difficulty for dive-bombers to actually knock out a tank with bombs alone. On 26 June 1941, for example, the whole of StG 2 had attacked a large concentration of Soviet tanks to the south of Grodno with bombs. But it was later discovered that only one tank had been completely knocked out, and that by machine-gun fire! New measures would obviously have to be found in future to deal with this problem, for, no matter how many tanks the Ju 87s destroyed, the Russians seemed able to replace them five-fold. At once research began to solve this problem.

The advances along the southern sector of the front were less spectacular than on the central front, but in the far north, the drive along the Baltic coast made rapid progress towards Leningrad [St Petersburg], which soon came within Stuka striking range. A considerable part of the city's defence came from the heavy naval gun support fire laid down by the warships of the Soviet Baltic Fleet, bottled up in its base at Kronstadt. This was the toughest nut yet that the German dive-bombers had to face, for the fleet was heavily protected by an enormous array of anti-aircraft weaponry, located both afloat and ashore. According to RAF theorists then, this target should have been totally impervious to dive-bomber attack – but the Stukas decided otherwise.

A lull in the ground fighting during August enabled the Ju 87 units I and II/StG 2 to be switched 250 miles to the north to rapidly co-ordinate strikes against these warships from bases established at Tyrkowo. The principal units of the fleet were the two old battleships, dating from the First World War, the *Marat* and *Oktobrescaja Revolutioa*. Although obsolete and unsuitable for engaging in modern naval operations, their powerful 12-inch guns were still formidable weapons for shore bombardment, and commanded the coastline to a depth of 16 miles inland. It was realised that normal dive-bomber payloads would be unable to pierce their heavily armoured decks, but it was hoped that repeated attacks would demolish their upperworks and make them untenable. Meanwhile, special deliveries of the new armour-piercing 2,200 lb bomb were brought up, and the Ju 87s prepared for the assault.

The first mission to take out these ships took place on 16 September against the *Marat*, which was firing inland from the deep-water channel between Kronstadt Island and Leningrad. Led by *Hauptmann* Steen, III/StG 2 attacked through thick cloud cover and achieved surprise, planting one 1,100 lb bomb on target. On the 23rd, the battleship was discovered repairing her damage at Kronstadt naval base, and by this date the heavier bombs were available.

Thus armed, thirty Stukas made their approach from 9,000 feet, without the benefit of cloud cover, and tipped over through a storm of flak. Steen went down into the inferno of fire and the rest followed him down. Hans-Ulrich Rudel followed his leader in with no dive-brakes and released his bomb from below 3,000 feet, despite warnings not to do so. He described this classic attack later:

> My Ju 87 keeps perfectly steady as I dive; she does not swerve an inch. I have the feeling that to miss is now impossible. Then I see the *Marat* large as life in front of me. Sailors are running across the deck, carrying ammunition. Now I press the bomb-release switch on my stick and pull with all my strength. Can I still manage to pull out? I doubt it, for I am diving without brakes and the height at which I have released the bomb is not more than 900 feet. The skipper has said, when briefing us, that the 2,000-pounder must not be dropped from lower than 3,000 feet, and to drop at a lower altitude is to endanger one's aircraft! But I have forgotten that! I

am intent on hitting the *Marat*. I tug at my stick, without feeling, merely exerting all my strength. My acceleration is too great. I see nothing, my sight is blurred in a momentary blackout, a new experience for me. But if it can be managed at all I must pull out. My head has not yet cleared when I hear Scharnovski's voice: 'She is blowing up, sir!' Now I look out. We are skimming the water at a level of 10 or 12 feet and I bank round a little. Yonder lies the *Marat* below a cloud of smoke rising to 1,200 feet; apparently the magazine had exploded.[4]

The *Marat* sank in shallow water with her fore section almost torn away. Although later some of her guns were brought into action for a time, she was finished as a sea-going unit. The dive-bomber attacks continued, Steen himself being killed in a later sortie, when his green-nosed Ju 87 was hit by flak. He attempted to steer his doomed aircraft into the cruiser *Kirov*, which was already damaged by his bomb. The *Oktobrescaja Revolutioa* was also hit, and many lesser vessels damaged to a degree. The urgent summons received from the southern front, however, called the dive-bombers thither before they could completely finish the job they had so brilliantly started.

Instead of pressing straight on to Moscow in August, the impetus of the German attack was switched to the southern front, and culminated in the Battle of Kiev, where German Panzer armies closed their pincers around over one million Soviet troops in a great battle of annihilation, which again saw the dive-bombers used to the full. Operating from the Konotop area, 250 miles south of Smolensk, in support of the 4th Panzer Division, the Ju 87s were in constant action as the surrounded Soviet armies attempted to break out, but by 26 September it was all over and yet another enormous victory achieved. Already, however, the days were growing ominously shorter as the Russian winter set in early.

The assault was then renewed toward Moscow on 2 October, in Operation Typhoon, and initially it, too, achieved the breathtaking success of earlier operations. Nine Soviet armies were eliminated in the great double battle of Vyazma-Bryansk, but after this the weather closed down and made operations from the primitive forward airfields more and more difficult. Strong counter-attacks by fresh Siberian re-inforcements against the German forces approaching from the north were only beaten off with great difficulty. The Stukas, flying from the Juchnow area, put in attack after attack and prevented a rout, but later, pressure forced the line back. Although advance elements of the German spearhead got within sight of the Kremlin domes, Moscow remained, like Leningrad and Hitler's grandiose visions, an unattainable dream.

Operating conditions became well-nigh impossible as mud gave way to sub-zero temperatures, for which the Germans were ill prepared. III/StG 2 at Rhew found that the engines would start, despite intensive care. The devoted work of the ground teams, out all night warming the engines at half-hourly intervals to prevent them freezing solid, was affected as the men began to suffer acute frostbite, and serviceability fell alarmingly, reducing some units to 30 per cent of their strength.

Stopped dead by the combination of the Russian winter and their extended lines of communication, the Germans were then almost overwhelmed by the massive Soviet attacks during the winter of 1941–2. For the first time the Germans were on the defensive, and only heroic fighting by the troops on the ground and the firm orders of Hitler for them to stand fast, not panic and fight it out, brought them through.

The Stuka, despite the conditions, did much to help in this, by attacking Soviet tank forces whenever they broke through, and they often had to fight for their own advanced airstrips as the Marauding T-34s threatened to overrun them, as was the case at Kalinin with II/StG 2 and I/StG 2.

Stuka *Staffeln* were now beginning to re-equip with the Dora, the first such reorganised unit to see action being I/StG 2 in Staraya Russa in January 1942, commanded by *Hauptman* Bruno Dilley. Other dive-bomber units had been earmarked for a return to the Mediterranean, where a renewed assault upon the island of Malta, followed, it was hoped, by its occupation, was planned, but when Soviet tanks tore a 100-mile gap in the German front line, these orders were hastily rescinded, as Friedrich Lang recalled:

I/StG 2, which belonged to VIII *Fliegerkorps*, was transferred in November 1941 to Böblingen, near Stuttgart. We had desert camouflage painted onto our Ju 87s and we were fitted out for Africa. At the beginning of January, we received orders to cancel everything and respray our Stukas white and transfer in the quickest possible way, group by group, to Duo (between Pleskau and Ilmensee) as the position at Wolchow and around Demjansk was becoming disastrous. In the transfer 3 *Staffel* lost two or three planes in a snowstorm near Elbing.[5]

In a further reorganisation that winter, IV (Stuka) LG 1 became I/StG 5 under the command of Hans-Karl Stepp, and when weather conditions in the far north became impossible for flying operations for a while, this unit was moved south for an interval to operate with StG 1 under Walter Hagen on the Leningrad Front, changing over to Doras at the same time. StG 77 also withdrew, *Staffel* by *Staffel*, to Böblingen for upgrading.

Somehow, the German line, although pushed back in many places, held on until the spring thaw brought relief and a renewal of the offensive. But, in the interim, the dive-bomber had made its power felt under *very* different conditions from those experienced by the German aircrews in the bleak and inhospitable Russian wastes, for by this time the Pacific was ablaze with war.

*   *   *

By contrast to the attitude of most pre-war aviation forces, the dive-bomber had pride of place in the *Nihon Teikoku Kaigun* [Imperial Japanese Navy], as two Japanese historians have pointed out:

> During the period 1939–40, the accuracy of Japanese level bombers was incredibly poor. It was so bad that it was doubtful whether one hit could be achieved when three or four groups of nine-plane formations released their bombs from a height of 10,000 feet against an evading battleship-sized target on the open sea.
>
> On the other hand, an attack by three dive-bombers against the same type of objective almost guaranteed at least one successful hit on target. High official circles were of the opinion that for attacking warships, dive-bombing and torpedoeing were the pre-ferred methods of attack.[6]

And despite considerable improvement in the high-level bombing accuracy by the IJN, this pre-war thought was fully borne out through-out the Second World War, and by aircraft of every nation. Accord-ingly, the Aichi D3A1 Val featured largely in the first, and many subsequent, attacks made by the Japanese, and the accuracy of this aircraft rivalled that of the German Ju 87 in the Pacific conflict that followed, before later heavy losses thinned the ranks of the highly trained élite group of dive-bomber aircrews through their misuse and mis-direction, in much the same way that the Germans and British Fleet Air Arm attacked the wrong targets earlier in the war.

The first strike was, of course, the opening shots at Pearl Harbor, and was launched from the flight decks of the six big aircraft-carriers of the *Kidō Būtai* commanded by Admiral Nagumo on the morning of Sunday 7 December 1941. The attack was made in two waves, and the first included fifty-one D3A1s under the overall command of Lieutenant Akira Sakamoto. Their particular task was to guarantee that American fighter cover over the US fleet anchorage was nil, and for this duty they split their attack in turn, into two phases, concentrating their fire on what they understood to be the two main American fighter airfields.

Sakamoto himself led off the attack with twenty-five Vals against Wheeler Air Base, dropping the very first bomb of the Pacific War at 0755. A second group of twenty-six Vals, led by Lieutenant Kakuichi

Takahasi, attacked the air base of Hickham Field, and also the seaplane base at Ford Island in the middle of the harbour, alongside which lay moored the great bulks of the US Pacific Fleet's battleships. The three American aircraft-carriers, prime targets for elimination if found, and which were the original first-choice targets, had already been reported as absent, much to the regret of the Japanese aviators. Because they were attacking parked aircraft and not warships, the bomb load of the D3A1s in this wave consisted of 250 lb fragmentation bombs.

Achieving complete surprise, the Vals made their dives onto their target against minimal opposition, and achieved devastating results. Hickham Field had reportedly housed all the heavy bombers of the USAAC in the area, and these were the only aircraft capable of striking back at the Nagumo force; while Ford Island was erroneously thought to hold the US Navy's main fighter contingent ashore. The information proved unreliable, most aircraft being on their home carriers or *en route* back to Pearl at the time of the attack, but even so the devastation was widespread after these dive-bombing attacks had ended.

The second wave of Japanese carrier aircraft included a further strong formation of seventy-nine D3A1s, under the inspiring leadership of the Navy's foremost exponent of dive-bombing, Lieutenant-Commander Takashige Egusa. Their priority target had been, of course, the American carriers, but in their absence they turned their attentions to various ships which had escaped the earlier visitations of the altitude- and torpedo-bombers. These included the battleship *Nevada*, which they caught trying to make a run for the open sea, hitting her repeatedly until she beached; the battleship *Pennsylvania* and destroyers *Cassin* and *Downes*, which they wrecked in dry-dock, and the destroyer *Shaw* in the floating dock, whose magazine they detonated, tearing her bows off. The second wave was, naturally, met by fully alert defences, and suffered accordingly. Even so, just one dive-bomber was lost from the first wave, with fourteen casualties from the second.

The methods employed by the Japanese Vals were interesting and had been highly honed prior the attack under Egusa's direction following his combat experience in China. They cruised in mass, in V-formation of threes by three, with top fighter cover (the incomparable Mitsubishi Zero) up and above their own formation. On reaching Hawaii, they climbed to gain sufficient altitude, around 8,000 feet, then came in over the mountains to the east of the harbour in single line ahead, following the movements of the flight leader, whose own aircraft was easily recognisable by the bright red tail and rear fuselage sections. In this their organisation was similar to the yellow undercarriage markings of the Stukas over the English Channel, as described earlier by Mahlke, and for the same reasons. Selecting their targets, they timed their dives so that no more than three or four seconds elapsed between each diving aircraft. In addition to the warships sunk and damaged, some ninety-two Navy and ninety-six Army aircraft were destroyed on the ground and in the air.

On the way back home from the Pearl Harbor strike, the 2nd Carrier Division was detached to assist in the capture of Wake Island. On 21 December, the carriers *Hiryū* and *Soryū* launched a strike of eighteen Vals from a position 200 miles north of Wake, but thick cloud negated their sortie. A second attack, led by Lieutenant Heijiro Abe, went in the following day, and also consisted of eighteen D3A1s. These had eight Zeke fighters for protection, but as these later concentrated on making strafing runs at low level, some defending US Marine Corps F4F Wildcat fighters managed to get in quick attacks. The Vals none the less dive-bombed the island gun batteries on 23 December, when the actual landings were made, and the island was quickly overrun.

The D3A1 dive-bombers were subsequently to be found in action all over the fluid south Pacific battle zone; reputed attacks included ninety of them hitting Rabaul on 20 January, switching to Kavieng, Lae and Salamaua in New Guinea and again at Rabaul on the 22nd, but they found few worthwhile targets. On the 24th and 25th they hit Ambon Island in the Celebes, and on the 4th they dive-bombed an Allied cruiser force south of Kangean Island, badly damaging the US cruiser *Marblehead* and hitting the heavy cruiser *Houston* on one of her after turrets, north of Bali. Sixty-eight Vals, hitherto held in reserve in the Home Islands, were released for operations in the Philippines and later the conquest of Java in the Dutch East Indies (Indonesia).

The most spectacular operation in which the Val featured after Pearl Harbor was the carrier strike on the northern Australian port of Darwin on 19 February. Seventy-one Vals took part and, in precision attacks, sank seven large merchant ships and the American destroyer *Peary*. A similar strike against Tjilatjap in Java on 3 March sank two merchant ships and damaged fifteen others.

In April the *Kidō Būtai*, now with five carriers, moved west into the Indian Ocean to seek and destroy the second British Fleet that had been assembled there under Admiral Sir James Somerville, to defend the Indian sub-continent. Fortunately for the ramshackle British force, the Japanese failed to locate them, but the dive-bombers attacked the ports of Colombo and Trincomalee, both in Ceylon (Sri Lanka), and also located two British heavy cruisers, *Cornwall* and *Dorsetshire*, which had been foolishly detached from the main fleet. On 5 April, around midday, a powerful force of eighty Vals was flown off the Japanese carriers under the overall command of Egusa to deal with this pair. The two cruisers were finally located, and despite one of them being fitted with radar, surprised, at 1350 hours. Ten minutes later the Vals attacked both ships over their bows and out of the sun. The accuracy of their dive-bombing was phenomenal, despite the violent twisting and turning of the two ships and barrage of their combined AA armaments. It was all over in minutes. One of the survivors from the battle, Lieutenant Geoffrey Grove RN, aboard *Cornwall*, later recalled the attack:

> We watched the planes like hawks, and, as the bombs came down, we flung ourselves on our faces. If the hit was close to you, you found yourself being bounced like a ball. We had three hits almost directly under us, and for one of them I was standing up and was enveloped in a great sheet of flame. I thought it was the end of me, but actually my clothing saved me and I was unhurt. Well, this couldn't last. We took something like fifteen hits in seven minutes and the poor old girl took on a bigger list than ever and started to settle.[8]

The *Dorsetshire* was pulverised in the same brisk, efficient manner, as one historian later noted:

> Commander Egusa's dive-bombers established an all-time record in bombing accuracy with the destruction of these two cruisers. Perhaps the bombing conditions were perfect – the cruisers were bombed from dead ahead and down sun, which was the blind spot; whatever the reason, every bomb literally either struck the enemy or scored a near-miss. So thick were the explosions that many plane crews could not determine whether they had actually released their missiles. Only after all our planes had assembled in formation and the pilots could visually check the racks of the other planes could we tell whether or not several planes were still armed.[9]

After striking at Colombo and Trincomalee on 5 and 9 April, when they sank the armed merchant cruiser *Hector* and the destroyer *Tenedos*, and damaged the submarine depot ship *Lucia*, the Japanese found another worthwhile target on the latter date – the British aircraft-carrier *Hermes*, the Australian destroyer *Vampire*, the corvette *Hollyhock*, naval auxiliary *Athalstane* and the tanker *British Sergeant*. All these ships were hustled to sea to avoid the air attacks on the harbour, but without any air cover. The ships called for help and RAF fighters were promised, but they never came at all. Some Fleet Air Arm Fulmars did finally arrive, but far too late, and, in a brief skirmish came off worst to the Vals, losing two of their number without loss to the Japanese! All were once more found by Egusa's dive-bombers, and all were quickly sent to the bottom of the Indian Ocean. One eyewitness, Lieutenant Dennis Brimble aboard the *Hermes*, gave this account of her last moments:

Suddenly, at a great height, appeared flight after flight of planes, estimated to number about seventy, and wishful thinkers thanked God for the RAF! But we were quickly disillusioned. They used the same tactics as the previous group, coming in one after another in a constant stream, so that, as one stick of bombs exploded, the next was already in the air from the following plane. The forward lift rose into the air to a height of approximately 20 feet, snapped its hydraulic system, dropped back onto the flight deck and half down the well to wipe out all those in the hangar who had been blown forward by the blast.

We were now on fire from end to end, and sinking. Still they came on, and word came at last: 'Every man for himself.'[10]

As the Japanese recorded: 'Egusa's men once again achieved an incredible percentage of direct bomb hits; so unusual was this accuracy, unparalleled even in future operations, that to calculate the number of hits, we had to count the misses and subtract these from the total number of bombs released!'[11]

Back in Britain, news of these disasters reawoke old fears that in neglecting the dive-bomber Britain had committed a major blunder. The Press was uneasy and, with some justification, suspected a massive cover-up. In the *News Chronicle* Air Correspondent Ronald Walker, with typical journalistic stupidity, placed the onus entirely on the wrong two services. He blamed, in fact, those who had fought for the dive-bomber: 'In the Navy and Army alike there still lingers the belief that the dive-bomber is not an effective weapon.'[12]

General Sir Gordon Finlayson was far more perceptive. Writing in the *Daily Sketch* about the continued lack of a British dive-bomber, he said:

Perhaps, one day, we may learn the real reason for our lack of this powerful weapon. We hope the reason is good: if so we will be delighted that the secret has been so well kept![13]

Up to this time, it had been the Japanese dive-bombers that had made most of the running in the mainly maritime war in the East. At the first major air-sea battle between the American and Japanese task forces, the Battle of the Coral Sea, which took place on 7 May 1942, the American SBDs were finally able to come into the picture more, and they gave at least as good as they got in this confused encounter. The first strike mounted by the Japanese carriers included three dozen D3A1s, and they sank the American oiler *Neosho* and her escorting destroyer, *Sims*, in mistake for an American carrier. When the forty-five SBDs from the *Lexington* and *Yorktown* struck back in turn, they too caught the wrong vessel, but at least it was a carrier, albeit a small one, the *Shoho*, which they soon put down. Smothered in hits and near-misses, she sank at 1135 hours, and Lieutenant-Commander Bob Dixon's excited radio signal to *Lexington* heralded a new era in the dive-bomber story and in naval warfare: 'Scratch one flattop – Dixon to carrier – Scratch one flattop!'

The next day the fight continued, with the main forces still searching for each other at long range. Thirty-three Vals scored a hit on the carrier *Yorktown* that penetrated four decks and killed sixty-six of her crew. Meanwhile, two dozen SBDs from this same vessel, along with twenty-two more from *Lexington*, got through to the Japanese fleet. The *Yorktown* strike was intercepted by Zekes, and VB-5 only scored one damaging hit on the *Shokaku*. They were followed by Lieutenant John Powers in the last plane, and he held his dive, even though hit by flak time and time again, finally dropping his bomb at 300 feet before smacking into the sea alongside his target. His bomb carved through the Japanese carrier's wooden flight deck, inflicting heavy damage. *Lexington*'s VB-2, under Commander William B. Auldt, made the final attack and scored a third direct hit. Despite this, the *Shokaku*, like the *Yorktown*, lived to fight another day.

The most famous carrier-to-carrier battle in naval history can here only be briefly mentioned due to lack of space. I have re-examined it exhaustively elsewhere.[14] This was, of course, the Battle of Midway, which occurred between 4 and 6 May 1942. The initial air strike launched from the now just four carriers of the reduced *Kidō Būtai*, against Midway Island itself, included thirty-six D3A1s led by Lieutenant Takeihiko Chihaya of *Akagi* and Lieutenant Masaharu Ogawa of *Kaga*. Each of the four big Japanese carriers had twenty-one Vals embarked, plus some spare aircraft, but this battle also marked the operational debut of the Yokosuka D4Y Judy dive-bomber also; two were embarked aboard the carrier *Soryū*, but were only employed as fast reconnaissance planes; the aircraft was still not fully operational in its dive-bomber configuration.

Return strikes from the island base itself included sixteen Dauntless dive-bombers of Marine squadron VMSB-241, led by Major Lofton R. Henderson, and eleven SB2U-3 Vindicators, led by Major Benjamin W. Norris. Henderson was a veteran dive-bomber pilot, qualifying as a Marine Corps aviator in 1929 and serving in Nicaragua in 1930–31 and as an instructor at Pensacola Naval Air Station, Florida, between 1931 and 1933. Both these dive-bomber formations arrived over the Japanese fleet from 0755 and were met by heavy AA fire and strong, fully alert fighter defences. Captain Elmer G. Glidden, leader of the second division in Henderson's group, gave me this eyewitness account of their attack:

The first enemy fighter attacks were directed at the squadron leader in an attempt to put him out of action. After two passes, one of the enemy put several shots through the plane of Major Henderson, and his plane started to burn. From the actions of the leader it was apparent that he was hit and out of action. I was leader of the second box, immediately behind the Major. As soon as it was apparent that the Major was out of action I took over the lead and continued the attack. Fighter attacks were heavy, so I led the squadron down through a protecting layer of cloud and gave the signal to attack. On emerging from the cloud-bank, the enemy carrier was directly below the squadron, and all planes made their runs. The diving interval was five seconds.[15]

Losses were severe, eight SBDs being shot down and no hits being obtained. The old 'Wind Indicators' followed them down, and selected the battleship *Haruna* as their target, again without success, and two Vindicators were destroyed. But the climax of the day's fighting came at 1207, when two of the three main SBD strikes launched from the three American carriers, *Enterprise*, *Hornet* and *Yorktown* (hastily patched up after the Coral Sea), caught the Japanese carriers by surprise. Although the *Hornet* dive-bombers, VB-8 and VS-8, under their Air Group leader, Commander Stanhope C. Ring, all missed the target, the other groups were more fortunate. Led by Commander Clarence W. McClusky, there were thirty-seven Dauntless dive-bombers from the *Enterprise*, with VB-6 and VS-6 commanded respectively by Lieutenant Richard H. Best and Lieutenant Wilmer E. Gallaher, and seventeen SBDs from the *Yorktown* under Lieutenant-Commander Maxwell F. Leslie of VB-3, which, although launching later, arrived over the target simultaneously with McClusky's team. They were able to attack and destroy three of the Japanese carriers, *Akagi*, *Kaga* and *Soryū*, in a series of devastating strikes.

Lieutenant Paul A. Holmberg flew with VB-3. 'Lefty' Holmberg was Leslie's wingman, and as Leslie had accidentally lost his bomb earlier, 'Lefty' became the first dive-bomber into the attack with a payload to drop. He recalled:

Fortunately for our dive-bomber squadron, enemy fighters were remaining at low altitudes as we approached, to cope with our torpedo-plane attack taking place at the same time. Therefore, we had no air opposition while proceeding to a point over our selected target at about 24,000 feet altitude. In the initial part of our dive (down to 12,000 feet) our flight path (dive) was at about 70 degrees (20 degrees less than vertical). This tactic enabled us to expedite the attack as no enemy opposition appeared. In the vertical phase, from 12,000 feet down to bomb-release, I was concentrating on adjusting the aircraft's heading to keep the cross-hairs of my telescope bombsight on a red ball painted on the forward part of the flight deck of the target ship. I concentrated on two things at this juncture: one was to watch the altimeter for 1,500 feet coming up, the other was to push the electric bomb-release button, and, at the same time, pull the manual bomb-release lanyard at 1,500 feet altitude. I did this to make doubly sure my bomb was released!

Next, I concentrated on pulling out of my dive so that I would be just skimming the water when I regained horizontal flight. Several seconds had passed after I had regained horizontal flight when my gunner (my rear-seat man) shouted joyously over the intercom that my bomb had struck the target and that I should look back to see. I did so with satisfaction – but just for a moment, for then I concerned myself with evading ship's gunfire that manifested itself by shell splashes in the water in my vicinity.[16]

His target carrier was one of the three big Japanese carriers hit in that attack, and all three burned and sank. The one remaining Japanese carrier now fought on by itself, and managed to make two attacks, the first one by Val dive-bombers alone. They took heavy losses, but enough got through to the *Yorktown* to score three direct hits. Later two torpedoes from a second air attack, and two more from a Japanese submarine, caused her to be scuttled, but not before the American had hit back and the SBDs had completed a memorable victory by dive-bombing the *Hiryū* and so damaging her that she, too, had to be sunk. The final victory of the dive-bombers in this battle was the destruction of the heavy cruiser *Mogami* and the heavy damaging of her sister ship *Mikuma* by Dauntless attacks from *Hornet* and *Enterprise*. The dive-bomber in the Pacific War had proved *the* decisive weapon.

Notes

1. Slessor, Air Vice-Marshal, *Use of Bombers in Close Support of the Army*, dated 6 May 1941. VCAS 2302 (National Archives, Kew, London, AIR 8/631).
2. *Report of Battle Pilot*, enclosed with VCAS 2302 (National Archives, Kew, London, AIR 8/631).
3. Mahlke, *Generalleutnant* Helmut, to the Author, op. cit.
4. Rudel, Hans-Ulrich, *Stuka Pilot* (Eurphorian, Dublin, 1953).
5. Lang, *Oberst* Friedrich, to the Author, op. cit.
6. Okumiya, Masatake & Horikoshi, Jiro, *Zero!* (Cassell, 1957).
7. Read his life story in Peter C. Smith, *Fist from the Sky*, Crécy Publishing, Manchester, 2006.
8. Tomlinson, Michael, *The Most Dangerous Moment*, op. cit.
9. Okumiya & Horikoshi, *Zero!* Op. cit.
10. Tomlinson, Michael, *The Most Dangerous Moment*, op. cit.

11. Okumiya & Horikoshi, *Zero!* Op. cit.
12. Walker, Ronald, *The Dive-bomber Does it Again*, article in the *News Chronicle*, issued dated 11 April 1942 (National Newspaper Museum, Colindale, London).
13. Gordon-Finlayson, General Sir R., *Dive-bombers – Why This Awful Delay?* article in *Daily Sketch*, issued dated 22 April 1942 (National Newspaper Museum, Colindale, London).
14. See Peter C. Smith, *Midway: Dauntless Victory*, Pen & Sword Naval, Barnsley, 2007.
15. Glidden, Elmer G., Captain, USMC, *Combat Report*, dated 17 June 1942 (USMC-AG-1265-kps).
16. Holmberg, Rear Admiral Paul A., to the Author, op. cit.

CHAPTER TEN

'I went into a loop'

After the decisive battle of Midway, the emphasis of the Pacific War shifted far to the south and to the chain of islands known as the Solomons Group. The Japanese were already expanding their conquests south-east down this chain of islands, constructing airfields as they went, and with the long-term aim of cutting Australia off from the United States. To forestall this, the US Marines landed on Guadalcanal and Savo Islands, and a long battle of attrition commenced, which saw much hard landing fighting, an enormous number of sea battles in confined waters involving battleships on down to PT-boats, and a hard slugging match in the air. Again, for striking power this was a war fought by the Val and Dauntless.

At the naval Battle of the Eastern Solomons, the dive-bombers of both sides' naval task forces played the leading roles. SBD strikes sank the small Japanese carrier *Ryujo* and damaged the larger *Shokaku*, while the D3A1s hit the *Enterprise* three times, but she survived. Another victim of the Dauntless in this encounter was the seaplane tender *Chitose*.

Marine Corps and Navy SBDs operated to great effect from the much-fought-over jungle airstrip of Henderson Field on Guadalcanal itself, inflicting severe casualties of the ships of the Japanese 'Tokyo Express' convoys and warship squadrons trying to penetrate the 'Slot' in order to land reinforcements. At the naval Battle of Santa Cruz, the Vals again led the dive-bombing attacks on the Japanese Navy's principal foes, the American aircraft-carriers. On 26 October 1942, two waves of Vals were sent against them, and at 0655 hours the first attack by twenty-two D3A1s, led by Lieutenant-Commander Mamoru Seki, found the US task force and attacked on their own. Their target was the carrier *Hornet*. An eyewitness described the last dive of Seki thus:

Lieutenant-Commander Seki's plane seemed to have taken several direct hits soon after he gave the order to attack. His craft was directly in front of mine as I went into my dive. I noticed the bomber enter its dive and suddenly begin to roll over on its back. Flames shot out of the bomber, and, still inverted, it continued diving toward the enemy ship.[1]

136

Seki's Val struck the *Hornet's* funnel and burst through the carrier's flight deck, and its bomb load erupted, bursting the ship's boilers. In addition, three direct hits were scored by other D3A1s, one aft to starboard, another exploding on impact with the flight deck, while another gouged its way down to the fourth deck level before detonating. The *Hornet* slewed to a halt, listing and disabled, and was then hit by two torpedoes from Japanese torpedo-bombers.

The second wave of Vals, twenty strong, and led by Lieutenant Sadomu Takahashi, was intercepted by US fighters, but enough of them got through to plant two direct hits on the carrier *Enterprise*, while other Vals dashed themselves vainly against the defences of the battleship *South Dakota*, flanked as she was by the anti-aircraft cruiser *San Juan* and the heavy cruiser *Portland*. Against this huge array of AA firepower, all their efforts broke, with heavy losses among the dive-bombers involved. One Val did score a direct hit on the battleship with a heavy bomb atop the battleship's 'A' turret, but this failed to inflict much damage on such a heavily protected target. Another Val scored a direct hit on the *San Juan*, and her flimsy decks offered little resistance; the bomb penetrated though to the ship's keel before exploding deep inside and jamming her rudder.

The return strike of SBDs found the Japanese carriers in turn at 0840. Two of the Dauntless scouts made a surprise attack through cloud cover and hit the carrier *Zuiho* aft with two bombs; these planes were piloted by Lieutenant Birney Strong and Ensign Charles Irvine of the *Enterprise's* VS-10. Meanwhile *Hornet's* strike, already in the air, had fifteen SBDs, while *Enterprise* got away another three and *Hornet* followed up with nine more. The first wave scored three direct hits on the carrier *Shokaku*; the second demolished the bridge of the heavy cruiser *Chikuma*, for a total loss of twenty aircraft. The crippled *Hornet* was then attacked by the last six Vals left from the carrier *Junyô*, led by Sub-Lieutenant Shunko Kato, and they hit her yet again, as did more torpedoes. She finally sank at 0135 hours on the 27th.

*   *   *

A world away from these intense 'ding-dong' life-and-death naval duels, the spring of 1942 witnessed the renewal of the *Luftwaffe* blitz on Malta by both German and Italian dive-bomber forces. This aerial assault grew to a crescendo as March passed into April. Enormous damage was done; many warships were sunk at anchor in the various creeks of Valetta harbour, and Malta became the most-bombed place in the world. To keep the island in the fight at all required major naval operations in order to try and fight through with convoys of essential food and supplies to keep the garrison and population going. These convoys were disputed by the Axis air forces and navies working from bases that outflanked the convoy routes all the way from either Gibraltar in the west or Alexandria in the east. By August 1942, the island's situation had become desperate, and the largest and most famous of all the Malta Convoys took place, Operation Pedestal.[2] One of three escorting aircraft-carriers, HMS *Indomitable*, was the victim of a massed Stuka attack on 12 August, which again took place close to the western end of the Sicilian Channel. In a scene remarkably resembling the fate of her sister two-and-a-half years earlier, this armoured-deck carrier was also left smoking and on fire from three direct hits and two very-near-misses inflicted on her by the Ju 87s of StG 3 operating from Trapani airfield. Nine Italian Stukas of 239 *Squadriglia* also took part in this mission. The commander of these Italian Stukas described their attack in this manner:

> About ten minutes before coming within sight of the ships, I made a left-hand turn in accordance with the pre-arranged flight plan: I checked my compass. I was at an altitude of roughly 2,000 metres. Some flak exploded around me and I realised I was right over the convoy, which must have moved considerably north in comparison to the spot where it had been sighted by our aerial reconnaissance. I ordered my unit to go into the dive, but I went into a loop because I had gone beyond my vertical line of my selected target and, in so doing, ended up at the rear of the formation.[3]

Cumbat later told me that his dive was made against 'an aircraft-carrier located forward of the central line of ships in the convoy'.

> During my short dive, we were surrounded by the outlines of shells from the anti-aircraft guns of all the warships. I dropped my load of bombs and pulled out at about 200 metres from sea level. During that critical phase Cavallo warned me, 'Fighter on your tail'. I had not yet reached my line of manoeuvre before two cannon blows ripped through the two wings and a machine-gun volley reduced my right fuel tank to the appearance of a soup strainer ....[4]
>
> We employed on our Ju 87s a private camera, operated by the gunner, to try to get some pictures during our attacks, but, as you can imagine, the results were very poor and not definite. From this attack I lost both my wingmen to the flak and myself did not obtain any witness of my results or documentation. That night at 0200 on the 13th, Catania Air Headquarters called me at base asking if I could confirm that my unit had scored hits on an aircraft-carrier, as the Germans were claiming it for their Stukas. I replied that I could not prove it either way, but should they obtain better information than I, then they should award it to one of my

two lost companions who were seen to complete their dives. I never subsequently checked further, all I know is that I lost two very brave and enthusiastic young pilots that day.[5]

Over in the Western Desert also, the tide of war swung first one way then the other. The Ju 87s it was that had paved the way for Rommel's most spectacular coup, the capture of Tobruk in June 1942. Yet another British humiliation at the hands of the Stuka, it led to a Motion of Censure of Churchill in the House of Commons. Rommel's initial thrust eastwards had at first been held up at Bir Hakeim. In support of his attack on this position, StG 3 flew up to three combat missions a day in the face of heavy fighter opposition. Lurid headlines appeared in the British Press:

> *100 Stukas Hammer Bir Hakeim.* From the top of a riddled German bomber, I watched 100 German dive-bombers swoop on Bir Hakeim. It was the greatest dive-bomber raid ever unleashed in the desert.[6]

Another British eyewitness of this assault, described more soberly StG 3 going about their work against the Free French defenders and unhindered by the 'dominant' RAF:

> While we're surveying the scene, the air becomes filled with a deep droning, which gradually grows to a tremendous roar. We scan the sky apprehensively, but it's some time before we can discern a group of aircraft approaching slowly and very high up from the west. There may be about twenty of them but a moment later Corporal Crotch excitedly points out another twenty, tailing them up. Then, twenty more come into sight, and another twenty, until almost a hundred planes must be crawling nearer with ear-splitting tumult and relentless precision across the sky. Our relief is great, as each group, in turn, wheels over the area of derelict vehicles, tilts into a dive of deafening crescendo and pours out bombs from a still high altitude. Ack-ack sprouts from various points to meet them, the earth goes up in a screen of smoke and sand, and a medley of infernal crashes punctuates the screaming of the planes as they dive, climb and veer away. It's an awe-inspiring sight, and we forget ourselves in watching it. Of course, it's Bir Hakeim.[7]

When the fortress fell, the men on the spot had little doubt as to one of the main reasons. 'Constant Dive-bombing' proclaimed the headlines in *The Times* the following day.[8] In the *Sunday Express* on 31 May, Major Oliver Stewart, the defence correspondent, predicted the outcome of future operations in an article entitled, 'Can we check Rommel without the dive-bomber?' He posed the following question for his readers: 'Here we have, therefore, a practical test of theory. Can the momentum be taken out of the enemy's thrust without the help of the dive-bomber?' he asked.[9]

It could not. Tobruk was invested once more. Rommel wasted no more time.

> In fact, Rommel had issued his orders for the attack on 18 June, the day after he had finally closed the ring by capturing Gambut. He had obtained Kesselring's promise of support from all the Stukas he could provide, which would attack the south-east sector at dawn.[10]

A German officer later described the methods used by the Ju 87s to crack this hitherto impregnable nut.

> The Stukas dropped their noses and swooped over our heads. They plunged at the enemy perimeter; bombs screamed down and crashed into the minefields. Rommel had thought up a new trick in the desert. He was not bombing the defenders, but blasting a way through the minefields. One crash would be followed by another, and a whole series; one bomb would detonate a chain of mines, like some atomic fission, continuing on beyond the first explosive shock.[11]

Much was made of this by the dive-bomber's critics, who claimed stridently that Allied losses from them at Tobruk were negligible. This, then, is why: the Ju 87s were not banging on the roof but prising open the back door. The result was the same: Tobruk fell.

When Tobruk surrendered as quickly as Bir Hakeim, the British public and Press exploded in pent-up frustration at this latest of a seemingly endless list of British defeats and disasters attributed to the dive-bombers of their enemies, the impotence of which the RAF continued to proclaim as it scored victory upon victory.

The Times of 22 June was, perhaps, the most restrained: 'Dive-bombing seems to have largely decided the issue at Bir Hakeim, and it is probable that it has been to a great extent responsible for the fate of Tobruk.'[12] This is stated passively, not wishing, even now, to rock the boat.

Others were rather more forthright. *The Star* on the same day said in its leader column: 'Most of all we were beaten by the dive-bombers ...',[13] while in the *Sunday Express* Major Stewart was predictably bitter in his article: 'Events in Libya last week, and especially the fall of Bir Hakeim, direct attention once again to the merits of the dive-bomber.' He listed these as 'blasting power, accuracy, psychological suitability'.[14]

Reviewing the situation, as the British continued to fall back toward Cairo and the Suez Canal, the *Sunday Times* of 28 June reflected:

> To that inferiority a third important contribution was made by the dive-bomber. As usual we had none and the Germans many, and as usual their special aptitude for making direct hits proved invaluable against difficult targets like tanks and strongpoints. We know from the defenders that it was the dive-bomber which overcame Bir Hakeim, nor does there seem any good reason to doubt the Germans' claim that it performed the same service for them at Tobruk.[15]

The author of this article, Scrutator, seemed to have a good insight also into the real reason for this state of affairs: 'There are people at the Air Ministry who will probably scorn dive-bombers to the end; but I have yet to hear of any soldier or sailor who does so after undergoing attack by them.'[16]

Another who spilled the beans was a Mr T.C.L. Westbrook, formerly with the MAP, who wrote to *The Times* on 27 June: 'Just lately many confusing and conflicting statements have been made about the lack of dive-bombers. The true facts are that the Air Ministry decided, before the war, against the use of them ....' He went on to spell out the earlier situation. 'In the early days of the Ministry of Aircraft Production it was impossible to order dive-bombers as (1) the British programme was full and production poor, and (2) the RAF did not want them.'[17]

This, of course, was too accurate for comfort and caused a flurry at the Air Ministry, as did another give-away of who was to blame. This came in a radio broadcast by Robert St John, NBC's London correspondent, to America on 23 June:

> Most experts here place a lot of blame for what happened in Libya on the *lack* of dive-bombers. And most of the Little People of England think that that's America's fault. The Air Minister has twice publicly declared that dive-bombers *were* ordered from America as far back as 1940 and haven't *yet* been delivered. But I know that American officials have pleaded with the British to *take* dive-bombers ... to use them ... to make them an important weapon of war ... as the Nazis have done. *American* airmen are impressed with what Nazi and Jap dive-bombers have done, and what ours *can* do. But the RAF had been reluctant to concede the effectiveness of dive-bombing. And that's rather ironical ... because a controversy has been going on lately in the columns of one London paper between various British pilots of the *last* war ... a controversy over *which one of them* originated dive-bombing. It

is a fact that dive-bombing was a British invention of a quarter of a century ago.[18]

All this revealing of secrets brought to a head the simmering arguments and the old counter-arguments that had long been raging behind the scenes during the previous years. As long ago as August 1941 the Prime Minister had warned the CAS that, 'There is widespread belief that we have not developed the dive-bombers because of the fear of the Air Ministry that a weapon of this kind, specially associated with the Army, might lead to the formation of a separate Army wing.'

The astute Prime Minister had, of course, hit the nail directly on the head, and the glaring failure of the cherished and revered heavy bombers of the RAF to destroy the two German battle-cruisers in the nearby French harbour of Brest, despite an enormous amount of effort and expenditure of bombs, had also brought a growl from him on the same lines: 'The policy of the Air Ministry in neglecting the dive-bomber type of aircraft is shown by all experience to have been a grievous error, and one for which we are paying dearly both in lack of offensive power and by the fear of injury which is prevalent afloat.'[19]

All of which brought forth once more the standard defence from the air marshals which have been reproduced earlier and from which this latest defeat had shifted them not one iota. Their head-in-the-sand stance was typified by the Secretary-of-State's reply during the Air Estimates speech of 4 March 1942: 'It would be a complete mistake to suppose that the Air Staff does not want them', was one remarkable statement, made, no doubt, in good faith but appalling ignorance. He added, 'Now we have obtained, with more efficient fighting aircraft, the mastery of the air in more than one theatre of war, we hope to find good use for them.'[20]

That mastery of the air was not very obvious over Tobruk, nor had it been over the English Channel just a few weeks earlier, when the whole German battle fleet steamed through it and more than half Bomber Command's 240 aircraft failed to even find the ships, and certainly did not hit them, attacking instead, in many cases, friendly warships in error. Not surprisingly in the immediate aftermath of that fiasco, Sinclair's words rang rather hollow as a consequence. Nor was he alone in making strange utterances. In the *Daily Sketch* in March, a Major-General Ernest Swinton slavishly followed the new official line, stating that, 'The fact is that official opinion has been definitely against employing these machines.' But even he was forced to concede that:

> The Germans, Russians and Japanese still rely largely on dive-bombing, while the Americans are building and using these machines on a very big scale. Now, all these people are realists,

and it is not conceivable that they would waste money, material and manpower on a weapon which had not proved its worth.[21]

Even more bizarrely, considering what had just taken place in the Indian and Pacific Oceans, a Commander H. Pursey RN stated that the Royal Navy was not enthusiastic, there being no dive-bombers serving afloat at this time: 'They are of more value for attacks on naval bases than on ships. One reason is that dive-bombers are best operated from shore bases rather than aircraft-carriers.[22]

An incredible thing to allege at a time when American and Japanese carrier-based dive-bombers were causing 90 per cent of all the damage in the Pacific War! The standard RAF arguments as to why they were the only Air Force in step in this argument were given another public airing in a long article in the *Sunday Dispatch* in May. Written by 'A Leading Authority in Close Touch With the RAF', it claimed to be 'The First Authoritative Light on the War's Greatest Public Controversy'. In fact, it was just another re-hash of the standard Air Ministry line, except that it contained the following gem: 'Tanks form an ideal air-raid shelter.' It also claimed, somewhat incongruously in view of its title, that: 'There is thus no controversy, but the Air Ministry knows the limitations of the dive-bomber better that those who have only seen it operating against them under conditions very favourable to it.'[23] Quite where *that* was if the RAF had total air control, as Sinclair had claimed, was rather hard to determine, so he did not do so!

The *Daily Mail* ran a leader in a May issue entitled 'Blind Spot', which made the point very tellingly:

> The Air Ministry, in spite of all the evidence, has not been fully convinced that this type of aircraft is an effective weapon. This may be the blind spot in an otherwise brilliant Service. The dive-bomber is not an especially complicated machine to produce, and it should be made available without further delay.[24]

*   *   *

The Air Ministry rode out the storm and kept building up for the first 1,000-bomber raids on German cities, their only real interest. This, they were convinced, would quickly bring the enemy to his knees, and all the current worries about fleets being sunk and armies being defeated and evacuated would all be irrelevant anyway! Whatever the public feeling on the matter, the fact was that, even if by some miracle the air marshals had suddenly seen the light and changed their deeply entrenched prejudices at this time, and had they been bold enough to admit they were as wrong in 1942 as they had been in 1941, 1940, 1938 or 1918, they would *not* have been in a position to do anything positive to rectify matters.

When it was revealed by the Air Minister himself that the RAF had American dive-bombers coming into service, the Press was taken in completely. The *Daily Sketch* carried an article by Gordon Webb which demonstrated how they had been fooled: 'The Americans claim that no other aircraft in the world is as efficient and so deadly for dive-bombing as the Bermuda [*sic*].' He added for good measure:

> Today the dive-bomber stands a proved weapon for these kinds of attack. It is good to know that, while we ourselves are so backward in its development, the United States have reserves of them upon which we can draw until we can develop our own and bring them into battle.[25]

Nobody at all mentioned the superlative British Hawker Henley, still being used as a target tug! Far from being the great white hope for dive-bomber supply, American industry was sadly lacking in results. Webb's dizzy euphoria aside, the dismal truth was vastly different.

* * *

In March 1942, the Allocation and Delivery Progress of the Bermuda and Vengeance aircraft was summarised in response to Churchill's query as to where the dive-bombers ordered in 1940 and 1941 had got to:

> Bermuda: Production output not anticipated before March 1942. All aircraft coming to UK for Army Co-Operation Command. Delivery to service say three months after arrival in UK – July/ August.
> Vengeance: Twelve aircraft accepted at factory to 10 March 1942. Allocation at present the subject of discussion at political level but previous to standstill order, the following were the dispositions: Canada (60), India (240), Australia (300) Unallocated (400).[26]

On contemporary types immediately available the CAS reported only three, and completely ignored the Douglas SBD/A24!

> The Vengeance and Bermuda are on order for the RAF. The Chesapeake (Vindicator), is a naval dive-bomber now obsolescent. Performance of the two types intended for the RAF is very similar but the Vengeance seems to be the most suitable; it is reported more robust and more pleasant to handle in a dive than the Bermuda. The Bermuda is reported to be heavy in the rudder and to suffer from slight buffeting of the tail when diving.[27]

It was further noted that: 'The Bermuda will replace the Blenheim in Army Co-Operation Command and will be used as a dive-bomber and bomber reconnaissance aircraft, and the Vengeance is intended to be employed as a light dive-bomber in India, Australia, Canada and South Africa.'[28] Hardly the critical centres of the war at the time, or ever!

On the naval dive-bomber position, Cherwell wrote to the Premier about the equally long-delayed Fairey Barracuda thus:

This aeroplane seems to have had an unfortunate history. There was a year between the selection of the design and the beginning of the construction of the prototype, and two years from this stage to the first flight, which showed the aerodynamic troubles leading to the redesign of the tail. This delay was caused partly by a change-over at the outbreak of war to the Merlin engine (probably justified), and the suspension of production for three months in the summer and autumn of 1940 when everything had to be sacrificed to pushing fighters into the front line. The great delay is most disappointing, but the performance of the machine seems good. Production seems to have been handled on peacetime lines, so that it will be nearly midsummer 1942, i.e. a year after the design was officially agreed, and more than four years after it was selected, before we get the first squadron.[29]

On 19 May 1942, a meeting was held at BAC between that organisation and an RAF delegation under Air Commodore E.B.C. Betts, because: 'It has been suggested that the Vengeance is an unpopular and unwanted aeroplane, that as a result of British indifference the output from the Vultee plant at Nashville is very much behind schedule and that it would be better to use the capacity for some more useful type of aeroplane.'[30]

A total of 500 British and 400 Lease/Lend Vengeance dive-bombers were under order from the Vultee plants at Douney, Nashville, and a further 200 British and 200 Lease/Lend aircraft from the Northrop plant at Hawthorne, California. 'The Vengeance was developed solely for British use, and the Americans took little or no interest in it until the discussions in connection with the Arnold/Portal Agreement, under which 350 were allocated to the US Army ....' It was admitted that:

Production is lagging badly behind the initial contract schedules, but this is not uncommon experience with a new type of aircraft. So far as the Vultee factory is concerned, it has been frankly admitted by the firm that this was fundamentally due to weak management, a defect which has since been remedied, largely at British insistence.

The meeting report concluded: 'Whether the type proves an oper-ational success or not, it must be remembered that the Vengeance is one of the only two single-engined dive-bomber types which we have on order for the RAF.'

The unexpected fall of Tobruk, on top of the loss of western and southern Europe, the Balkans, Malaya, Singapore, heavy naval losses in the Indian Ocean and Mediterranean, etc., all piled up to a dismal chain of military incompetence for which the British government could not evade responsibility. It all prompted a Motion of Censure on the Churchill Cabinet's handling of the war to date. It was not a happy picture, and naturally, the total lack of British dive-bombers was the subject of some of the severe criticism in the House.[31] Swallowing his own misgivings on this, for he was fighting for his political life, Churchill took the politicians way out and veered round to the defence of the RAF line in his own speech:

> I can only say that the highest technical authorities still hold very strong opinions on either side of this question. Of course you cannot judge whether we ought to have had dive-bombers at any particular date without also considering what we should have had to give up if we had them. Most of the Air Marshals, the leading men in the Air Force, think little of dive-bombers and they persist in their opinion. They are entitled to respect for their opinions . . . .[32]

He continued:

> . . . because it was from the same source that the eight-gun fighter was designed which destroyed so many hundred of dive-bombers in the Battle of Britain and has enabled us to preserve ourselves free and uninvaded [sic].

It was a brilliant speech overall, despite the fact that it was mainly smoke and mirrors and the obvious nonsense it contained. What, of course, the RAF would have had to do without had it adopted the dive-bomber would *not* have been eight-gun fighters, as the RAF kept on insisting (in retrospect), but hundreds and hundreds of those totally useless Battles and Lysander aircraft. Also, of course, the eight-gun Spitfire and Hurricane owed very little indeed to the air marshals, and far more to the sheer dogged persistence of their designers, whom the gentlemen at the Air Ministry cold-shouldered pre-war as they were only interested in heavy bombers! Nor were 'hundreds' of Ju 87s shot down in the Battle of Britain, only fifty-four in fact. But all these truths mattered little then beside the fact that Churchill easily won the vote. His future as war leader was assured, leading to both the 'Area Bombing' policy, which pleased the air marshals, and the 'Unconditional Surrender' policy, which satisfied the American President. While the debate was not really an exclusively dive-bomber issue, it allowed the steam to be taken out of it, but although the immediate crisis was over, the great dive-bomber controversy was not!

* * *

While the various factions in Great Britain incestuously argued and debated the place, or lack of it, of the dive-bomber in the UK arsenal, the increasingly bitter war being waged in the Pacific was centred almost entirely on that type of aircraft. Throughout 1942 and into 1943 the SBD and D3A2 had slugged it out mainly on their own, although both machines were of elderly design and due for replacement. But by the end of 1943 the new generation of dive-bombers belatedly began to appear on the battlefield in increasing numbers. The change-over from peacetime footing to war production had not only affected the production of the Bermuda and Vengeance, but had not assisted the introduction of the Curtiss SB2C Helldiver or the Yokosuka D4Y1Judy either.

In the case of the latter aircraft, the Japanese were unable to solve the problem of wing flutter in the Suisei until the spring of 1943. Only then could the Judy be used in her proper role and not just for recon-naissance as hitherto. The Val and Dauntless designs, just like the Stuka, had, perforce, to be stretched and modified still further while awaiting the arrival of the new aircraft. The US Army half-heartedly toyed with their version of the Dauntless, the A-24 Banshee, using a few operationally in the Dutch East Indies and later with the 531 Fighter-Bomber Squadron at Makin, before turning to the 500 made-over P-51 Mustang fighters which, fitted with slatted dive-brakes from the V-72 Vengeance, became the A-36 Apache dive-bomber and operated with high success in the Mediterranean in 1943–4.[33] In the case of the far more enthusiastic US Navy, the long-awaited Helldiver from Curtiss at Columbus, Ohio, was beset with enormous teething problems. This aircraft first joined the fleet aboard the carrier *Essex* with VS-9 as early as December 1942, but innumerable difficulties caused one carrier captain, Captain J.J. Clark of *Yorktown (II)*, to recom-mend the entire programme be scrapped! Not until July 1943 was a Helldiver unit formed that could be regarded as fully operational.[34]

Again, the Army Air Corps variant, the A-25A Shrike, was ordered, and no fewer than 3,000 were asked for, but constant modifications and changes in policy meant that those that were eventually built had no employment and ended their days as target tugs, a fate which seemed to be the sorry fate of every unwanted dive-bomber type the world over! In the south-west Pacific, the RAAF used the Commonwealth Wirraway as a makeshift dive-bomber in Malaya and Papua New Guinea, until the Vultee Vengeance eventually arrived, and then it was employed briefly, but most effectively, on combat operations. The New

Zealand Air Force adopted the SBD Dauntless and, again, used them to very good effect, alongside the US Marine Corps units in the Solomon Islands campaign.

Dive-bomber operations, both island and carrier based in the Pacific in the years 1943–4, were so numerous and diverse that only the salient details can be given here.[35] The trend overall was that, as their losses mounted, the Japanese dive-bombers were more and more flown by semi-trained personnel, and thus their accuracy and power to influence battle outcomes diminished, and indeed sharply declined after 1942. Moreover, the increasing size and protective power of the new US fleets made attempts by the penny-packets of Japanese dive-bombers to penetrate their overwhelming fighter screens, assisted by radar interception, and to pierce their massed AA batteries, well-nigh impossible. (In Task Force 38 alone, for instance, the ships' AA firepower far exceeded the total AA defence of the *whole* of Great Britain!) After several such air-sea battles had been fought and lost, the Japanese dive-bombers dashing themselves in vain against such defences, the practicality of such attacks was, for them, shown to be futile. The Japanese then went over to suicide attacks, the reasoning being that, as a pilot stood little or no chance of returning from a sortie, anyway, at least he could take out an enemy warship with the deliberate sacrifice of his own life as a *Kamikaze*. But this was a wasting asset, even if an effective one.

Conversely, the huge expansion of the American fleet gave it dive-bombers in abundance, even excess. The American Navy could mount saturation attacks of this nature whenever it chose. But this expansion also involved an enormous influx of fresh pilots, but their longer training time ensured that there was no fall in accuracy as afflicted their Japanese opposite numbers, although they were never as proficient as the old pre-war veterans. Thus, although the Americans now attacked with hundreds of Helldivers instead of dozens of SBDs, ship tonnage sunk showed no great upward surge, although bombs dropped mushroomed. It was not until toward the end of the Pacific War, when their main surviving targets, the heavy ships of the Japanese Navy, lay immobilised in their home anchorages, did the majority of the Japanese battleships finally succumb, in the same way as had Germany's.

After the Japanese had been forced to evacuate the garrison from Guadalcanal, the Allies initiated a step-by-step advance up the Solomons chain to isolate Rabaul in New Britain, Japan's main base in the south. SBDs island-hopped from airstrip to airstrip, striking hard at the Japanese warships, mainly cruisers and destroyers which were employed in either reinforcing or evacuating their troops from the islands. These dive-bomber missions were supplemented from time to time by strong carrier-based raids from the growing US Task Groups, but no major fleet action developed during 1943 as the focus shifted north.

In January and February 1943, several such dive-bombing attacks on 'Tokyo Express' squadrons were made. The heavy casualties inflicted upon these ships stung Admiral Yamamoto into retaliation, and on 7 April 1942 Operation I-Go air offensive was launched by the Japanese Navy in an attempt to wipe out the American forces in the South Pacific area. Every available dive-bomber was dispatched, including many landed from the carriers of the fleet. For four days they pounded Allied airstrips and attacked shipping, and a great victory was proclaimed. The truth was very different: results were actually negligible, and were grossly over-estimated by the Japanese themselves. In reality, the Americans lost only half the number of aircraft that the attackers did, and included in that Japanese loss tally were many D3A2s and their irreplaceable aircrews. The Japanese carrier fleet had therefore been denuded to no avail and was compelled to withdraw to replenish both men and machines, and for a while the Val practically vanished from the skies of the southern Pacific.

This left the US Marine Corps and RNZAF Dauntless squadrons to carry on dive-bombing missions in their theatre on their own, which they set about with a will. In attacks on Munda, Australian coast-watchers pinpointed new gun emplacements as soon as the Japanese constructed them, and the SBDs duly took them out.

Just how effective they proved was confirmed by Commander Eric A. Feldt RAN in his book *The Coastwatchers*: 'Indiscriminate bombing of jungle positions is generally harmless, but this precise delivery of high explosives on selected targets was something else again.'[36]

Despite much initial distrust from friendly troops on the effectiveness of dive-bombing, and the dangers to themselves of close support, the USMC used this campaign to develop its own techniques, which were on a par with the German Ju 87 units for accuracy of delivery, when once perfected.

With eight officers and eight radiomen, Air Liaison Parties were set up, under Major Wilfred Stiles, equipped with four command cars, each of which was fitted with an SCR-193 radio, and an Aldis lamp, pyrotechnic equipment and Isenburg cloth for panels. In the jungle fighting the enemy might be only yards away, and their pillboxes and coral foxholes were tough enough to withstand all but direct hits. The first such mission was laid on by twelve SBDs on 12 July, but proved a failure. Thereafter, the Marines gradually gained proficiency at this form of dive-bombing.

On 1 August 1943, eighteen Dauntless dive-bombers and eighteen Grumman TBF Avengers, acting in the glide-bombing configuration, hit Japanese gun emplacements at Lambeti Plantation in support of the 43rd Division. On the 25th a mass dive-bombing attack mounted by fifty-four SBDs and fifty-three TBFs, with Marine, RNZAF and land-based Navy aircraft all taking part, silenced Japanese AA positions on Bibilo Hill.

Fresh reinforcements of D3A-1s and 2s were flown off the Japanese aircraft-carriers on 28 October on the orders of Admiral Koga, in another effort to halt the American advance. Forty-five Vals were reported on Rabaul's airstrips at this date, and they mounted an all-out assault against the American beach-head on Bougainville in November. But they suffered heavy losses once more, for 75 per cent of the Japanese dive-bomber aircrews were killed. The few survivors were again withdrawn, and this was to prove to be their last big effort of 1943.

On the formation of Marine Air Wing (MAW) Four in late 1942, the Marine SBD squadrons moved into the Central Pacific in the wake of further landings. This force included MAG-13 with VMSB-151 and VMSB-241, and MAG-31 with VMSB-331 and VMSB-3341. In December 1943, these aircraft were operating from Tarawa in the Gilbert Islands against the Japanese airfields in the Marshall Group, and in March 1944 they shifted over to Kwajalein, striking at the enemy airfields on Wotje, Manoelap, Mili and Jaluit. These SBDs were later joined by the famous 'Ace of Spades' squadron, VMSB-231, commanded by Major Elmer Glidden, veteran of both Midway and Guadalcanal.

Speaking of their work on 27 December 1944, Rear Admiral De Witte C. Ramsay, Chief of the Bureau of Aeronautics, described their methods thus:

> Over 70 per cent of their targets have been 50 feet or less in diameter whereas normal dive-bomber targets are 200 feet in diameter. The targets in the main were Japanese gun positions, which were eliminated one by one ....
>
> The Marine squadrons involved tried several techniques but the most effective for the Corsair seemed to be a 70–80 degree dive at high speed.[37]

A very powerful new Marine Corps fighter-bomber, the Chance-Vought F4U Corsair, was being increasingly utilised in the dive-bomber role by shore-based Marine units as the war went on, gradually replacing the Dauntless in almost, but not quite, all units.

The Corsair was an outstanding aircraft, both as a fighter and as a dive-bomber. It was first employed in the latter role in the Marshall Islands on 18 March 1944, when eight Makin-based Corsairs of VMF-11 dropped 1,000 lb bombs on AA positions at Mille. The US Navy squadron, VF-17, had also experimented with this big fighter in dive-bombing in February during attacks on Rabaul, in which both Navy and Marine pilots used their own improvised bomb racks. The wheel had come full circle from 1918.

Subsequent experiments revealed that the F4U could be safely and efficiently employed as a dive-bomber in dives of up to 85 degrees. The plane's six .50-calibre guns were used for staffing in the latter stages of the dive.[38]

The incredible Corsair could, in fact, lift twice the bomb load of the specially designed Dauntless, but some pilots stayed faithful to the old SBD right to the end, one such being 'Iron Man' Glidden.

Notes

1. Okumiya & Horikoshi, *Zero!* Op. cit.
2. For the definitive description of this battle see Peter C. Smith, *Pedestal: the convoy that saved Malta*, Goodall, Manchester, 2002.
3. Cumbat, *Generale B.A.*, *Betwixt Sea and Sky*, August 1942, original typescript made available to the Author.
4. Cumbat, *Generale B.A.*, to the Author, 9 May 1977.
5. Cumbat, *Generale B.A.*, *Betwixt Sea and Sky*, op. cit.
6. *The Times*, issue dated 12 June 1942.
7. Crimp, R.L., *Diary of a Desert Rat* (Leo Cooper, 1971).
8. *The Times*, issue dated 13 June 1942.
9. Stewart, Major Oliver, article 'Can we check Rommel without the dive-bomber?' in the *Sunday Express*, issue dated 31 May 1942.
10. Carver, Michael, *Tobruk* (Batsford, 1964).
11. Schmidt, Captain H.W., *With Rommel in the Desert* (Harrap, 1958).
12. *The Times*, issue dated 22 June 1942.
13. The *Star*, issue dated 22 June 1942.
14. Stewart, Major Oliver, 'Again we missed the Dive-bomber!', article in the *Sunday Express*, issue dated 28 June 1942.
15. *Scrutator* in an article in *The Sunday Times*, issue dated 28 June 1942.
16. *Ibid.*
17. *The Times*, issue dated 27 June 1942.
18. St John, Robert, NBC Broadcast for Tuesday 23 June 1942.
19. *PM Personal Minute*, to CAS, dated 27 August 1941, M448.1 (National Archives, Kew, London, AIR 8/430).
20. *Extract from Air Estimates Speech*, dated 4 March, 1942 (National Archives, Kew, London, AIR 8/631).
21. Swinton, Major-General Ernest, article 'Dive-bombers – the Army and Navy Views', in the *Daily Sketch*, issue dated 3 March 1942.
22. Pursey, Commander H., RN, article 'Dive-bombers – the Army and Navy Views', in the *Daily Sketch*, issue dated 3 March 1942.
23. The *Sunday Dispatch*, issue dated 10 May 1942.
24. The *Daily Mail*, issue dated 21 May 1942.
25. Webb, Gordon, 'Our New Dive-bombers', article in the *Daily Sketch*, issue dated 20 February 1942.

26. CAS *Minute*, Appendix A, March 1942 (National Archives, Kew, London, AIR 19/ 264).

27. *Report on US Dive-bomber situation* (National Archives, Kew, London, AIR 20/1763).

28. Cherwell to Prime Minister, dated 25 March 1942 (National Archives, Kew, London, AIR 8/631).

29. *BR Secret/US Confidential Memo*, dated 20 May 1942 (National Archives, Kew, London, AIR 19/233).

30. *Ibid.*

31. On the questions and replies during this debate on dive-bombers see *Hansard*, issues dated 1 and 2 July 1942. Dive-bomber queries raised by the following MPs: Aneurin Bevan (Ebbw Vale), Mr Molson (High Peak), Miss Ward (Wallsend), Sir William Davidson (Kensington South) and Mr Garro Jones (Aberdeen North). Defending the Air Ministry position were the Minister of Production, Mr Lyttelton, and Wing Commander Grant-Ferris (St Pancras), as well as the Premier himself.

32. Prime Minister to the House of Commons, 2 July 1942, *Hansard*, op. cit.

33. See Peter C. Smith, *Straight Down!: The North American A-36 dive-bomber in action*, Crécy, Manchester, 2000, for their story.

34. See Peter C. Smith, *Curtiss SB2C Helldiver*, Crowood Press, Ramsbury, 1998, for the full story.

35. Peter C. Smith, *Jungle Dive-bombers at War*, John Murray, London, 1987, gives the full account.

36. Feldt, Commander Eric A., RAN, *The Coastwatchers*.

37. Sherrod, Robert, *History of Marine Corps Aviation*, op. cit.

38. *Ibid.*

CHAPTER ELEVEN

'Keep nosing over and dropping those bombs'

C aptain Elmer G. Glidden USMC from Hyde Park, Massachu-
setts, was a graduate of the Hensselaier Polytechnic Institute,
with a degree in aeronautical engineering. Like a great many
other young men, his obvious future appeared to lie in the services,
and he was appointed an aviation cadet in December 1939, undergoing
his flight training at US Naval Air Station Pensacola, Florida. He was
appointed a second lieutenant and naval aviator in November 1940,
and transferred to Hawaii later. Typical of his generation of airmen in
the USA, he had his debut of combat at the Battle of Midway, as we
have seen from his combat report. That harrowing experience of battle
against the odds would have been enough for most dive-bomber pilots,
but for Glidden Midway was just the beginning!

Glidden served with distinction in many other areas, and he and
his Dauntless grew into something of a legend in the Pacific War. On
the occasion of his 100th dive-bomber mission, the company house
journal of the Douglas Aircraft Corporation published an article on this
'forgotten' ace, still plugging away at the enemy in his own modest
fashion.

In the South Pacific the dive-bombers battered the Marines' and
Army's way from Munda to Rabaul. They were the first in action
against the Japs and the first to land on the new strips as they were
built.

The Douglas SBDs that started this long trip back to Tokyo are
still in there punching, and many of the pilots who struck the first
blows with SBDs are still flying the rugged Dauntlesses and still
pinpointing enemy targets. Their chief targets now are in the
Marshall Islands, where day after monotonous day the Marine
Corps keeps up the business of pulverising bypassed Jap bases.

It was on this run last August, that what is probably an all time
record for dive-bombing missions was set. The record, 100 dive-
bombing attacks by one man, was set without fanfare. Probably
not more than a dozen people knew a record was being made.

153

The man who made the record was Major Elmer G. ('Iron Man') Glidden, a truly rugged pilot. He genuinely shuns heroics and once told one of his wingmen, 'I know what I do and you know what you do. What's the difference who else knows it?'

From a patrol plane, First Lieutenant Louis Olszyk watched Major Glidden lead his flight of SBDs of Brigadier General Louis Wood's Fourth Air Wing, saw him peel off and nose towards enemy beach positions.

'Layers of cloud formations enveloped him on the downward journey', wrote Olzyk. 'Then he pulled out and levelled off. He left his mark below, his one 500 lb bomb and two 100 lb bombs sending up a geyser of debris, smoke and dust from the Jap atoll.'

Back on the ground of his home field, the scene was typical. There was no fanfare and, at first, only an occasional congratulatory handshake. Glidden had kept the number of his missions a secret, with only First Lieutenant Lytton (Bud) Blass of Garretsville, Ohio, who served with him on Guadalcanal, and members of the flight office knowing the score.

When others learned of his 100th dive and expressed awe at the number,[1] Glidden dismissed them with: 'If you keep flying long enough, the number just automatically piles up. You don't have much else to do or say about it except to keep nosing over and dropping those bombs.'

Records reveal, however, that Glidden's performance has been nowhere as easy as he puts it. Less than ten pilots who served with him on Midway and Guadalcanal are in squadrons today. Approximately one-half of them have been killed; others are victims of war neurosis or relegated to desk jobs.

Even malaria and dysentery failed to keep this man on the ground at Guadalcanal. He flew missions as far as 250 miles from the base when he should have turned in for hospitalisation. Then, as now, he talks away all attempts to place him in a desk job.

Glidden is an elusive target for the Japs. His plane has been hit several times, though never seriously. He himself hasn't as much as a scratch. Only one person of several operating squadrons in the Marshalls exceeds the Major's 73 dives made there. At Guadalcanal, in 25 dives, he lavished devastation on enemy cruisers, destroyers, landing barges and ground troops. He took over command of the squadron – the famous Ace of Spades – after the commanding office was killed in action.

How many missions Glidden will end up with by war's end is hypothetical. His squadron has several months of its present tour still remaining and Glidden is all for moving on with the war. 'I was in on practically the beginning of the war', he explains,' and I want to stay on for the kill.'[2]

If all the above sounds like a typical news story of the time, then perhaps to place Glidden's work in proper perspective it should be recorded that he won two Navy Crosses for his combat at Midway and Guadalcanal and that we was awarded the Air Medal after his 104th dive-bombing mission. The citation on that occasion read as follows:

> During the period March 1944 to August, he flew numerous reconnaissance missions over Japanese-occupied atolls in the Marshall Islands area, conducted frequent anti-submarine warfare patrols, and led a total of 63 dive-bombing attacks through enemy anti-aircraft fire against enemy surface craft and vital ground installations, inflicting severe damage and destruction on his targets.

Nor was that the end of the Glidden saga, for he was still serving and flying with the Marines in Vietnam!

Throughout 1943, the SBD had continued to be the mainstay of the US carrier-based dive-bomber arm, but the Helldiver made her operational debut on 11 November with VB-17 commanded by Lieutenant-Commander J.E. Vose. 'Mose' Vose had, like Glidden, flown the Dauntless at the Battle of Midway and also at Santa Cruz; and now he led the first strike of her successor in action against Rabaul. Twenty-three SB2Cs took part in that historic mission.

The air-sea war raged on with unabated fury. In a carrier raid on 5 November, twenty-two SBDs joined in a mass strike at the same target, severely damaging four heavy and two light cruisers. A counter-strike by the Japanese Navy included twenty-seven Vals, but the bulk of these were annihilated by fighters and flak, and not a single hit was scored on any ship of the US task force. The Helldiver gradually replaced the Dauntless, but the faithful old SBD was still flying from two carriers during a heavy attack on the Japanese fleet base of Truk mounted by a task force that included no fewer than nine aircraft-carriers, made in February 1944. At the huge naval Battle of the Philippine Sea in June 1944, eight-one Judy and twenty-seven Val dive-bombers flew from the decks of nine Japanese aircraft-carriers, while a total of fifty-seven SBDs were still included among the great mass of Helldivers launched from fifteen American carriers which were engaged. This battle, dubbed 'The Great Marianas Turkey Shoot', so easy was it for the Americans, virtually saw the end of Japanese carrier-borne dive-bomber operations, as they were all but wiped out and achieved nothing. The Judy and Val continued operating, but mainly from shore airfields and increasingly as Kamikazes, while the once proud carrier fleet was reduced to bait to lure the American carriers away from the Japanese battleship forces, as at Leyte Gulf.

At this period of the war in the Pacific, as well as in Africa and Europe, the distinction between the dive-bomber and the fighter-bomber became increasing blurred, with big fighters conducting dive-bomber missions, and it marked the beginning of the end of the latter as a specially designed type, although dive-bombing itself became more and more common, increasingly becoming more accepted and widespread in its application. Surprisingly enough, it was destined to be the last starter in the specialised dive-bomber field which was to achieve new successes with the method. By this time in the war, the Soviets were starting to pay back in kind all the suffering that they had taken at the hands of the Stuka, and pay it back with interest.

It is worthy of note that after the Battle of Kursk in the summer of 1943 the true exclusive dive-bomber declined in the *Luftwaffe*, whereas in the Soviet Air Force the dive-bomber *par excellence*, the speedy Pe-2 *Peshka* (as the PB-100, after further tests, had gone into service under this designation), was *increasing* in stature as a front-line aircraft almost daily. Over 460 of these twin-engined dive-bombers were ready for service even as early as June 1941, but Russian pilots with the skill and ability, and who were familiar with the correct dive-bombing techniques to utilise them effectively, were few and far between. Methods had, therefore, virtually to be developed and taught from scratch and evaluated in the field of battle. This was initially made more difficult due to the rapid retreat of the Soviets, and also the fact that the Pe-2 was a far more potent aircraft than the slow Tupolevs and suchlike medium bombers they were replacing. The Soviet tendency, therefore, at least during the first year of combat, was for many squadrons equipped with Pe-2s to rather mis- or under-use the *Peshka's* full capability. This truly awesome dive-bomber was, perforce, more flown as a medium bomber than in her true role to start with. As time went by, of course, natural dive-bomber pilots emerged and became legendary, such as F.G. Fedorov of the 9th Bomber Air Regiment, who was briefed to carry out a detailed analysis of the Pe-2 in the 1942 battles, and Ivan Polbin, who proved himself to be the outstanding Russian dive-bomber pilot, with a natural flair and ability to get the best from the inherent accuracy of the method. It was Polbin who led the 150th Bomber Air Regiment in some of the earliest Soviet dive-bombing missions and who took it to a whole new level of expertise later.

As might be expected, the higher echelons of the RAF were not even impressed by this aircraft's performance, especially as it had so convincingly disproved all their pre-war theories about aircraft of clean aerodynamic design being unable to carry out dive-bombing! In March 1943, for example, the Assistant Chief of the Air Staff was writing: 'The

Pe-2 is usually employed in high dive-bombing', but he added, 'We have no knowledge of the dive-bombing technique they employ in operating the Pe-2, nor has the Pe-2 been popularised as has the IL-2.' He went on to further state: 'About the Pe-2 we have no information to indicate that its contribution is in any way outstanding.'[3]

This was, at the very least, a highly disingenuous statement, some might term it an outright untruth, for the Air Staff knew very well, and *had known for at least two years* prior to this statement, *exactly* what the Pe-2 was capable of. As might be expected, nothing whatsoever was going to convince the British air marshals that *any* dive-bomber was useful, but they had no valid excuse for such barefaced affrontry as this ACAS statement, for as early as September 1941 they were in receipt of a highly detailed report from Squadron Leader Lapraik, after he had given the Pe-2 a complete examination and flight testing in Russia. His report gave very precise and excellent details of just what the *Peshka* was capable of and what she was like to fly, the only such account in English. Let us quote from it.[4]

The Lapraik report started off unambiguously enough: 'One of the most notable aircraft produced in Russia', he enthused, adding that, 'This aircraft has already been extensively employed on operations and is of a type with no counterpart in the RAF.'

From his description, which the ACAS appeared to have 'forgotten' two years later, the following information says in no little depth what the Pe-2 was like as a machine and to fly.

The Pe-2 was a twin-engined low-wing monoplane of metal construction of conventional stressed-skin composition. The tail had twin fins and rudders and was remarkable for the pronounced dihedral on the tailplane. The dive-brakes were of the 'Venetian blind' type and attached to the main spar, being electrically operated. Two M-105 (Hispano-Suiza type) 12-cylinder liquid-cooled engines powered the plane, which could carry four 100 kg bombs internally with alternative wing loads of two 500 kg or four 100 kg bombs.

The pilot and navigator entered the aircraft through a trap door in the bottom of the fuselage. The pilot moved forward to his seat, which was on the port side of the fuselage, the back of his seat swinging to the side of the fuselage. The pilot was seated well forward and responsible for bomb-release and also, to some extent, the radio, by means of a four-position switch by his left elbow. The navigator was seated just behind and to the right of the pilot. Besides navigation, this man operated the top gun and emergency undercarriage system. The radio operator was also the lower gunner and was completely shut off from pilot and navigator.

'The test pilot thought the layout of the cockpit very good', Lapraik wrote, and while taxiing was 'very easy but rather uncomfortable as the undercarriage is harsh', the take-off itself was considered 'easy and straightforward' using 15–20 degrees of flap. In level flight, the Pe-2 was reasonably light and effective throughout the whole speed range: 'Although longitudinally unstable, the aircraft is stable directionally and laterally.'

The dive was made on test without the dive-brakes, to the limiting speed of 360 mph, and the aircraft handled well, there being no change in trim and no sign of vibration. Small movements were made with the controls, but all seemed reasonably light, although they did get stiffer as speed was gathered. The recovery was easy, the aircraft regaining level flight in 820–985 feet. 'One of the more interesting aids to dive-bombing was the electrical device which showed a red light if acceleration during recovery was above 7 g.'

Lapraik did not use the dive-brakes, as his passenger was not strapped in, but the Soviet experts described their technique in this aircraft to him in the following manner:

> The throttles are eased back and the diving brakes selected. The brakes extend fairly rapidly and as they extend they cut out the normal trimming device and trim the aircraft nose-heavy. On the release of the bombs, the trimmer is automatically returned to its original position and the aircraft recovers from its dive. For practice dives without bombs, the trimmer is returned to its original position by a small white push-button on the shelf near the diving brakes' selector switch.

There was *no* provision for level bombing. Lapraik's report also mentioned that:

> The shock-absorbing qualities of the undercarriage are not good and the machine is inclined to 'hop' along the ground. A slightly tail-up landing is advised by the Russians; the brakes are good.

The view was generally good, but forward view was reported as 'excellent owing to the tapering nose and a large glass panel in the floor by the nose'. This panel had a red line painted on it, which, it was presumed, simplified the pilot's approach to the target.

With this magnificent dive-bomber available, Russian proficiency grew by leaps and bounds, especially after extensive combat and trials had ironed out initial hesitancy. Colonel Ivan Polbin himself evolved the classic Pe-2 tactic during combat in 1942, when his unit had distinguished itself at the defensive battle of the Verkhne-Businovki pocket in July 1942 and later at the Stalingrad counter-offensive. Here, the 2nd Bomber Air Corps (BAC), under Colonel I.L. Turkel, had flown from forward bases in round-the-clock missions to hold off a German relief column in December 1942.

Polbin's tactics became known as *Vertushka*, 'The Dipping Wheel'. The dive-bombers would circle the prescribed target, and then break off from their Vee-of-Vee configuration, one at a time with a 1,500–2,000 ft interval between each aircraft, and approach the target at an angle of dive of 70 degrees. This presented the defence with a continuous line of dive-bombers approaching at high speed, thus saturating their fire. As the first Pe-2 began her pull-out, the second would be approaching the point of bomb-release and the third commencing its final attack dive.

At the decisive Battle of Kursk in July 1943, both German and Soviet dive-bombers were very heavily involved. The Soviet 2nd and 17th Air Armies flew continuous sorties from 5 July with both Pe-2 and IL-2 aircraft. As a result, on 7 July it was reported that the 7th and 9th Panzers lost seventy tanks in twenty minutes, the 3rd Panzer lost 270 and the 17th Panzer was also hard hit. Slessor might not want to see any RAF aircraft 'skidding around Kent' looking for tanks in case of invasion, but the Russian generals were *very* happy indeed to see the Pe-2 doing just that, and with such a good kill ratio. Only sixty tanks remained effective out of an initial force of 300 by the end of the attack.

On the German side of that vast front line, the Ju 87s were no less committed; some 850 sorties were flown by the Stukas on 6 July, and these claimed to have knocked out sixty-four T-34s, with the newly formed cannon-armed *Kannonvogel* units, firing tungsten-tipped AP shells, being particularly potent in this respect. Losses in aircraft on both sides were also heavy, due to the enormous concentration of flak, especially by the Soviet armies in that sector. Cross-battery duelling between the huge numbers of heavy artillery pieces employed by both sides also proved something of a novel, if deadly, new hazard for the dive-bombers when flying at low level during their dive recovery phase, but it was even more so, naturally, for the conventional ground-strafing aircraft. Even so, among the famous German dive-bomber aces who fell at Kursk were Horst Schiller of I/StG 3 and Walter Krauss of III/StG 2.

The Russians held the German onslaught, thanks to excellent knowledge of their enemy's plan of attack, and, after much severe fighting, were even able to open their own counter-offensive at Orel on 11 July. Before this attack the Germans it was who now fell back. Non-stop dive-bomber sorties by the Ju 87s at full stretch once more held the line from total collapse in many places, and so this defeat was not quite the massive disaster that Stalingrad had been, but none the less Kursk marked the end of the German offensives in the East and the beginning of the Russian advance that only ended on the streets of Berlin.

The vulnerability of the now ageing Stuka was fully realised, but its promised replacement dive-bomber, the Me 410, never did materialise in any meaningful numbers, and so they had to soldier on. Production of the Ju 87 therefore continued, with many new variants for night-fighting and ground-attack capabilities, but in lieu of anything else, the trend in the last twelve months of the war was to convert to the Focke-Wulf Fw 190 *Jabo* fighter-bomber for dive-bomber attacks. Thus the Germans, like the British with the Supermarine Spitfire and the Americans with the massive Republican Thunderbolt, followed the US Marine Corps Corsairs and started using heavy fighters as dive-bombers. This switch of carrier was reflected in the *Luftwaffe* by the change in the designation of the Ju 87 units, from StG to SG (Ground Attack) from October 1943 onwards.

Soon afterwards, a steady replacement programme of the Fw 190 commenced, but its implementation was slow. I/SG 5 in Norway went over in January 1944, followed by II/SG 2 in February, but by June 1944 only III/SG 2, under the indomitable Rudel, was left using the Ju 87 *Gustav*, continuing to do so until the very end of the war. The displaced Stukas, other than those fitted with tank-busting cannon not pensioned off, continued to undertake combat duties, being reallocated to specially equipped *Nachtschlachtgruppen* as night harassment bombers, and these actually also conducted some special daylight dive-bombing missions on both the Eastern and Western fronts in 1944–5, of which more anon.

Germany's dwindling number of Allies followed suit. The Hungarian 102/I unit changed over to the Fw 190 late in 1944, converting to it from the Ju 87D it had flown since July 1943. The Rumanian 3rd and 4th Groups, however, were still flying their Dora-3 and Dora-4s when that country abruptly switched sides the same year. Similarly equipped were the Bulgarian and Croatian dive-bomber forces in 1944–5.

*   *   *

During 1943 and 1944, the development of the fighter-dive-bomber concept was steadily increasing in favour, as we have noted, in the Pacific, in the Mediterranean, on the Eastern Front and in Europe, with the British, Americans, Germans and Italians all adapting big, modern fighter aircraft to bomb carriers once they found that they could dive vertically. None the less, established dive-bombers like the Ju 87 continued to be much in evidence in the North African finale and on into the autumn of 1943–4. The final uses of the Stuka after El Alamein saw operations in Tunis, when both the British from the east and the Americans from the east closed in on the last German bridgehead and received several very bloody noses from the Ju 87 in the process, her swan-song in Africa, as it were. Able to continue working from former Vichy-French concrete runways when the more tender Allied aircraft were grounded by poor weather and washed out by the rain, the Stukas were able to operate extensively. Never exceeding a total strength of fifty to sixty machines, the Ju 87s, based in both Tunisia and Sardinia, gave the Allies several pauses for thought before Tunis finally fell in May 1943. The unexpected re-emergence of the old Ju 87, which had been written off so many times before, once more caused unrest in the Press and Parliament in the UK.

After the Motion of Censure debate had included questions on the dive-bomber scandal in midsummer 1942, the Air Ministry had hoped that their viewpoint, even if not universally accepted as valid, would now no longer be subject to public debate, having the Premier's public, if not private, backing. But the hoped-for lull failed to happen. Major Stewart returned to the attack in July of that year with an article in which he claimed that, 'Criticism has fulfilled its purpose.'[5] With Sinclair's earlier statement as ammunition, he claimed that the fact that the RAF, while doubting the usefulness of dive-bombers, would find some use for them was a major climb-down.

> Air Ministry resistance to them, and the failure of some air officers to take full note of the special features of the dive-bombing technique, led to their being placed low in the order of priorities. Now, a step forward has been taken in overcoming these prejudices. Dive-bombers are being delivered. Only one thing must be looked on with suspicion. There seems a tendency to hedge about how these aircraft are to be used when we get them. In publications which voice Air Staff views, it is repeated that the dive-bombers we are to get are to be modified and used for other purposes. Any official hedging on this matter now would be a grievous error. The dive-bomber must not be modified into some milk-and-water fighter-bomber. The fighter-bomber is a compromise machine which has its uses and was finely handled by our pilots in Africa. But it has shorter range, less blasting power, lower accuracy and higher vulnerability to light anti-aircraft weapons than the genuine dive-bomber.[6]

He was right to be suspicious, for, as was to be expected, the Air Staff still did not accept any of his arguments, although Stewart's informed comments (after all, he had actually conducted dive-bombing himself as a young pilot and knew what he was talking about) struck some raw nerves in the accuracy of his predictions of their true intent. They therefore again brought up their heavy guns to refute him.

In a long, full-page article published in September 1942, Air Chief Marshal Sir Hugh Dowding, who had been shunted off to the sidelines after the Battle of Britain for not conforming, was wheeled out to centre stage once more to briefly articulate the tired old Air Ministry view on the dive-bomber and its value. Although he was forced by facts to concede that 'the dive-bomber is a terrifying and devastating weapon', it was also, he asserted, 'a vulnerable one'. Among the many points he reiterated were a few particularly fallacious ones. 'Dive-bombing, nearly vertical, can be performed only by a highly specialised machine, designed and built for the task ...', and '... dive-bombing demands specialised training. It should not be particularly difficult to devise a scientific instrument to allow for the effects of wind on dive-bombers, but, as far as I know, none exists at the moment ....'[7] He ignored the fact that for seven years pre-war the Admiralty had repeatedly asked the Air Ministry for a dive-bombing sight but had been fobbed off repeatedly and never got one.

Thus, although Dowding presented the case against the dive-bomber in great depth, and probably uniquely to the general public in such a manner, in the process he inadvertently revealed himself equally out of touch and badly briefed on such aircraft as the Soviet Union's Pe-2, for example, or on the studies of the Swedish and German dive-bombing devices the RAF had had the opportunity of examining in 1939–40, and which they had found efficient.

Another thorn in the side of the RAF top brass on this issue was Mr Westbrook's letter, mentioned earlier, criticising the fact that the Dauntless had not been bought by Britain when offered. This caused a minor stir for, at first, despite Midway and the Pacific fighting, the Air Ministry did not even appear to know to which aircraft he was referring! Did he mean the Boston?, one witless senior officer was moved to enquire. Sinclair's Private Secretary sought to steer him aright:

> As regards the Douglas dive-bomber, this is certainly the A24 and not the Boston as you suggest. I have asked the ACAS(T)'s people to get in touch with you to try and ascertain whether any consideration was given to order the type.[8]

He was also concerned at the Robert St John broadcast, which claimed the Americans had indeed offered to supply the dive-bomber that was currently winning the war in the Pacific to Britain in 1941. DOR replied:

> The only Douglas dive-bomber of which I have any knowledge is the A24, which is the SBD-3 (Dauntless). General Lyon of the American Embassy informs me that this aircraft is officially known by them as a light bomber and that it is used in America as a dive-bomber.

Indeed it was! He continued:

> I have no record that the A24 has ever been considered for us for RAF use.[9]

However, after some reflection, it seemed as if Mr Westbrook had been right after all, for the RAF had indeed been given the opportunity to order the Dauntless in April 1941. 'At that date, you will recall, we had decided that sufficient dive-bombers were already on order and we wanted any productive capacity available to be used to increase the production of heavy and medium bombers.'[10] Ah, yes, what a surprise! In fact, the reply that had been sent at the time stated bluntly: 'Not interested in A24 dive-bombers. Please reconsider possibility of using the capacity for heavy bombers.'[11]

Similar doubts had been expressed on the accuracy of the St John broadcast, it being stated that, 'We know nothing of this Press statement. If true, it would be about the first time on record of American officials having been pleased with us to take American aircraft!' But, again, despite the heavy sarcasm, the Dauntless offer showed that it, also, was true after all. In preparing a suitable reply for Lord Trenchard to deliver, it was stressed that, 'As for the Douglas dive-bomber already in production, which Mr Westwood mentions, it would certainly have taken time to adapt this to suit our equipment.'

The continuing success of the Ju 87 in North Africa also caused some difficulties explaining away:

> What, however, Lord Trenchard can say about the success of the German dive-bombers is a difficult matter ... I do not know on what grounds he could base an opinion that the Stukas achieved very little success.

Which was not surprising!

An amusing sequel to all these smokescreen statements trying to prove black was white came in an article in the *News Chronicle* in which Tedder was quoted as telling the assembled journalists that:

> Concentrated day bomber raids – 'Boston Tea Parties' we call them – are more devastating from a morale-breaking point of view than the dive-bombing the enemy visits us with. For one thing, bombing by Bostons is more impersonal. You know the Stuka's bombs are for you when he spirals and begins to scream down in his dive; but the Boston just flies on overhead giving no sort of hint of the target he is after until the bombs have dropped a carpet pattern over the desert. You don't know the Boston's bombs are for you until the first bomb hits the ground beside you ....'[12]

This schoolboy howler of an answer was apparently given, and based upon, a statement put out by the Scientific Adviser's Department of the War Office, and was repeated in a report thus: 'Once the dive-bomber has started his dive, it is clear against whom his attack is directed. Others can stand by and watch.' But *they* had added the rider:

On the other hand, at least as far as the British air forces are concerned, it is fair to say that the dive-bomber has not had nearly so much research and experiment on it as have our other types. Further progress may lead to still greater accuracy.[13]

Major Stewart was among many who, once he had stopped laughing, seized on this gaffe with alacrity:

One of the most amazing reasons ever advanced for the official resistance to the dive-bomber, by the way, was that troops on the ground can tell at once where a dive-bomber's bombs would fall, so that, unless the bombs were coming near them, they could get on with their work, whereas with a level or glide bomber nobody knew where the bombs would fall! This attempt to argue that inaccuracy is desirable for its own sake is the funniest of all attempts to justify the official attitude.[14]

With which we can surely agree. Even Churchill was metaphorically forced to throw up his hands in despair. 'We cannot just leave the statement as it is', he cautioned the CAS. 'He *meant* well, but the impression created is quite the reverse of what was intentioned.' Dowding was duly returned to store.

In March 1943 Air Force Intelligence had noted the declining numbers of Ju 87s being used by the *Luftwaffe* in North Africa, and claimed that many Press statements concerning dive-bombing were wrong. Squadron Leader Smith wrote to ACAS:

It is clear that the use of the term 'Stuka' as applied to dive-bombing aircraft is still not understood. 'Stuka' is a German abbreviation of the word *Sturzkampfflugzeug* and is used by them exclusively in reference to the Ju 87 dive-bomber; for the sake of simplicity we have followed the German application of this word.

But it was Smith who was wrong, for the GAF applied the word *Sturzkampfflugzeug* to *all* their dive-bombers, and it was the *Allies*, by general usage, who came to regard it as only applying to the Ju 87! He continued: '... from our knowledge of past tendencies in the GAF and in the light of the military operations in which we have so far been engaged, there is little evidence to support the view that aircraft of the Ju 87 type would, in fact, have been of such great value of us so far during the war.' Presumably then, he was implying that the use of Lysanders, Gauntlets and Swordfish as emergency dive-bombers in France and North Africa during 1940 was something long planned for!

The misinformation continued. The development of the Me 210 had been raised, suggesting that a continued German interest in dive-bombing was being maintained. Not so, claimed the same report, 'It is, in fact, little more than an up-to-date version of the well-known

Me 110', which would have surprised the Messerschmitt design engineers struggling to make this aircraft's dive-bombing capabilities effective. Smith added: 'There is no evidence that it has ever been intended for use as a dive-bomber [*sic*].'[15]

Wrong again! While it is certainly true that the original specification issued in 1939 was for an improved Me 110, dive-brakes had been fitted in the Me 210 V2 and V4 prototypes, and diving trials had been conducted with them in 1940. Although the dive-brakes were later removed, dive-bombing trials continued with the V12 prototype, and the early production models of this aircraft were all built with dive-bombing as one of their main functions; with a maximum bomb load of two 1,100 lb bombs as their payload. Plans had been promulgated pre-war to establish at least twelve *Stukagruppen* equipped with this aircraft to replace the Ju 87. In the end, due to difficulties with the engines, only the Hungarian Air Force actually used their Me 210C as a dive-bomber in wartime combat.

Another totally incorrect statement came from the Air Ministry at this time. The North American A-36 Invader had formed two dive-bomber units in the USAAF, and they had performed with great success in Sicily and at the invasion of Salerno in 1943. The RAF could not believe that such high-speed, modern aircraft could carry out dive-bombing despite all their own predictions, and issued statements to the effect that the A-36 was not a dive-bomber, but merely a Mustang fighter-bomber. When it was politely pointed out to them that these aircraft were fitted with dive-brakes, the story was released to the Press that these dive-brakes were never used but always wired shut! So successful was this fiction that most post-war accounts of the A-36 repeat this myth as fact. Interviews by this author with the pilots who actually flew the Invader, as she became nicknamed, found that they hardly ever, if at all, wired the dive-brakes shut, but used them properly throughout the Italian campaign.[16]

*   *   *

In contrast to the stream of anti-dive-bomber statements pouring out of the Air Ministry in 1942–3, those at the sharp end of things had a somewhat different perspective from their Whitehall masters on the best way to fight the war. A signal from AHQ Bengal to AHQ India presented rather a different viewpoint on the issue:

> I cannot exaggerate the importance I attach to the early arrival of Vengeance dive-bombers in the command. Present equipment of Blenheims and Hudsons, though satisfactory for Medium Altitude bombing, are *quite unsatisfactory* for attacks on ships at sea or in harbour .... *Had dive-bombers been available, I consider that our object*

*at Akyab on 9 September could have been achieved at less than half the effort.** Therefore submit that 82 Squadron should be moved into 221 Group, form there and undertake their first operational training there. Would gladly release a Blenheim squadron in exchange if this is considered necessary.[17]

The complications such an admission would make to the official Air Ministry propaganda spin were realised and highlighted in a memorandum sent to Wing Commander G. Houghton at North West African Air Force Command in April 1943, and signed 'Stansgate'. Referring to his signal of March, which claimed the complete ineffectiveness of the Stuka dive-bomber, which in itself was considered 'excellent', the publicity boys were warned that claims from India on the success of the Vultee Vengeance were likely to cause a clash of interest!

You will appreciate that we are employing the Vengeance in India with no little success and we shall therefore need to be careful in our reference to the ineffectiveness of the dive-bomber and its alleged obsolescence. I realise, of course, that your references were specifically to the Stuka, but it might be difficult for us, if challenged, to maintain that we intend to represent that German dive-bombers only are things of the past.[18]

AHQ's signal in June 1943 brought this conflict of truth to a head:

Propose releasing Vengeance as being operational here. Not claiming it's anything but dive-bomber but wish two points made. First, that Burma is one place where dive-bomber used properly as compared to Stukas in North Africa. We have not lost one Vengeance in operations and it has been able to do its job effectively and with impunity. Secondly, Burma, as distinct from desert, is ideal dive-bomber country where targets are concerned, camouflaged and surrounded by woods and hills.[19]

The reaction in Whitehall was totally predictable: 'Vengeance dive-bomber publicity presents many pitfalls from standpoints both of security and publicity.'[20] Having a successful machine on the strength was to be hushed up as it conflicted with doctrine!

Before their viewpoint is considered further, some examination is necessary of just what the Vultee Vengeance was like to fly and how it was assessed by the test pilots who flew it first. Fortunately we have an eyewitness report on this much-maligned aircraft that is independent of the usual derogatory hyperbole.

It was in June 1943 that the Bombing Development Unit at Feltwell flight-tested a Vengeance, and they delivered a very critical report.[21]

* Author's italics.

While it was admitted that, 'The only BDU pilot experienced in dive-bombing technique has recently been posted. The trials are therefore likely to be considerably prolonged while other pilots learn the technique ...', the aircraft itself was not initially well thought of. 'Serviceability has been so phenomenally bad that only 7 hours 35 minutes had been flown.' None the less, they made the following points:

> The Vengeance handles very well in a dive. The air-brakes are efficient and it would be difficult to attain a speed of more than 300 mph. Aileron turns are easy, the aircraft is stable and the pull-out is good, taking less that 500 feet without undue 'g' force. The wing obscures the downward view considerably, making it difficult for the pilot to judge the moment to go over into the dive. This is important as it is the biggest single factor in attaining accurate bombing.
>
> The Vengeance handles moderately well. It is rather heavy, both in the air and on the controls, but it can be forced to manoeuvre fairly quickly. Take-off and landing are simple. For a two-seater aircraft with a 1,600 hp engine, the Vengeance has a bad performance, it being rather worse, in almost every respect, than the Battle.[22]

After further testing to examine the time taken to train a fresh pilot in the technique of aiming, they used a pilot who had never flown a Vengeance and who, also, had never carried out dive-bombing in any aircraft. From this they concluded, contrary to the opinion expressed by Dowding:

> It appears that there is no great difficulty in teaching a pilot to dive-bomb and attain average results of between 50 to 70 yards. To reduce this figure to 25 to 35 yards requires regular practice.[23]

In August 1943, these trials continued, and the following points were listed:

> To nose straight over onto a target ahead of the aircraft is uncomfortable, needs considerable forces on the control, gives a greater speed in the initial part of the dive with consequently difficulty in aiming the aircraft, and lastly, means the target is out of sight for a considerable period, making the judgement of the moment to nose over very difficult.[24]

It was therefore recommended that the dive should be entered by a semi-stall turn:

> The leading edge of the wing of the Vengeance is considerably forward of the pilot, and his downward view is restricted to that

extent. If, however, the approach is made slightly to one side of the target, finishing the level flight with a gentle turn-in, the target can be kept in view to within 3 or 4 seconds of the correct moment to begin the dive.[25]

It was found vital to get the aircraft correctly aimed as soon as possible after 'cartwheeling' over. 'Only very small adjustments to aim can usefully be made once the aircraft has settled into a dive of, say, 75 degrees.' No bombsight was fitted, nor was one considered necessary. The best aids were said to be:

1. A broad white line painted along the top of the fuselage from the windscreen to the NACA cowling of the engine.
2. The edge of the cowling itself.[26]

The bomb door and dive-brakes were found to be rapid in action and did not need opening until just before going into the dive, and it was quite acceptable to close the brakes while coming out of the dive.

No. 45 Squadron was the first RAF Vengeance unit to see combat. Their first mission took place on 27 November 1942 in support of the Arakan offensive. During a brief period of operations the Vengeance carried out five offensive dive-bombing missions. Their targets included enemy-occupied villages and enemy-defended positions, the target being indicated by smoke on the latter. On each sortie, six Vultees took part, flying in a box of two Vics of three. Approach was made from between 10,000 and 12,000 feet. About 5 to 8 miles from the target, the leader formed up, with the second Vic of three dropping back to about 100 yards astern of him. Both Vics then changed to 'echelon starboard', the second stationed astern of the first formation. About 3 miles out the R/T order 'Bomber-doors open' was given by the leader, who opened his.

The dive was commenced from 10,000 feet; the leader approached so that the target moved up the left side of the nose of the aircraft and disappeared under the leading edge of the mainplane, at the wing root. Fifteen seconds after this, he rolled his aircraft to the left until 'it was vertical or slight past vertical', opening his dive-brakes just after he was committed to the dive; No. 2 opened his while rolling in, and No. 3 just prior to the roll. This gave an interval between aircraft of about 1,000 feet. The angle of dive was between 70 and 90 degrees. 'If the angle of dive is less than 70 degrees, accurate bombing is difficult.' Bomb-release was at about 3,000–4,000 feet. In all these attacks, *a very high degree of accuracy was achieved and losses were nil* [Author's italics].[27]

In India, then, there was no doubt at all about the efficiency of the dive-bomber and every confidence in its future. But not so in Whitehall.

Notes

1. Of course this is in the United States; on the Eastern Front Ju87 aircrew were flying four sorties a day, as normal routine, and many Stuka aces clocked up over 800 combat missions, but this was not widely understood in the West who still thought 100 missions were exceptional.
2. Olszyk, Lieutenant Louis, *Milwaukee Journal*, issue dated 23 September 1944.
3. *Memorandum*, ACAS though D of L(O), dated 3 March 1943 (National Archives, Kew, London, AIR 20/4249).
4. Lapraik, Squadron Leader, *P.E.2 Twin-Engined Dive-bomber, Report*, dated 11 September 1941. Air Intelligence A.I.2(g) IIG/132/2/27 (National Archives, Kew, London, AIR 40/29).
5. Stewart, Major Oliver, *Still Kicking Against the Dive-bomber*, article in *The Sunday Times*, issue dated 5 July 1942.
6. *Ibid.*
7. Dowding, Air Chief Marshal, Sir Hugh, 'The Truth About Dive-bombers', article in the *Sunday Graphic*, issue dated 6 September 1942.
8. PS to Secretary-of-State for Air and S9, dated 29 June 1942, M3997 (National Archives, Kew, London, AIR 19/233).
9. DOR to ACAS(T), dated 29 June 1942, ACAS(T)/25/T (National Archives, Kew, London, AIR 19/233).
10. S9 to PS of Secretary-of-State for Air, dated 30 June 1942. ACAS(T).25/T (National Archives, Kew, London, AIR 19/233).
11. MAP 4877/13/4, dated 13 April 1941 (National Archives, Kew, London, AIR 19/233).
12. Extract from *Army Requirements of the Royal Air Force for Direct Support in Battle*, dated 30 November 1942.79/Misc/1277 (National Archives, Kew, London AIR 20/4249).
13. *Ibid.*
14. Stewart, Major Oliver, article in *Evening Standard* (London), issue dated 27 February 1943.
15. Air Intelligence 3(b) to ACAS, dated 3 March 1943 (National Archive, Kew, London, AIR 20/4249).
16. Peter C. Smith, *Straight Down!* Op. cit.
* *Authors italics.*
17. AHQ Bengal to AHQ India, dated 11 September 1942 (National Archives, Kew, London, AIR 23/4361).
18. Air Intelligence 3(b) to ACAS (National Archives, Kew, London, AIR 20/790).
19. AHQ India to Air Ministry, dated 3 June 1943 (National Archives, Kew, London, AIR 20/4249).
20. Dated 12 June 1943 Sec.X.49 (National Archives, Kew, London, 20/4249).
21. BDU Report; Part I: *Tactical Trials on Vengeance Dive-bomber*, and Part 2: *Dive-bombing in Vengeance*, dated 4 October 1943. BDU.18 (National Archives, Kew, London, AIR 19/233).
22. *Ibid.*
23. *Ibid.*
24. *Ibid. – Memorandum*, Bombing Development Unit, BDU/S.98/AIR.
25. National Archives, Kew, London, AIR/19/233.
26. *Tactical Memorandum* No. 35, AHQ India – *Vengeance Operations in Arakan* (National Archives, Kew, London, AIR 23/3288).
27. *Tactical Memorandum* No. 35, AHQ India – *Vengeance Operations in Arakan* (National Archives, Kew, London, AIR 23/3288).

CHAPTER TWELVE

'The plane baulked and reared'

Even more irritating to the detractors of the dive-bomber than the success of the Vengeance on its operational debut was another series of victories for the much-derided Ju 87 Stuka obtained in the autumn of 1943 against all predictions of her imminent demise. When Italy surrendered in the summer of that year, the whole vast region adjacent to the Aegean Sea was left open to whosoever could exploit the situation first. American political reluctance and blindness to the strategic importance of the Turkey and the Balkans, coupled with suspicion of British 'Imperialism', forced Churchill, who had no such cosy illusions about ultimate Soviet intent, and Britain to go it alone with hastily improvised forces. The strategically important islands of Cos, Leros and Samos were all hastily occupied, but the most important island of them all, Rhodes, which had vital airfields, had a strong German presence *in situ*, and these quickly disarmed the much larger Italian garrison. Thereafter, at Hitler's behest, they flew in reinforcements of troops and aircraft from all over Europe. The Ju 87s of the StG 3, after subduing the Italian defenders of the Greek islands of Cephalonia and Corfu, quickly moved into Rhodes and soon began to assert German aerial dominance.

In a series of carefully planned operations, the Germans proceeded to bomb, and then occupy, every disputed island in the area, driving out the British and Italian troops in fierce fighting in which the Stuka yet again paved the way for the paratroops by destroying gun batteries and strongpoints, while, at sea, efforts by the Royal Navy to reinforce and supply the British-held islands from distant Alexandria in Egypt left them open to massed dive-bomber assault, during which they suffered losses almost as heavy as at Crete two-and-a-half years earlier, and under very much the same circumstances.[1] Cruisers, destroyers, landing ships and small craft were all sunk or heavily damaged by Ju 87 precision attacks, and the British were quickly ejected from the area, which barred the approaches to the Dardanelles. This sharp demonstration of German air power proved the Stuka was as effective as ever in such circumstances, no matter how much the RAF might bluster otherwise.

Small wonder, then, that Air HQ India's enthusiastic reports of their own successes with the Vultee dive-bombers, although far more modest in scope, touched raw nerves and were badly received in London. In response the Air Ministry warned India that, 'It is important, therefore, to avoid resurrecting misguided ideas by exaggeration of the relative importance of the dive-bombing technique generally among our many other methods.'[2]

Where established facts were disproving their own preconceived standpoint, it was very clear which was to be given higher priority! 'Regarding public policy aspect, you will remember dive-bombing has been the cause of acute and misguided controversy here and when release is first made it will be most important to frame publicity so as not to cause renewal of misapprehensions and controversy here.'[3]

They therefore enforced a strict blackout on any news release on the successful use of the Vengeance, which they considered was 'somewhat premature'.[4]

Peck went even further, for in a memorandum to the Deputy Director of Public Relations (Press) he stated, 'We thought our best line to this end was to point out the flexibility of the Vengeance as a light bomber capable of different methods of attack and concentrate on successful achievements of the Vengeance rather than on success of the dive-bomber technique as contrasted with other methods.'[5]

AHQ India was, naturally, not altogether pleased at being instructed to adopt such misleading methods, and replied to Peck that he just couldn't have it both ways:

> Existence Vengeance as dive-bomber widely known here and use. Suspicion can do more harm than good if our release of information pretended that it was anything else. Moreover, after months of hard work maintenance and aircrews have overcome severe technical difficulties and perfected Tactical technique. They would be quite unable understand any belittling results of their efforts. Stories from North Africa and Britain about dive-bombers being 'dead' have not been calculated to improve our crews' morale. Publicity now will help counteract any tendency personnel may feel they are flying a type in which the Air Ministry has little confidence.[6]

The makers of policy remained quite unmoved by all this; reputations were, after all, at stake! In a Secret Memorandum they again reaffirmed their opposition to any extension of use of the dive-bomber. Although they admitted that AHQ had reported that the Vengeance 'was a good dive-bomber and by reason of accuracy could be used with effect against small, lightly defended targets', they went on to state that it had limited radius, poor defensive armament and slow speed, bad forward view and was no good for low-level or high-level bombing. Despite what their people in India might feel, they therefore concluded:

> It is considered that the employment of the dive-bomber of the Vengeance type would be most uneconomical if used against targets in Europe. The use of specialised dive-bombers of the Vengeance variety against targets such as enemy transports or troop concentrations is not justified and would be of little operational value. The admirable dive-bombing qualities found in the fighter dive-bomber, coupled with its fighter performance, accuracy, range and bomb-carrying capacity, considerably outweigh the advantage in the use of Vengeance dive-bomber in operational squadrons.[7]

So, although forced to concede dive-bombing itself was a valuable tool, the RAF were *not* about to use dive-bombers to conduct it if they could possibly avoid it!

During 1943, the development of the fighter-dive-bomber had indeed spread in all air forces, as we have seen. In American Air Force eyes, their earlier unhappy experience with the A24 operationally during the chaotic days of the crash of the Dutch East Indies had coloured their thinking on the subject and had led to the postponement of dive-bombers being introduced into the USAAF, despite massive, if unfulfilled, orders for adaptations of various Navy types, the Banshee and the Shrike, and custom-built machines, the Buccaneer and the Vengeance. A major factor was the failure of most of these type of dive-bomber to actually materialise due to production difficulties in the brand-new aircraft plants with their largely untrained workforce. This supply blockage only further worsened an unhappy situation, when Army versions of the Helldiver and Bermuda (VA-42) failed to arrive on time. Then the Vengeance (A-35A) also failed to show up on time, and suffered from a poor power-plant due to indifferent manufacture. The brief flowering of the one undoubted and undisputed success, the 500 A-36s, was put aside, and orders were not repeated, not even to sustain the six squadrons' normal operational losses. Instead the 'Thud' (bomb-carrying Republican Thunderbolt) took over the job and equated to the GAF's later adaptation of the less-resilient Fw 190.

Specialised dive-bomber research work in the USAAF was finally abandoned after one final attempt to produce a viable product for the job, the Vultee XA41. This would have been a very large aircraft capable of toting up to 7,000 lb of bombs. Weighing 23,000 lb 'all-up', it was powered by a single 3,000 hp engine. However, by the time it was put forward all Army Air Force interest in such highly specialised dive-bombers, which had never been much and largely sprang from one man only, 'Hap' Arnold, was dead and buried.

In Italy, prior to the collapse of the Fascist government, fighter-dive-bombers vied with other projected types to replace their ageing Ju 87Ds, but few ever left the drawing-board or the designer's blue-print stage. The Avia LM02, for instance, was a typical Italian idea. This was to be a special glider-dive-bomber, built for the express purpose of attacking the huge amount of Allied shipping that was usually concentrated at Gibraltar. The aircraft was to be of all-wooden construction (despite the fate of the SM84s which had rotted away in the Mediterranean heat after just one mission) and was to be fitted with the Junkers slatted dive-brakes. The concept was for this aircraft, equipped with a pair of 820 kg bombs, to be towed across the western Mediterranean by an SM79 bomber to a release point about 20–30 miles from the Rock. The glider would then be unhooked, carry out its dive-bombing mission and then make a water landing off Algeciras, with the pilot being rescued (if he survived all the various hazards) by a waiting Italian submarine!

Rather more realistic was the conversion of the Reggiane Re 2002 fighter to make shallow dive-bombing attacks at angles of about 45 degrees with a single 250 kg bomb under each wing. This concept actually made it to operational service, being credited with sinking three Allied freighters in July 1943.

American use of the North American P-51 as a dive-bomber again raised the whole question of the lack of RAF dive-bombing capability in the Houses of Parliament. One MP, Mr Purbrick, raised the question on several occasions, as on 21 January 1943.

'Have any of our fighter bombers been equipped so that they can also dive-bomb?' he asked the Minister, who had to confess that they had not. 'Would it not be advisable to have some of those fighter-bombers so equipped that they could also serve as dive-bombers under suitable conditions?' The Minister's reply was again illuminating in what it inadvertently revealed: 'No, Sir; because the effect of that would be very unfair to the pilots who have to fly these aircraft.'[8]

Undaunted, Purbrick returned to the fray later, asking on 3 February:

In view of the fact that a fighter aeroplane was equipped to enable it also to dive-bomb, and was tested and confirmed by the Air Ministry over eighteen months ago to the effect that such equipment did not interfere with its performance as a fighter, will there now be further investigation of the matter, with the object of enabling our fighter-bombers also to dive-bomb under favourable circumstance?

Behind the scenes the Assistant Chief of the Air Staff (TR), Sorley, was
minuting S6 that:

> In spite of the absence of any evidence on our part that the
> Mustangs delivered their attacks in steep dives, Mr Purbrick is
> evidently under the impression that they did so. As you know, he
> is the member who is constantly asking questions why aircraft are
> not fitted with dive-brakes, and so I think it would strengthen our
> position if we answered this question by simply stating, 'No, Sir,
> the aircraft which carried out these attacks were *not* fitted with
> dive-brakes.' On his own confession, therefore, he would make it
> evident that aircraft can attack in steep dives without the aid of
> dive-brakes.[9]

A somewhat different statement to the views being expressed by the
RAF in 1938 and ever since! It was also untrue that the A-36s were
not fitted with dive-brakes, that was what made them different from
the P51. I was told by Mark Savage, one of the A-36 pilots with
16 Squadron, that Jack R. Collingwood, the officer who maintained the
Group's War Diary in combat in Sicily, had made a particular point to
verify this:

> One question I keep asking pilots who flew the A-36s is about the
> dive-brakes. A number of books and articles would state that the
> pilots would have them wired shut. I don't recall *any* of our pilots
> doing it. In fact, I can remember we had some dignitaries on the
> field one day when we sent several aircraft to show them how the
> A-36 was used on dive-bombing. I myself was impressed and
> learned why the Germans called them the 'Screaming Demons'.[10]

Having shifted its ground somewhat, the Air Ministry still held out
against dive-bombing, while quoting the exact opposite reasons it had
used against them in 1943 to what they had five years earlier. The Air
Minister's Private Secretary admitted that, 'The dive-bomber question
becomes more awkward with the American retreat in Tunisia [after
attacks by Ju 87s]', adding, 'It seems to me that a statement for public
use is likely to be a pretty tricky one ....'[11]

Unfortunately, the eventual expulsion of the Axis from North Africa
only took the heat off them for a short while because the A-36's success
over Sicily and the Straits was even more evident than the Vengeance's
successes in India, and much more visible to the general public. There
still exists a Pathé News film showing one of the American A-36
Invader squadrons extending their dive-brakes and peeling off over
Calabria to dive-bomb artillery positions. Visual evidence like this of
our principal ally just could not be hidden, no matter how much the
Air Ministry wanted it to be.

Meanwhile the highly embarrassing non-arrival of the dive-bombers ordered so long ago by Lord Beaverbrook had also came to a head in 1943. Earlier indications of how things were developing were contained in exchanges of correspondence on this thorny subject. Nine months earlier, on 26 June 1942, Sinclair had written to Churchill:

Lord Beaverbrook expressed his complete agreement with my view that our failure to obtain the dive-bombers which he ordered in July 1940 was due to the inefficiency of the American producers. He told me that, so inefficient were the American plants that the American Government had to take them over.[12]

Due confirmation came that August, with a memorandum from Hugh Molson to Sinclair:

Geoffrey Mander tells me that the true explanation is that the long delay in the delivery of these dive-bombers was due to the American company [Brewster] falling down on their contract. I want to urge that this should be plainly stated in fairness to you, because there is a feeling that the delay was due to obstruction on the part of your department. Geoffrey Mander says that this is due to the unwillingness to put any blame upon the Americans.[13]

By 5 March 1943, the saga reached another stage, with a very gloomy forecast from the British Air Commission in Washington DC. Both contracts with Brewster for the Bermuda, totalling 750 dive-bombers, should have been nearing completion, but, 'The progress on these contracts is thoroughly unsatisfactory throughout ... it is still obvious that completion before 1944 is impossible.' On the costs involved, these were spiralling alarmingly:

There have been many increases in labour rates, the last of these was recently awarded by the War Labor Board with retroactive effect to April 1941 and is estimated to involve an addition to the cost of contract A.642 alone, of approximately 2,000,000 dollars. The effect of the other labour increases has not yet been accurately assessed by the firm, but it will certainly involve some millions of dollars over the whole 750 airplanes.'[14]

The report went on to list other problems:

The position is further complicated by the fact that on the reconstruction of the firm last year, the U.S. Navy Department guaranteed a loan to them of M.30 dollars, much of which must be written off if the firm have to sustain the losses which will inevitably be involved if they get no concessions or awards on our contracts.

This affected the British orders only, as the US Navy used different contract terms. In the opinion of the Commission:

> It seems desirable to consider immediately, whether the Bermuda type is of such importance as to justify our continuing the contracts. If it is not, it is suggested that we consider putting the break clause into effect or transfer to the US Navy of as much as possible.[15]

The VCNAS was informed that this report:

> ... is bringing the question of the continuance of the Bermuda very much to a head. As far as I know it, the position is that we are far from being clear of trouble with the Bermuda, and in fact, the latest report stated that the bolts securing the wings have been found to be cracked in 10 per cent of cases where examination has been made. This, coupled with all the other shortcomings of the aircraft being delivered from production in an incomplete state, does not make for a speedy and satisfactory introduction into the Service ....[16]
>
> If it were not for the political factor that the Bermuda is the only dive-bomber which we have for introduction into the Service, and that this has been repeatedly stated as being put into effect, I would advocate that we should cut our losses and wash our hands of the Bermuda, if this could be done. The interminable argument about the dive-bomber still goes on, and as far as I know we have not got a decisively killing argument against it. Until we have one, I had hoped that the Bermuda would end the controversy, if only by virtue of the fact that we could say that we have a dive-bomber, although we can't use it [sic].[17]

This crystallised the Air Ministry's whole attitude, but, of course, was hidden from the public. The Pe-2 was a success for our Russian allies – the Ministry knew nothing about it; the Vultee Vengeance was a resounding success for RAF crews in combat in India, but the Ministry, rather than rejoice, hushed it up; the Ju 87 was continuing to humiliate us in Tunisia and at Leros – the Ministry refused to acknowledge the fact; the A-36 was a success for our other main ally in Sicily and Italy – the Ministry insisted, quite incorrectly and despite film footage, that they were not *really* dive-bombing; the Bermuda was in trouble on the production line – the Ministry thought it a great pity, but only because they wanted it for a smokescreen and not to be used!

However, Brewster's inefficiency must have come as a blessing in disguise. The VCAS wrote to Sinclair that, 'We have thus reached the position that an aircraft *which we hoped to employ* [Author's italics] [sic] in 1941 will be starting flying trials in this country more than two years later.'[18]

He proposed that they take the War Office into their confidence, to draw up an agreed plan of action:

We are due to form four dive-bomber squadrons in the United Kingdom. Some 200 Bermudas have already been delivered and more are bound to come along before the contract can be cancelled. Thus, apart from the fact that the Bermuda is not fit to fly, there is nothing to stop four squadrons being formed immediately and maintained for a considerable time.[19]

If the War Office failed to back them up, then 'We should continue our efforts to make the Bermuda airworthy, with a view to employing it for some non-operational purpose.' He admitted that news of the curtailment of the Bermuda contract would, 'no doubt cause a minor political sensation', but consoled the Minister by pointing out that, 'The problem will be made slightly easier by the fact that for some months we have been gently deflating the dive-bomber in Parliament.'[20]

The Minister was uncompromising: 'If a blunder has been made in ordering the Bermuda we must not be restrained by any fear of political embarrassment from refusing to order crews to fly aircraft which are not battleworthy and from cancelling the remainder of the contract.' But other options might be open to them. 'On the other hand [that good old politician's phase signalling an imminent compromise], we must not lightly jump to the conclusion that the Bermuda cannot be made operationally fit.' If they could, then all well and good; if not, then perhaps other uses could be found for them. 'A squadron or two for attacks on shipping and perhaps a squadron to accompany a tactical striking force with the single role of dive-bombing ....' It was also added [presumably with a view to their own political insurance] that 'It would be useful to ascertain exactly where the responsibility lies for the Bermuda order.' The reply continued:

There is, on this file, a most formidable list of defects on the Bermuda. It is three years since it was ordered; during that time Washington has been swarming with RAF officers. Surely it was the business of some of them to be in touch with the Brewster Company and to assure themselves that the Bermuda was being produced according to our requirements?[21]

Finally he recorded his neck was on the block:

I have told Parliament, after consultation with the Air Staff, that we wish to have light bombers with dive-bombing characteristics. I have said that they would certainly be useful against ships, and that they might be useful on land. If the Bermudas are not battle-worthy, cannot we get some other type of dive-bomber from the United States ...?

A meeting was duly held on 23 March 1943, at the VCAS office, to discuss all this, and a memorandum from the Deputy Director of Ordnance (Aircraft) that same day, pointed out the obvious. There were 1,300 Vengeance dive-bombers on order, and India would not require anything like that number. 'We could, if necessary, divert to this country, sufficient Vengeances to build and maintain four Army Support Squadrons for an indefinite period ....' On whether the A-31 or the improved A-35 should be purchased from America, it was pointed out that the former had ceased production in April, but that the A-35 would be available.[22]

The Vice-Chief of the Air Staff agreed with this and advised that the Delegation should stop, or curtail, shipments of the Bermuda, that the MAP be advised to operate the break clause as soon as possible, that Vengeance aircraft should be diverted to the UK for four squadrons, that the War Office should be informed thus and that all work on the Brewster should be halted.[23]

All well and good, but this was not fated to be the last word on the Bermuda saga!

*   *   *

By mid-1943, the Allies were everywhere (except the eastern Mediterranean, Burma and China) finally on the offensive, and one of the main prerequisites of successful dive-bomber operations insisted upon, viz. that of complete control of the air over the battlefield, was either an absolute reality, as we have seen in India, or rapidly becoming one, as in Italy, over the Eastern Front and in the Pacific. In all these theatres of war save the two latter, prior to the Normandy invasion of France in June 1944, the Royal Air Force was committed (much against their natural tendency) to a policy of close co-operation with the Army, Dive-bombing, if not dive-bombers, was therefore forced upon them by degree, and, ultimately, came to be utilised most successfully indeed.

With a shift in emphasis away from the gruelling stalemate in Italy and toward the build-up for the Allied landings to liberate western Europe, there was a gradual run-down of the Italian-based Desert Air Force as the winter of 1943 drew on. The Spitfire wings were no longer much needed for their original fighter protection mission, there were so few enemy aircraft to oppose, but more and more, they sought new employment via new methods of how to attack pinpoint targets isolated in mountain gorges and steep-sided river valleys which level bombing could not touch. Thus their combat emphasis changed bit-by-bit into an improvised dive-bomber role as a logical development of the well-tried 'Cab Rank' system, but adapted for mountain terrain. To see how this came about let us look in detail at one such unit.

When 324 Wing RAF returned to Italy in October 1943, it was spared the fate of its two companions, disbandment, and was, instead, re-trained for specialised ground-attack work, and, in particular, dive-bombing. No. 43 Squadron was part of this wing, and it is through the eyes of Flight Sergeant Dennis Young, a young Spitfire pilot in that squadron, that we here examine the methods, techniques and typical combat profile from 1943 onwards.

'No. 43 Squadron was part of four such, which were flying Spitfire IXs in 324 Wing, Desert Air Force (DAF) at this period', Dennis Young told me.[24]

Ours was a totally mobile Wing: everyone lived from tents and caravans, and the main impression of life for these units in that terrible Italian winter of 1943–4 was of mud, cold and acute discomfort. Although listed as being equipped with Mark IXs for all of this period, in actual fact, as D-Day drew nearer all, or most, of these aircraft were taken away from us and we were mainly re-equipped with Mark VIIIs. There was a general feeling that, back home, we were regarded very much as a 'Second Rate' area of the war after mid-1944.

Young and his fellow pilots had no previous training whatsoever in dive-bombing, of course, prior to joining the squadron, 'unless you counted dumping smoke bombs out of ageing Harvards in Rhodesia!' His own training was strictly that of an orthodox fighter pilot and was done in Tiger Moths at Salisbury Airport, Rhodesia.

When the decision was taken to utilise us as dive-bombers, my squadron set up an offshoot lash-up unit for training eight to ten pilots at a time in a three-week course. This training unit was part of the Wing and was based at Perugia. Two light service bomb racks were fitted under the wings and smoke bombs were used. We practised against a floating raft of a target, about 6 feet square approximately, moored on the nearby lake. We soon got quite proficient at it, although it did not go down well with the locals, who still fished the area. To have four Spits flashing down scattering smoke bombs in the water was hardly conducive to getting a good catch for market!

Once training had been completed, the pilots rejoined their squadrons, No. 43 operating from airfields at Perugia, Ancona and Riccione. Here, the airstrip was laid on the wide beach alongside the *Piarrale*

Lunghomare, and consisted of PSP interlocking steel plates. Young remembers that they had no trouble with high tides, but that strong crosswinds made it a hazardous spot for landing. On the actual bomb payload, he recalled:

> 250 lb bombs were first employed, but these proved poor in actual combat service and not very accurate to drop. We then carried a single 500 lb bomb under the fuselage and this was accurate. This was our main weapon, but, as I recall, we also did some experimental drops with napalm toward the end, in makeshift containers, which was a tricky load to handle.

The 500-pounder was fixed beneath the Spitfire's body on a medium-service bomb rack, which had two adjustable arms to hold it, and it was released by an electrical switch.

> There was a small button, which you merely jabbed, fixed to the ring, like a firing button in fact. If, perchance, your bomb hung up on you, then you cursed a bit and started pumping away with your foot at the other release. This was a steel rod in a bush, spring loaded, and it was purely physical. One just stamped hard on it continually until something gave, and your bomb fell clear. We were not in a frame of mind, when that happened, to care too much were the bomb finally went, but as long as we were north of the 'Bomb Line'[25] it didn't matter much.

No proper bomb sights, as such, were utilised. Sometimes lines were marked on the cockpit, but this was not popular. If, as frequently happened in that winter weather, these became dirty or oil-ingrained, they gave the impression of an incoming aircraft on the edge of one's vision. More normal was the locating of a dot on the hood at a position to give the correct angle to the distant horizon. The Spits were placed on trestles and the angle calculated and marked.

Tactics, as always, depended on the target. At this period of the war the Allies' overwhelming air strength was used quite liberally to aid the Army, and so it was not uncommon for the Spitfires to be sent against even lone snipers ('I remember on one mission, two of us completely demolished a church, just to root out one sniper. We went in so low and close I could see individual soldiers taking aim at us!'), but more often than not, it was against solitary tanks hidden in haystacks, specific houses known to be strongpoints ('On another mission we were even given the number of the house in the street we were to demolish: it contained Gestapo people and it was duly taken apart.'), and the like. Aircraft not a battlefield weapon? Slessor was probably appalled; he was certainly proved to be very much mistaken!

The most common mission type of all was the 'Rail Cut', the severing of the rail links between strategic centres, and sometimes the demolition of the railway stations themselves. These latter targets were unpopular for they were usually strongly defended. The main opposition encountered was of course German flak, which was most unpleasant and usually accurate.

> 88 mm or 105 mm flak batteries were our commonest foe and nasty they were. The Germans posted them about in deadly little clusters around important positions, but there were also static flak zones, through which one had to fly to reach the target. I particularly remember a fixed barrage over the River Po, which we always had to negotiate. The black bursts were not so bad as the smokeless stuff, which you didn't usually see anyway in the sky. It exploded like a bright red ball, and if you saw *that*, it was normally too late anyway!

Two main approach formations were adopted for Spitfires divebombing. Neither used any fighter cover at all – 'You were your own fighter cover' – and these were four- and six-aircraft boxes. The most common in No. 43 Squadron was the four-Spitfire formation, known as the 'Fluid Four'.

In this configuration, the four Spitfires flew in box formation, about 200 yards apart as maximum spacing. The two leading aircraft flew straight and true at normal heights of 18,000 to 20,000 feet, while the rear pair weaved from side to side, slightly *en echelon*, on their flanks, and varied their height also. The starboard leader was usually the CO of the unit or leader of the attack group, and all four aircraft carried bombs. An alternative formation to this was the six-aircraft box, with the front three and mid-after Spits flying straight and true, and, again, the two rear flankers weaving, as in the 'Fluid-Four'.

Only rarely did a single aircraft go off on its own, while the two-plane unit was the preserve of the 'Cab Rank' system. In general, 'Cab Rank' liaison with Eighth Army 'Rover Paddy' control systems, was reserved for 'nasty' little targets, and again, were not popular. It was difficult and wearing.

> You would sit in pairs, ready to go, in a lay-by at the end of the runway until the flares went up and off you went. You had to fly with a map in one hand, listening and talking to your guide and trying to identify one scruffy village from another. We were only 15 miles behind the front line in most cases and knew the area quite well, but it was still no fun trying to make out a grid reference with your goggles steamed up and the people down below doing their best to kill you.

Once the leader had located the target, and if the reception committee of flak was not *too* dense, the whole formation, still in its four-plane box, would circumnavigate the target to assess it.

Once that was done to the leader's satisfaction, the box would go into line-ahead formation and deploy for the final dive. Parallel to the target the leader would go into a hard bank (more often than not to port) and centre the dive with the sun behind him. The outward flight to the zone would normally be made at an unhurried 250 knots, but, once in the normal dive path; 80–82 degrees was the norm for No. 43 Squadron Spits, and speed quickly built up.

The leading aircraft would go into the target, over and down across in seconds. The propeller-boss was used to align the target in the final dive, and it was raised until the target vanished under the Spitfire's nose, usually between 4,000 and 2,000 feet, rarely lower. There would be a partial black-out for a split-second, but, with the tail trimmed heavy by use of the elevator trim-tab operated by a small wheel, the aircraft would lift out of the dive and go straight out and away as fast as possible.

At a few seconds' intervals, Nos 2, 3 and 4 would follow the leader into the target at slightly different converging angles to throw off the defence. None the less, being the last aircraft in was no sinecure, as the German gunners and their predictors were very good indeed. Tail-end Charlie in fact was not allocated, as might be expected, to the junior pilot; quite often, in fact, one of the more senior officers, who would have a few personal tricks and ideas up his sleeve, to avoid giving the flak a 'nil-deflection' shot, would take this position.

Rendezvous was made 'anywhere out of the way'. The Spitfire carried 20 mm cannon, and these could be pumping out during the attack if the target justified it, as obviously rail cuts normally did not. Young considered that it was usual for this type of four-plane attack to always get at least two spot-on hits out of the four bombs, with two close.

> You could do an enormous amount of damage with the cannon, but against railway lines it was hardly worth bothering, unless that is, you felt particularly naughty. Then, if you were cutting between two stations, you could continue up the line to the local station of a typical little country village and flatten the entire area within seconds.

I asked Dennis Young about the speed that built up in the final un-braked dive, and the inevitable black-out.

> I estimate we were getting up to 600 mph, but of course it was off the clock. We had several cases in No. 43 Squadron of buckling at the wing roots of the Mk VIIIs after a dive-bombing attack. Of

course, Spits were not built for this kind of work at all and had no special bracing. There was a big 'g' force at the end of the dive. One went into the straps. One felt very heavy, you were forced down, you felt your face, eyes and mouth, drawn down. You saw red, then grey, then flickered right out to nothing. Within a split-second you found yourself flying on untoward. After a long series of such missions the strain could build up.

There was, of course, no automatic pull-out in the Spitfire:

I don't think they were necessary, although I saw one or two chaps go straight in and never appear to attempt a pull-out. Until you are down to 200 feet or so, it is very hard to judge distances on the ground precisely at that kind of speed. But you had to force a Spitfire down into that steep a dive, it took an effort, and so they usually came up all right.

The casualty rate in No. 43 Squadron Dennis Young remembers as 'ghastly', and in going through his photograph collection certainly almost every one brought a response like, 'that was before his last mission', 'he didn't survive', 'his girl let him down back home, he didn't want to come back and he was dead within a few weeks'. This may be emotional, as they were his close friends, but there is no doubt that dive-bombing in a Spitfire was no easy war. The wheel had come full circle for the RAF from those far-distant Orfordness trials with the Spitfire of her day, the equally legendary Camel fighter!

Finally, to round off this chapter, Dennis Young described to me a dive-bombing mission that was almost his last. It was a 'Cab Rank' sortie, but with four aircraft, and Young this time was nominated as the unenvied 'Tail-end Charlie'. They were briefed to strike at a stoutly defended target near Treviso, in Northern Italy, towards the end of the war.

It was yet another 'Rail Cut' and I was flying No. 4 on this mission, when we went into line astern. There was lots of flak about, you could see it everywhere, thick black bursts of 88. I watched our leader go in, through, out and away. Then I watched as the other two went into their dives, through the bursts, and then I followed them down.

I wasn't hit, and I didn't see anything, but the plane baulked and reared and I knew that I had been damaged. I did a very shallow run and got out as fast as I could. As I came away, my faithful old FTR felt bad, very rough indeed. I had taken shrapnel in the engine somewhere and the pneumatic system. I had fired back in my dive with the cannon, uselessly, but it made me feel better, but they didn't fire. I thought, if they are out, what about my wheels, would they lower, can I land, I didn't know.

I looked around for my companions, but they were long gone. There was nothing in sight as far as I could see. The flak was astern, far away, and the sky was empty. I called on the radio to the other three, but there was no reply. I nursed the old bus along on my own. I thought, this is your lot, as I got over the sea. It looked awfully cold down there and I didn't want to ditch.

So there I was, no guns, no companions and, for all I knew, no wheels. I had already smashed one Spit up on a previous mission, putting it nose-down in a ditch, and this particular aircraft was the favourite mount of another pilot in the squadron I kept borrowing. 'Don't scratch it!', he had implored as I had left. It didn't look too bright for him either!

I flew down to Rimini and called up the tower. I explained what had happened, that I couldn't risk putting my crate down on that short runway. They told me to lower my flaps, which I did. They worked all right, but I had no brakes. They sent me packing, some 15 miles down the coast to a USAAF Marauder base, where they had built a strip for themselves a mile long. Luckily, of the four frequencies on my VHF set, the Yanks were using one of them and I explained my dilemma to them. They said it was OK to come in shortly, but as they did so my engine gave a couple of pops and a loud bang. Thinking about my wheels, brakes and guns, I had forgotten about my fuel. I was bone dry!

There was no alternative. I went straight in – down wind! As I zoomed onto the deck I glimpsed, in a fleeting moment, another Spit taking off, whoops! We missed each other by a matter of feet. The runway seemed to go on and on, but with no brakes the Spit just kept on rolling and rolling. This is it, I though yet again, another write-off.

I reached the end of the runway and ran off onto the sand. But the nose didn't tip up this time, just fell gently back, and I was down in one piece.

Meanwhile, the pilot of the other aircraft had put his plane into a screaming split-arse turn and thundered down onto the runway again, revving it right up to where I sat limply in the cockpit. Up went his cockpit and up he shot. It was my luck to have scared the pants off a visiting group captain from another unit.

He tore me off the most colossal strip and it was some time before he ran out of words in which to describe me and my ancestors, and I was finally able to explain my position. After he had heard me out, he was as nice as pie!

*   *   *

In France and the Low Countries, the final Allied version of dive-bombing by aircraft of the Tactical Air Force, which had been set up in November 1943, was implemented. Typhoons, Spitfire Vs and Xs and Mustang IIIs were all used by the RAF for this task. From March, 1944, these machines trained in the role in readiness for the Normandy landings, but suffered heavy casualties from German flak. The greater publicity was given to the rocket-firing Typhoons, which were credited with enormous powers of destruction and with the bulk of the German tank casualties during the battle of the Falaise Gap. Only much, much later, did careful analysis re-attribute much of the carnage to Allied artillery fire.

Dive-bombing still featured, with the Bombphoons being particularly efficient in this role, as were the USAAF's P-45 Thunderbolts, both these big fighters being capable of lugging very large bombs and dive-bombing with them at the steepest of angles without suffering inherent structural damage as had the more lightly built Spitfires and Mustangs. Their first operational missions in this configuration showed that they were more willing to take advantage of the dive-bombing approach to lessen losses and attain the necessary degree of precision. On 5 March 1944, for example, Thunderbolts of the 366th Fighter Group carried out a very exact dive-bombing attack against the airfield at St Valery, but with a bomb load consisting only of 250 lb weapons. Similarly smaller bombs were also used on early Bombphoon missions, but gradually, as confidence grew, the payload was increased, first to a single 500 lb bomb and then, ultimately to toting a 1,000-pounder.

In the days immediately following the invasion, Spitfires dive-bombed gun emplacements in the Calais area and also used this method against pinpoint targets like the V-1 rockets' launching sites (Operation Crossbow) throughout 1944. When the Germans started launching the true missile, the V-2 rockets, an even sterner task faced the Allied units. Only a direct hit on a V-2 launching site would do, and despite all their years of opposing the method as an effective method, and of declaring modern fighter aircraft could not do it, the RAF relied on both to try and put a stop to the Germans' latest horror weapon. Later to achieve fame as a BBC radio and television presenter, Flight Lieutenant Raymond Baxter flew dive-bombing Mark XVI Spitfires with No. 602 (City of Glasgow) Squadron on these sorties, which unit, along with No. 452 (Australian) Squadron, bore the brunt of these missions by No. 12 Group working out of RAF Coltishall, Norfolk, from December 1944 right through to March 1945. Baxter flew his first dive-bombing mission on 4 December, when he attacked a V-2 site, and soon they were flying two such missions a day. This little-publicised dive-bombing campaign was known as Operation Big Ben.[26]

The Spitfire dive-bombing of V-2 sites, which were usually constructed right in among Dutch civilian housing, in the manner of Islamic terrorists locating the Kazutaka rockets in Lebanon nowadays, called for a high degree of skill and precision. They were probably among the most important dive-bombing targets ever tackled, and yet they remain almost unknown, scorned by people like Alanbrook and expunged from RAF history. We have had to wait sixty years for some dedicated probing by two young air historians[27] for the full facts to come to light, and we should be grateful for their work.

Another dive-bomber was in action over France during this period, non other than the SBD, 'unsuitable and obsolescent'. Two such groups carried out these attacks, both belonging to the Free French forces, the *Aéronavale* and *Armée de l'Air* respectively, which had been supplied with both the SBD and the A-24. Thus the Dauntless extended her famous reputation yet further. SBDs had already made their European debut operating against German coastal shipping in Norwegian waters from the American aircraft-carrier *Ranger*, and proved far more efficient at this job than the medium bombers of Coastal Command. Now land-based Dauntless made attacks on the bypassed German garrisons dug in along the French coast.

In November 1944, two *Flotilles* of dive-bombers had been formed at Agadir, Morocco, with thirty-nine SBD-5s supplied by the Americans. After a brief period of training, thirty-two of these aircraft, forming the GAN-2, flew to Cognac and gave dive-bombing support to Free French ground forces engaged in mopping-up operations against the German-held Atlantic ports, seeing action at Royan, Le Vedon, Pointe de la Courbre, Pointe de Grave and the Ile d'Oléron. Between December 1944 and May 1945, these SBDs flew a total of 1,500 sorties and dropped 500 tons of bombs. Only five Dauntless aircraft were lost to flak during this whole six-month operating period.

The USAAF equivalent of the SBD, the A-24B, scorned by the RAF as unsuitable for European operations, was also in action with the Army unit GBI/18 *Vendeé*. Based near Toulouse in September 1944, they began operations against retreating German columns in southern France. They then moved up to Brittany, being based at Vannes with sixteen aircraft and conducted dive-bombing missions against the German forces isolated in the Lorient–St Nazaire pocket. Between December and May 1945, they lost a total of just four aircraft carrying out these last dive-bomber attacks on French territory.

Notes

1. For the only full and complete account of the campaign in English see Peter C. Smith & Edwin R. Walker, *War in the Aegean*, Stackpole Books, Mechanicsburg, PA, 2007.

2. AM to AHQ India, dated 12 June 1943, Sec.X49 (National Archives, Kew, London AIR 20/4249).

3. *Ibid.*

4. *Ibid.*

5. *Ibid.*

6. AHQ India to Air Ministry, dated 30 June 1943, AOC 561 (National Archives, Kew, London, AIR 20/4249).

7. Secret Memorandum: *Notes on Tactical Qualities of the Dive-bomber*, dated 9 September 1943 (National Archives, Kew, London, AIR 20/4249).

8. *Hansard*, issue dated 21 January 1943.

9. ACAS (TR) to S.6, dated 19 February 1943, TR/35/319 (National Archives, Kew, London, AIR 20/1873).

10. Jack R. Collingwood to Mark A. Savage, 20 September 1990, see *Straight Down!* op. cit.

11. PS to S-of-S, S.6 and ACAS, dated 19 February 1943 (National Archives, Kew, London, AIR 19/233).

12. S-of-S Air, to Prime Minister, dated 7 August 1942 (National Archives, Kew, London, AIR 19/233).

13. Hugh Molson to S-of-S Air, dated 7 August 1942 (National Archives, Kew, London, AIR 19/233).

14. *Report* by BAC Washington DC, dated 5 March 1943 (National Archives, Kew, London AIR 2/5504).

15. *Ibid.*

16. *Memo*, ACAS(TR) to VCAS, dated 8 March 1943 (National Archives, Kew, London, AIR 2/5504).

17. *Ibid.*

18. VCAS to S-of-S Air, dated 16 March 1943 (National Archives, Kew, London, AIR 2/5504).

19. *Ibid.*

20. *Ibid.*

21. S-of-S to VCAS, dated 21 March 1943 (National Archives, Kew, London AIR/2/5504).

22. *Memorandum*, DDO(A) to ACAS(P), dated 23 March 1943. LM/2795/DDO(A) (National Archives, Kew, London AIR 2/5504).

23. *Memorandum*, VCAS to S-of-S Air, dated 27 March 1943 (National Archives, Kew, London, AIR 2/5504).

24. Dennis Young in interview with the Author, 12 May 1977.

25. The 'Bomb Line' is self-explanatory, it merely being the mythical point drawn across Italy, north of which bombing was permitted without fear of hitting one's own forces. God help the Italian civilians, of course, but that was before 'Civil Rights' became more important than freedom from the Totalitarian Dictatorships!

26. See Air Ministry Secret Report, *Air Defence of Great Britain, Volume 6 (formerly Vol. 7) – The Flying Bomb and Rocket Campaigns 1944–45*, HMSO, London (National Archives, Kew, London).

27. Craig Cabell and Graham A. Thomas, *Operation Big Ben; the Anti-V2 Spitfire Missions 1944–45*, Spellmount, Staplehurst, Kent, 2004.

CHAPTER THIRTEEN

'The huge ship presented a beautiful target'

There was a strange period in the middle of the war, when the Fleet Air Arm, which had once been in the forefront of naval dive-bombing development, for a long time was left without a single front-line dive-bomber embarked in any one of its aircraft-carriers, just at the time when this type of aircraft was establishing itself as the major naval weapon of 1941–4. From mid-1941 until 1944, the only limited dive-bomber potential possessed by the world's leading naval power lay in the antiquated Fairey Swordfish and Albacore torpedo-bombers. Their dive-bombing missions, to be sure, were carried out with great skill, daring and panache, especially in the Western Desert, but this merely emphasised just how much of a poor relation the Fleet Air Arm had become, with these plank-winged, wire-strutted anachronisms from another age creaking across the skies and contrasting humiliatingly with the Dauntless, Helldiver, Pe-2, Vengeance and Ju 88. Even the Ju 87 and the D3A2, old as they were, presented a much more modern and workmanlike image, despite being an older design!

The very last Blackburn Skuas had finally been phased out of front-line service early in 1941. No. 801 Squadron flew the last combat missions:

> By mid-1941, we had become maids-of-all-work for attack missions, both shore and carrier based. Just before some of the old hands of 801 were hived off and embarked with Fulmar IIs in the brand-new *Victorious*, we had reached the art of hitting ships pretty well, indeed, for sure. We had all sorts of esoteric tricks in store for the wily Hun, even to the extent of hitting ships tucked into the shelter of cliffs in the deep fiords of Norway. This entailed a splendid curved approach, where the bomb was implanted with a nice 'in-swinger' type of movement.

But, like the other Skua units aboard *Ark Royal*, No. 801's days were numbered, and this vital dive-bombing expertise was thrown away. Before that, they had one last flurry of activity:

The squadron embarked from time to time [aboard the carrier *Furious*], either for strikes off Northern Norway or to provide strike/fighter or search roles for special convoys taking RAF fighter aircraft to West Africa for onward reinforcement for Wavell's war efforts. It was during this period we were sent to RAF St Eval for the 'Salmon and Gluck' effort, which in turn was ended when the German Air Force counter-attacked St Eval and severely mauled our poor old Skuas while parked near the control tower.[1] [This occasioned the cheers of the Skua pilots, who felt very bitterly that their RAF Coastal Command masters had no understanding of dive-bomber operations, and totally misused them.]

An Admiralty offer to Admiral Somerville of Force H, to station a squadron of Skuas ashore at Gibraltar, so that he could embark them from time to time when he needed a dive-bomber element, fell through due to the inefficiency of the authorities ashore at the Rock, who could not provide accommodation for them![2] With the departure of the Skua, relegated to target-towing duties, naturally, there was no replacement dive-bomber to take its place. The usual requirements for Fleet Air Arm aircraft, which made them so inferior to all other types, was that they had to combine as many different roles as possible in one air-frame, and these usually made them poor in most of them. This think-ing had resulted in the adoption of the Fairey TSR Barracuda being fitted with Fairey-Youngman flaps to give a dive-bombing capability, but, as we have already seen, this aircraft was so long delayed in gestation as to be herself semi-obsolescent on arrival in service in 1943, as the specification, given in reply to a prodding Churchill memor-andum, revealed:

> The Barracuda is a single-engined three-seater aircraft, designed for operations from aircraft-carriers as a torpedo-bomber-reconnaissance and dive-bomber. It is very manoeuvrable and easy to handle and is said to be an excellent aircraft for the role[s] for which it was designed. Although extensive diving tests have not been completed, trials have shown that the aircraft is steady in a dive and easily kept on target. Release of bombs during the dive has no effect on control ....
>
> Considering it as a shore-based aircraft, the range (910 miles) is inferior to the normal shore-based torpedo-bomber. As a dive-bomber, although it can carry four 500 lb bombs, its speed and range (524 miles with 2,000 lb bombs) are inferior to either the Bermuda or the Vengeance. It is also inferior in armament.[3]

Further information was given at this time on the Barracuda specifi-cation, as follows:

It presents an excellent all-round view for the pilot; it is very man-oeuvrable and easy to handle. Take-offs and landing are simple. The landing run is between 630 and 750 yards to 50 feet, according to bomb load. Comprehensive diving tests have not yet been made, but the aircraft has been dived up to a speed of 280 mph with a load of four 500 lb bombs and the bombs have been dropped singly in the dive.[4]

This high-winged monster incorporated the Fairey-Youngman flaps below the trailing edge, a high-mounted tailplane and an ungainly undercarriage. The Barracuda has been compared in elegance with a pregnant stork! These special flaps were inclined 30 degrees to act as dive-brakes, and were particularly effective, but their outward result was to make an ugly aircraft worse, and overall performance was poor compared to foreign dive-bomber types. The old adage, 'If it looks right, it'll fly right', took on a special significance with the ungainly Barra. Designed to Spec. 24/37, as a replacement for the Albacore, the original power plant had been the Rolls Royce Exe engine. Although two prototypes flew in 1940, it was not until 1942 that the first pro-duction model got off the ground. This massive delay was due to the dropping of development work on the Exe and switching-over to the adoption of the Merlin engine instead.

As also recorded earlier, the suspension of all work on her during the Battle of Britain further penalised her, and the Barracuda never really recovered from this series of setbacks. By the time she joined the fleet, her marked and obvious inferiority to the now-available Lease-Lend Grumman Avenger quickly became apparent. Only twenty-five Mk 1s were built, before the more powerful Merlin 32 engine, develop-ing 1,640 hp, was phased in, together with a four-bladed instead of a three-bladed airscrew. The prototype first flew on 17 August 1942 and first entered squadron deployment in January 1943 with No. 827 Squadron, followed by No. 810 Squadron in February, and the Barracuda finally equipped up to a maximum of twelve FAA units by January 1944. Thereafter she began to be replaced by the more workmanlike TBM Avenger.

The Barracuda had a poor maximum speed of only 228 mph and a ceiling of 16,600 feet. Although fated to be in front-line service for naval dive-bombing for little more than a year, the Barracuda is assured of a special place in the history of dive-bombing for the famous attack made upon the German battleship *Tirpitz* in her Norwegian lair, early in 1944. On the face of it, this seemed like promising to be a repeat of the *Scharnhorst* fiasco, against an even tougher and stronger opponent, but the Royal Navy this time attacked *en masse* and with more powerful weapons, and it turned out to be one of the classic dive-bombing missions of the war.

By early 1944, the Royal Navy had built up a sufficiently powerful force to contemplate taking on the most difficult and well protected of targets in a massed dive-bombing, and they were therefore sent against this 45,000-ton monster, which by her very baleful presence close to the supply convoy routes to North Russia had adversely affected the war at sea for two years, even though she rarely actually put to sea. The task of immobilising her (they knew they could not sink her by dive-bombing alone, and she could not be got at by torpedo-bombers) was entrusted to the Home Fleet, and extensive preparations began.

Intensive training programmes were initiated using a target at Loch Eriboll to simulate Kaa Fiord where the *Tirpitz* lay at anchor in Norway. Live bombs were issued during these trials to find out which combination of explosives might achieve the best results. It was fully realised that, while dive-bombing alone would not sink the battleship, they could inflict so much damage on her upperworks as to keep her under repair and inoperational for a considerable period. Torpedo-bombing, the obvious solution, was out of the question due to the position of her berth, which prevented a sufficient unimpeded torpedo run, and the surrounding nets and booms.

It was decided to utilise a mixed bomb load, delivered to the target by successive formations of aircraft for cumulative effect. Barracudas from Nos 827, 828, 830 and 831 Squadrons were to attack in two waves, and were provided with a strong fighter escort comprising Grumman Hellcats of No. 800 Squadron, Seafires from No. 801 Squadron, Wild-cats of No. 898 Squadron and Corsairs of No. 1834 Squadron. In total, forty-two dive-bombers were to be sent in, with an escort of eighty fighters. A large proportion of these fighter aircraft were to be em-ployed in the role of flak battery and flak ship suppression, strafing these batteries afloat and ashore to saturate the AA defences and create diversionary targets. For this the fighters were to employ tracer and AP ammunition on a 50:50 ratio.

The first group of Barracudas carried the 500 lb MC Mk II bomb with instantaneous fuses and with a 0.07-second interval on distributors, with the object of obtaining air bursts from the second and third bombs of the stick, whose ripple detonations and shrapnel would neutralise the ship's own AA guns topside and cause casualties to other exposed personnel by detonation above deck level.

The further aircraft carried 500 lb SAP Mk V bombs, with 0.14-second-delay fuses, enough of which were to be dropped to ensure the maximum number of hits and thus inflict between-deck damage, with-out penetrating the armoured decks of the leviathan. The 600 lb A/S Mk 1.1 bombs carried by other of the Barracudas were hydrostatic, and, like the SAP, stick spacing was 65 feet between the bombs on the ground, with the objective of obtaining more than one hit in each successive attack and so cause continuing damage to adjacent compartments, while the A/S bombs were to rupture the hull by alongside explosions, the water-hammer effect.

The largest weapon to be carried in this attack was the 1,600 lb Mk 1 AP bomb fitted with 0.08-second-delay fuses. This might penetrate several armoured decks if released from above 3,500 feet, but as fewer of these larger weapons could be carried, the percentage of hits was expected to be lower. The attack was to be made along the length of the *Tirpitz*, range errors in practice being double those of line. The height of release was to be 2,500 feet for the 500 lb bombs. The first strike was to commence diving from 8,000 feet (angle of dive 50–60 degrees), the second wave from 10,000 feet (angle of dive 45–55 degrees).

Detailed briefing by squadrons separately was completed at sea two days before the strike, but officers had already well familiarised themselves with the target from a mass of detailed maps, charts, photographs and scale models provided. Last-minute briefing took place one hour before each strike took off, and a last-minute board with estimated geographic position of the departure point was displayed as the aircraft took off.

Under the command of Admiral Sir Michael Denny, the fleet assembled at the rendezvous point 250 miles north-west of Altenfiord on the evening of 1 April. The Barracudas were embarked aboard the fleet carriers *Furious* and *Victorious*, the fighters aboard the escort carriers *Emperor*, *Pursuer* and *Searcher*. The battleships *Anson* and *Duke of York* provided heavy cover should the *Tirpitz* sortie out to snap up these tempting targets in bad weather, and the big ships had a close escort of four cruisers and fourteen destroyers.

By 1700 hours on 2 April, all the aircraft were fuelled and serviceable, and bombing-up was carried out on deck and in the hangars at 1800. The long-range fuel tanks of the fighters were fuelled at 0100 hours on the 3rd. A film of anti-freeze grease was applied to all leading edges, but the light winds at take-off point ruled out the application of de-icing paste, as the bomb-load was critical. The second strike was ranged on the deck overnight; the first being kept below and warm. At 0200 hours the second wave ran up engines and were in turn struck down, and the first were ranged on deck. At 0215 all aircraft for both strikes were brought up on the after lifts.

All this meticulous preparation contrasts with the earlier hastily organised attempt against the *Scharnhorst* in these waters four years earlier, and demonstrated how the Fleet Air Arm had carefully assimilated all the many mistakes made at that time. They were to be rewarded in spectacular fashion.

Aboard *Victorious*, flying off of the first range, ten Corsairs and twelve Barracudas, commenced at 0405 hours and was completed by 0415. The second range, of similar composition, completed flying off at 0534, although one Barracuda from this group failed to start and another crashed on take-off. No difficulty was experienced in good visibility, in either forming up or the departure of these strikes. Smoke floats were dropped to enable the fighters to form up during the first 10 miles of the outward leg. The first strike departed from the fleet 1 mile west of *Victorious* at 0438 hours on a track of 139°. They held this course for nine minutes to allow the fighters to form up. The weather was clear, with extreme visibility. At 0447 this strike began to climb, being within 25 miles of its landfall, Loppen Island, which was picked up by both strikes without difficulty. The first strike crossed the coast at 0509 hours, map-reading its way to the west of Lang Fiord and then east, down the valley to the target anchored in Kaa Fiord. No flak was met until the strike was within 3 miles of *Tirpitz*.

The route was, again, easy to find, the fiords standing out sharply against the snow-blanketed land around them; the second strike, of course, was aided by smoke from the first group's attack. All radio equipment worked perfectly, and the first strike's leader was able to pass position and details of the target to the second on his way in. Up to 25 miles from the coast, the Barracudas hugged the waves at a height of only 50 feet, with the fighters riding a little higher. The coast was crossed at 7,000 feet, and the approach made at 8,500 feet, as planned.

Two German destroyers and a supply ship were spotted in Lang Fiord, but failed to open fire as the first wave sped past them, and at about 15 miles from the target the dive-bombers commenced their initial dives at about 200 knots. At 5,000 feet, 3 miles out, they sighted the *Tirpitz* and the wing leader gave the order to deploy.

A synchronised wing attack was to be carried out, and a further deployment took place in the final approach phase. The port wing took advantage of hill cover at 3,000 feet, but the starboard wing had no cover at all; however, flak was light. On the final run-in and dive, considerable, but inaccurate, flak came up from both ships and shore batteries, and the latter were heavily strafed by the Wildcats and Hellcats. *Tirpitz* herself appeared to cease firing by the time the second wave attacked, due to the hits achieved by the first wave, exactly as hoped for.

The twenty-one Barracudas of the first wave completed their bombing runs within the space of sixty seconds exactly. Although the smoke screens started to operate as they arrived in sight, it failed to obscure the target for most of the aircraft of this group. Surprise was, in fact, complete.

Lieutenant-Commander R. Baker-Faulkner, the wing leader of No. 8 TBR, reported his attack thus:

About 10 miles from the target, I disposed 830 Squadron aircraft astern of 827 Squadron's twelve aircraft. Deployed starboard half of 827 Squadron shortly afterwards according to wing synchronised tactics. Sighted target in position expected, then dived to keep hill cover, sending all Wildcats and Hellcats to strafe guns and target. I then lost sight of all aircraft and carried out a dive from stern to stem of target, releasing bombs at 1,200 feet.[5]

No fighters appeared to dispute the issue and the second wave arrived unmolested. The first bombs dropped at 0529 and the second group attacked half an hour later, anti-aircraft fire being heavier but the smoke screen still not very effective. However, many of the Barracudas, in their eagerness to score hits, bored in lower than intended, the Germans later reporting that most bombs were released between 600 and 1,200 feet, and so no bomb actually penetrated the battleship's main armoured decks. None the less, she was smothered in direct hits and near misses, five AP and four HE from the first wave, and five more hits from the second wave.

Sub-Lieutenant J.D. Britton RNVR, of 830 Squadron, reported:

Dive to 2,000 feet before releasing bomb (a 1,600 lb). During the dive *Tirpitz* was seen to be constantly hit by various bombs, and a large explosion amidships appeared to be caused by 1,600 lb AP bomb. The *Tirpitz* was enveloped in large red flames, and smoke amidships. *Tirpitz* was stationary and heading up Kaa Fiord about 330 degrees.[6]

Sub-Lieutenant E.M. King RNVR was the last pilot to attack, and he stated:

On approach to target, long-range flak from ground batteries was fairly heavy, correct for height, but erratic for range and line. Just before entering dive for attack, observed black smoke and a belch of flame mast high. This was followed by a further, but smaller, eruption slightly further forward, possibly on 'B' turret. Target outline was discernible through the clouds of smoke, but assessment of damage was impossible.[7]

Only one Barracuda was lost in this brilliant dive-bombing attack. 'It is believed that this aircraft carried out its attack in spite of being hit, as it made its getaway with the remainder and was seen diving vertically onto the mountainside in flames.'

Aboard the *Tirpitz* they left an inferno. Although her main armoured deck was not penetrated, her upper works were in a shambles, and her light AA positions and compartments above the main decks were pulverised. Among her crew in these vulnerable positions 122 were killed and 316 wounded. She was put out of action for three months following this attack, which was pressed home with determination and courage by the young FAA dive-bomber aircrews, eager to prove themselves. Shades of their Skua forebears in these same waters would have surely approved of the manner in which their young counterparts had carried out this excellent attack.

The success of this attack led to it being repeated, with further, though much smaller, assaults, in order to keep *Tirpitz* inoperational, and further dive-bombing by Barracuda forces from various Home Fleet task forces took place against the battleship on 15 May, 14 July, 22 August and 24 August 1944. In these later raids, another direct hit was made with a heavy bomb. However, these assaults met with much better prepared defences and were thus not so successful. The Royal Navy had, in fact, reverted to 'penny packets' once more, with the inevitable result. All experience had shown that for dive-bombing, the best results were achieved with massed attack: numbers were essential.

Meanwhile, the emphasis of the air-sea war for the Fleet Air Arm had shifted back to the east, firstly to the Indian Ocean and subsequently, in 1945, to the Pacific. Here the Barracuda aircraft of Nos 810 and 847 Squadrons from the carrier *Illustrious*, in conjunction with Dauntless dive-bombers from the US carrier *Saratoga*, made attacks upon Japanese-held oil-storage tanks and oil refineries at Sabang, Sumatra, between 16 and 21 April, and again, with Nos 815 and 817 Squadrons flying from *Indomitable* and Nos 822 and 831 Squadrons from *Victorious*, against the same type of targets in the same locality, throughout the winter months of 1944–5.

By January 1945, most of the air groups in the Royal Navy's reconstituted East Indies Fleet aircraft-carriers had changed over to the Grumman Avenger for dive-bombing missions, and the Barracuda left the stage.

* * *

The Grumman TBM torpedo-bomber had made a spectacular mark in the Pacific war, after her terrible debut at the Battle of Midway, with the US Navy's vast task forces, sharing with the SBD, and then the SB2C, the majority of all the Japanese warships destroyed between 1942 and 1944. Although built first and foremost as a torpedo-bomber, the Avenger's capacious weapons bay was capable of lifting internally a 1,000 lb bomb without difficulty, and increasingly, as suitable torpedo-bomber targets dwindled in numbers, she was employed as a shallow dive-bomber, especially by the US Navy and Marine Corps and then by the Royal Navy, still without a proper dive-bomber, during the later stages of the Pacific War.

Over 1,000 of these sturdy and reliable aircraft joined the Royal Navy during this period, and here they were used as glide-bombers, dive-bombers and anti-submarine aircraft, rather than in their intended torpedo-bomber role.

Bearing a notable outward resemblance to its much small fighter stable-mates, the Wildcat and Hellcat, the Avenger was a highly successful design. She was a three-seat, all-metal monoplane, powered either with a single 1,850 Wright Cyclone GR-2600 (Mk 1) or a single 1,750 Wright Cyclone R-2600-20 engine, which gave her a maximum speed of between 259 and 262 mph. She first joined the Fleet Air Arm on 1 January 143, with No. 832 Squadron, and by the end of the war was equipping no less than fifteen squadrons.

Perhaps the Avenger's most spectacular exploit as a dive-bomber with the Royal Navy was the strikes she made against the Japanese-held oil refineries of Pladju and Songei Gerong, situated close to Palembang in Sumatra, on 24 and 29 January 1945, during the passage of the newly established British Pacific Fleet, which was transferring its base from the Indian Ocean via Australia to join the US Navy's drive on Okinawa on the way to Japan.

With the fleet carriers *Illustrious*, *Indefatigable*, *Indomitable* and *Victorious*, the battleship *King George V*, four cruisers and ten destroyers, the BPF left Trincomalee in Ceylon on 16 January, and after riding out two tropical storms off Sumatra was in a position to launch the first strike, at Pladju, on the 24th. Each Avenger was armed with four 500 lb HE bombs, and a covering force of fighters escorted them in. In addition, Fairey Fireflies, a new aircraft, armed with rocket projectiles, accompanied them on the mission. Although the force was intercepted by Japanese Army fighters from nearby training airfields, the Avengers pressed home their attack in the face of heavy AA fire and through a balloon barrage.

One of the Avenger pilots on that raid was Sub-Lieutenant Halliday, and in an interview that he later gave me at the Royal Naval College, Greenwich, this graphic eyewitness description of what it was like to dive-bomb in an Avenger emerged:[8]

> We were all very well briefed on our objectives; we had studied photographs of the area and models constructed aboard the ship, and when we arrived over the plant, the individual landmarks were easily identified. My own target, a cracking unit, stood out as a large cylindrical silver object. The type of attack chosen was really a cross between dive and glide bombing; it was the only way to neutralise a pinpoint target. It was essential to hit the

cracking unit, and not just plant a bomb somewhere near it. To achieve the right degree of accuracy we had practised this form of attack in our training. The bombs had to be released at a set height, using a sight, and if one veered from that at all the inaccuracies crept in and you would not hit the target. The main difficulty was that this was a fairly well-defended target by any standards, and it is very difficulty to concentrate on your target when you know that people are firing things at you – and the Japanese always used a large amount of tracer to make sure you could see something.

In other words, you had one or two diversionary things to think about, but once you started your attack, everything else had to be ignored; it was the pilot's job to hit the selected target on the ground come what may, and this we tried to do. It meant that the bombers could not take avoiding action, but must go in straight and true, relying on our own fighters to keep the enemy off our tail.

The Japanese were very cunning in their use of the balloon barrage. It was not floating at a set height, but they waited until we were committed to our attack and then allowed the balloons to come up. The balloon came up quite fast to meet you and in my opinion this was deliberate Japanese policy and not because they were caught by surprise. It was well calculated to put a dive-bomber pilot off. The pilot had to make a quick decision as to whether to press home the attack through the balloons, which meant flying below the level at which they would be stabilised or attempt to pull up above them.

Everyone quickly appreciated that if the attack was to be of any use we would have to press on down, which we all did. We were closing the target in a committed dive, so you were left with two options; you either dropped your bombs high, which immediately meant that the accuracy would be very much less, or you went down through the cables and dropped them at the right height. It is impossible, of course, for the pilot to see the cables, but you can see the balloons and you know that the cables are below, though you do not know exactly where. It is a very unpleasant experience, from the point of view of the pilot, to be flying along one moment with an aircraft flying perfectly normally beside you – and then suddenly a wing goes and the other plane spins down. We lost quite a few aircraft that way.

If you hit a cable very much outboard, you might survive; but you could only afford to lose about 2 feet off the wing tip, striking anywhere else inboard of that towards the wing root and that was the finish. The whole wing would go, and the plane would spin crazily into the ground.

Only two Avengers, in fact, were lost in this first attack. The second strike was launched at 0732 on the 29th from a gap in heavy squalls, each of the carriers putting twelve Avengers into the air to strike at Songei Gerong. Again, all the targets were well plastered. Sub-Lieutenant Halliday was hit and shot down in this attack.

> I was hit on my way down to the target, but I didn't realise it, until I pulled away, and saw three or four neat holes in my wing and flames coming out of the holes. I just burnt steadily all the way back to the coast – I did not expect to make it, as it lay 90 miles back to, and on the far side of, a mountain range. I was flying very low down when I was hit and realised that I would have to gain altitude to clear these mountains before I could reach 'friendly territory'. I had a lot of trouble; neither the wheels nor the flaps would lower, the hydraulics had gone, and the engine began playing up – it would only run, for some unknown reason, at a fantastically high rate of revs, and every time I throttled back, it threatened to stall and stop altogether, but I just kept going as I was. I flew like this for half an hour, with the wing blazing away like a torch and I cannot understand why it did not drop off miles back. Anyway, I reached the sea and to my intense relief saw a destroyer below me. I banked down past her, fired a Very light and pancaked close by her. She proved to be HMS *Whelp* and they had us all safely aboard in double quick time.

Four Avengers were lost over the target, but these two raids inflicted heavy damage on the two plants, whose production was never fully restored to the war's end. Interception by the Japanese fighters was largely ineffective.

> The only protection the Avenger had was a ball turret, and the enemy did lose a few aircraft to these, because they were slightly incautious about attacking aircraft with these turrets – they probably had not come across them before.
>
> I feel that this first raid pointed to an enemy who was waiting, but was not as alert as he might have been. After all, it was a very obvious target and they must have been expecting a visit some time. They were well aware of our carriers operating in the Indian Ocean. The second attack certainly found the enemy very much more alert; they were waiting for us and we were intercepted much further out. Even in the brief time between the two raids, the enemy could easily deploy reserves in from other areas.

A feature of the Royal Navy attacks was the introduction of the standard US Navy operational procedure of employing a senior pilot as Air Co-Coordinator for the mission.

This officer is an experienced and senior officer, usually a Group Commander. He patrols the battle area in his own aircraft, usually a single seater fighter .... The Air Co-Coordinator has to know in detail the plan of the operation and to be as familiar as possible with the terrain in which it is to take place. He is in communication by R/T with the Air Observers and the Support Aircraft Commander in the Headquarters Ship ....

The value of the Air Co-Coordinator is evidenced particularly during the most fluid stages of the assault. He can readjust the planned air support, and divert an attack to a different target when necessary. Flights of aircraft are constantly in the air, on call for bombing and strafing missions, and can be allocated their missions by the Support Aircraft Commander, usually through the Air Co-Coordinator. The system is similar to the 'Cab-rank' system. The Air Co-Coordinator is the agent in the air of the Support Aircraft Commander, and while the latter has the final decision on the allotment of ground targets to air attack, the Air Co-Coordinator is often called on to co-ordinate or divert the actual support missions, as he is in the best position to see how the battle is developing.

Although the Royal Navy never, in fact, used real dive-bombers in combat after the disbandment of the Skuas, but relied on torpedo-bomber adaptations, like the Barracuda and Avenger, or on fighters, like the Firefly and Corsair, to dive-bomb with, a later evaluation was in fact done on the standard American type, the Curtiss SB2C Helldiver. The Royal Navy pinned all its hopes on obtaining this aircraft for the final drive on Japan, and even started training the first Helldiver squadron, which was to have embarked aboard *Furious* for another crack at *Tirpitz* first. However, the Navy was finally thwarted in that intention by the US Fleet Admiral King, who so liked the Helldiver and so disliked the British that he ordered that all SB2Cs had to be allocated first to even US Navy reserve units before any could go to the Royal Navy. Despite strong protests about this unfriendly policy by Lord Alexander, the First Lord of the Admiralty, to Winston Churchill himself, the British were unable to reverse this decision.[9] So the BPF went off to battle at Okinawa, and then Japan, without them.[10]

*   *   *

And so, in the end, the Vengeance was the only Lease-Lend American-built dive-bomber to actually serve in combat with British armed forces.[11] But what of the Bermuda?

It will be recalled that as early as March 1943 the continued delays and postponements of the Brewster Bermuda programme, coupled with the continued total Air Ministry opposition to any type of dive-bomber, had led to an opportunity to end this commitment by London. In a general summary of the situation as it appertained in 1943,[12] it was revealed that, when the original contract, which had been placed by the French government, was taken over by the British government, modifications to make the aircraft more suitable to RAF needs were, quite naturally, required. These changes in specification were made between August and December 1940, the bulk of them being within the knowledge of the Brewster Corporation by the time the last batch of four hundred was ordered. The delivery date had therefore at that time been extended to enable these modifications to be carried out, and at the same time Brewster put in hand orders for the US government, and also for the Dutch government in exile.

The Bermuda production plan was further complicated by the placing of contracts by the US Navy to build sub-contracted Corsair fighters, and there was a British Lease-Lend interest in this aircraft also! Partly due to the additional work load, and partly due to a succession of labour troubles, deliveries on all these contracts were delayed, and the US Navy Department found it necessary to change the management, so poor was it, and put in their own nominees. This failed to have the desired effect, and it was not until 1 September 1942 that the first machine for the RAF appeared.

This highly unsatisfactory situation was constantly reviewed by the US Navy and the British representatives on the spot, and yet further management changes were effected early in 1943 by putting the dynamic Henry Kaiser in control. As he felt it was impossible to bring the Corsair into early full production until the Bermuda was completed, he made it a condition that the US Navy would resist any change in existing production orders.

When the first Bermuda reached England, extensive tests were conducted, as we have seen, and the plane was found badly wanting. It was then realised that by the time full production was complete the aircraft would be obsolete, anyway. As we have noted, earlier steps were then taken to try and enforce the 'break' clause and, at the same time, to break the news to the British Army and replace the Bermuda with any surplus Vengeance dive-bombers.

This was, in fact, implemented in 1943, and, as a final result, the Army, which in 1940–42 had been pleading for dive-bombers, finally changed their view in line with earlier Air Ministry recommendations and rejected them as unfit for European combat needs. This was rather a hollow victory for the Air Ministry, however, which left them neatly hoist with their own petard.

The initial letter sent to the War Office spelt out the situation on the Bermuda, but offered the Vengeance instead (A-31 or A-35), and completely reversed the earlier statements on their comparative merits, the new line being: 'The Air Council have no doubt that the decision to substitute the Vengeance for the Bermuda will not in any way decrease the value of the squadrons nor delay the date at which they become available for operations.' They added, somewhat remarkably considering their earlier declarations, that, 'Their performance is markedly superior to that of the Bermuda.'

The Director of Air at the War Office replied,[13] asking whether, as the Vengeance and Bermuda were classed as dive-bombers, they would be thus employed: 'It is desired to know whether these aircraft will be used in the role they were originally designed for, namely, dive-bombing in the true sense of the word, or for low and medium level bombing as carried out by light bombers, or in both roles.'

The DMC, eager to please, confirmed that the RAF would promise to employ the Vengeance squadrons 'for dive-bombing, since this is the role for which these aircraft were primarily designed. This does not, however, preclude their employment on level bombing if particular circumstance makes this desirable.'[14]

This, despite the reports from India and the test centres, that dive-bombing was the *only* suitable role for the Vengeance! None the less, the Air Ministry appeared to be at last swallowing their pride and finally giving the Army what it thought it wanted, while still, of course, leaving a door open to use them in other ways. It must, therefore, have come as all the more of a shock to them, albeit a pleasing one, when they found that the Army had now reversed its original decisions and its direction at the same time. Now that it was, finally, offered dive-bombers by an Air Council that had hitherto resisted their introduction at every turn, the Army, in reply, stated that it no longer wanted them! 'The C-in-C 21 Army Group is of the opinion, which he states is shared by the AOC Tactical Air Force, that there is no military requirement for the introduction into the TAF of dive-bomber aircraft of the Vengeance type.'[15]

This was an unexpected, but fortuitous about-face by the Army, and the RAF could now quickly kill off the dive-bomber concept once and for all, as it had all along been eager to do. It lost no time in doing so. At a meeting on 2 August 1943, to consider the organisation and equipment of the TAF, Air Marshal d'Albiac and his two Group AOCs not surprisingly 'expressed themselves most emphatically against being equipped with the Vengeance dive-bomber'.

The DCAS wrote to the Secretary-of-State, who had been enquiring about the position of the Vengeance in the RAF, that, 'In amplification, I have placed a short enclosure on this file, setting out the tactical reasons which led us to abandon the dive-bomber type of aircraft, the gist of this note being that the fighter-bomber type of aircraft combines, to a certain degree, the characteristics of the dive-bomber with that of the fighter, and is far more preferable on grounds of economy and flexibility.'[16]

They could not possibly have consulted any of the men at the RAF. Arthur Murland Gill, the CO of No. 84 Squadron operating in Burma with enormous success, who had until that time flown the long-nose Blenheim in Greece and the Far East, was to tell me that there was just no comparison between the RAF medium-type bombers and attack, and the Vengeance:

> The Vengeance was a big brute of an airplane, about five and one-half tons, with a Wright Double Cyclone engine. It was built like a tank, all metal, no fabric anywhere. Although there was only manual controls in those days and you always had to yank hard, the controls of the Vengeance were relatively light. It rolled nicely, and was stead as a rock in the dive. Built for the job.
>
> When we were flying Blenheims in the desert – and also when we had Blenheims in the Far East – we carried only four 250s, that's all. We did long, 1,800-mile, 13-hour flights to drop four 250 lb bombs, and usually after dark. We had little hope of inflicting much damage! It seemed such a waste of effort. Dive-bombing with the Vengeance in Burma, however, taught us what it meant to be accurate! For example, to take out vital bridges, I could usually send just a couple of Vengeances in with the almost guaranteed certainty that the bridge would be demolished, whereas with the Blenheim I could take the squadron against the same target day after day and rarely, if ever, score a hit.[17]

Originally the pilots of No. 84 had to learn dive-bombing from scratch: there were no manuals, no experts. But they dedicated themselves to the task, which, originally was concentrating on warship targets in case the Japanese returned to the Indian Ocean once more, as they had done in April 1942. When Midway ensured that that was not going to happen, No. 84 was going to be sent to support the Arakan campaign, but then that was abandoned and it was allocated close support of Orde Wingate's 'Chindit' forces as flying artillery operating behind enemy lines.

> We had to 'sell' our skills to the Army. They were familiar with the accuracy of German air support, but had never seen anything like it from the RAF, which had never bothered with dive-bombing before. Naturally, they were suspicious. Wingate was a dedicated genius, a professional down to his fingertips. He would listen, provided he was convinced you knew your job as well as he knew his. We demonstrated this to him by results. As we were all

very young men, he first thought of us as a bunch of carefree young kids, but, when we started hitting the things he wanted us to hit, and doing it pretty consistently, he became convinced, and stood firmly behind us. Unfortunately, his early death resulted in dive-bombing again losing his influential support in Army circles.[18]

During the three years I commanded No. 84 (Dive-bomber) Squadron in India, Ceylon and Burma from 1942–1944, I led 1,476 operational dive-bomber sorties against the Japanese in Burma. There were three other RAF dive-bomber squadrons equipped with the Vultee Vengeance – Nos 45, 82 and 110, and, later, two Royal Indian Air Force Squadrons. No. 82 Squadron operated in Southern Burma, the others in the North. Our targets were Japanese troop concentrations, supply dumps, airfields, bridges used by Japanese supply lines, Japanese-occupied villages, bunker positions, etc. We usually knew which division or brigade we were supporting, but never the regiment or unit (for security reasons). No. 84 Squadron also supported General Wingate's 3rd Indian Division after they were flown deep into Burma in 1944 and acted as their long-range artillery. We also supported our units during the Battle of Kohima and the Battle for Imphal, often dropping our bombs some 100 yards from our own troops dug in (which, I have been told by soldiers who were there, was a very frightening experience!).[19]

d'Albiac and his consorts had already made their minds up, and no opportunity was given for the Army in Europe to see what the Vengeance could do, even had there been any squadrons as well versed, trained and dedicated to dive-bombers as No. 84 and her sister squadrons in Burma. There was just no will.

DCAS added to Sinclair that the surplus Vengeance aircraft would be used in another role, and, with the tradition of the Henley and Skua behind them, it was not hard to guess what this would be: '... we are converting our quota of Vengeance to fill a very long-felt want in target-towing units ....' Mention of a 'fighter-dive-bomber' in the enclosure apparently left a loophole, which was quickly closed. 'What is the "fighter-dive-bomber?" Are we going to put dive-bombing brakes on some of our fighters (as the Americans do on the Mustang),' asked the Secretary of State, 'and if so, on which and how many of them?'

DCAS hastily replied that:

... the term 'Fighter-Dive-Bomber' employed by DAT in the note at enclosure 'A' is somewhat of a misnomer, and should more correctly read 'Fighter Bomber. Dive-brakes are fitted to enable an aircraft to dive at a steeper angle at reduced speed to ensure stabilisation in dive with a view to greater sighting accuracy. It is not our intention to fit dive-brakes to fighter bombers, but without them the Typhoon bomber dives at 80 degrees at speeds sometimes in excess of 450 mph and achieves consistent accuracy.[20]

The Bermuda/Buccaneer proved not that easy to get rid of. Representation was made to the US Navy Department by the BAC in Washington DC about termination of the contract, 'but in view of the undertaking given by the Navy Department to Mr Kaiser, the Navy Department felt unable to accede to our request to cancel or agree to take over the outstanding deliveries themselves.'[21] The contracts continued, therefore, until September 1943, when 450 of the first order, and eighteen of the 300 of the second order had been delivered. 'At that stage the Navy Department and Mr Kaiser had changed their views as to the need for further Bermudas to be made and the second contract was accordingly terminated under the Break Clause.'[22]

Out of a total of 468 Bermudas delivered in all, ninety-eight were transferred to the USAAF and the balance of 370 were considered for employment as, again, hardly a shock, target towers, 'but it was found that modification work was so extensive as to be uneconomic, particularly in view of the fact that another, and more suitable, aircraft was then available for use.'[23]

The final bill to be met by the Treasury for this ill-fated aircraft, which nobody in the UK could ever use, was $48,807,226.34 (the 34 cents on almost forty-nine million dollars was a nice touch by some Brewster accountant with a sense of humour!), and $21,014, 898.90 for the second.

The Bermuda dive-bomber had played no part in helping Great Britain defeat a German invasion, nor in helping defeat the German Army as part of our own invasion four years later, but it had certainly played a significant part in contributing to the post-war bankruptcy of this nation, from which it has only just recovered after sixty-two years![24]

If the British disdained to use the Brewster dive-bomber, even as a target-tug, the US Navy utilised them to good effect, if not in front-line combat, then as dive-bomber training aircraft, so can it have been *that* bad an aircraft? George M. Lane from Baton Rouge, Louisiana, flew the Buccaneer in this capacity during the war at US Naval Air Station Vero Beach with 341 Group, and he has no doubt that it was!

All my memories of the old Brewster Buccaneer seem to be rather negative. It was a notably unstable aircraft, and the tail assembly had the unfortunate tendency to rip off during dive recovery. Also, woe betide the unfortunate pilot who tried to tighten up on the turns going in for landing. I was following Dom Demasi when he overshot the runway on his crosswind approach and tried to correct by making a tight turn – the sight of those crisp black bodies stayed with me for years after that![25]

Other correspondents, including Donald B. Cooney, had fonder memories of the Brewster: he considered the aircraft one of the best of the new dive-bomber types, rating her higher than either the Dauntless or the Helldiver. His views have to be respected as he flew numerous combat missions in the South Pacific after conducting his advanced dive-bomber training with the Buccaneer in Florida. In the end, bad factory management killed off any opportunities for the Brewster to make her mark one way or the other during the Second World War.

*   *   *

How, then, stood the dive-bomber during the final year of the war? Dive-bombing itself was more widespread than ever before. All the combatant nations engaged in hostilities were practising it. But in Germany the Stukas were reduced to the *Nachtschlachtflier* and the Gustav tank-busters. Some three hundred Ju 87Ds had been converted for night-flying, mainly by the incorporation of instrumentation and having their flame-dampened engine exhaust led back over their wing-roots at the Menibum plant near Hamburg. Seven NSG wings were equipped with these conversions, each with sixty aircraft, and they operated quite successfully on the Eastern Front, in northern Italy and over France, Belgium and The Netherlands, as well as during daylight in the final German offensive in the Ardennes in December 1944. The *Panzerknacker* also, with its two underwing-mounted cannon, continued fighting to the very last day of the war as a front-line unit.

The other Axis partner, Japan, her carriers expended as bait or laid up in port through lack of fuel, employed the old D3A2 Val largely in the Kamikaze role, but the new, fast Yokosuka *Suisei* was every much a pedigree dive-bomber, and able, with luck and skill, still able to penetrate the defences of the American task forces besieging the homeland to inflict some serious injury, and the carriers *Franklin* and *Bunker Hill* were both very badly damaged by this dive-bomber in the closing stages of the Pacific War.

On the Allied side, as we have seen, the French introduced the Dauntless to European operations, while the RAF continued to employ the Vengeance in Burma, the Spitfire in Italy and the Spitfire and Bombphoon in western Europe in this role, although not advertising the fact. The Royal Navy had failed to obtain the Helldiver as it had wished, and the Barracuda had been phased out, leaving only the

Avenger to be utilised as a makeshift bomber. Home-built aircraft continued the Fleet Air Arm tradition of trying to be all things at once, with the Fairey Spearfish and the Blackburn Firebrand being toted as having dive-bomber potential, but not actually appearing until long after the war was over, leaving the Royal Navy no further forward than in mid-1941 in that vital respect.

In the Soviet Union, the Pe-2 had gone from strength to strength, with new tactics and better training, following a detailed study carried out on the 'Dipping Wheel' tactic by Colonel A.G. Fedorov. Tests on bombing ranges following examination of existing techniques were then translated into actual combat in the field by Fedorov himself at Roslav. Three Pe-2s concentrated their initial 60-degree dive-bombing runs on the enemy flak positions defending the German armoured formation, while the rest of the Soviet dive-bomber group circled out of range, confusing the gunners. Then a second section broke away from the circuit and attacked, then another, then another, breaking out of the *Vertushka* wheel and diving steeply onto the main target. This technique was so successful in practice that it was thereafter incorporated in a document prepared by Fedorov as the standard Pe-2 attacking technique.

By the beginning of 1945, the Soviets were on the borders of the Reich and preparing yet another titanic offensive toward Berlin itself. The fortress city of Breslau stood in their way and there were German armies and civilians trapped along the Baltic coast. All these were attacked and overrun and all German resistance was broken. The Pe-2s led the way with precision attacks on strongpoints, but the cost was a high one. The master exponent of Pe-2 dive-bombing, Major-General Polbin, was himself killed leading a dive-bombing attack on this front on 14 February 1945, his 40th birthday. Last-ditch attempts to defend Berlin saw all manner of aircraft thrown into the fray by the Germans, including some Ju 87s, but they were as pebbles before the oncoming Soviet tidal wave.

With the fall of Germany in May, after vicious house-to-house fighting in Berlin, during which the Pe-2s flew with maps in hand, just as the Ju 87 had once done at Stalingrad, many of the Soviet dive-bomber units were hastily moved eastwards in readiness for the offensive against the Japanese Army in Manchuria. The accelerated date for this attack, motivated politically by the American attacks on the Japanese homeland, meant that the Pe-2s were thrown in before they were fully prepared, but they quickly proved their superiority from July 1945 when the Soviets swept all before them and advanced on down into the Korean peninsula.

The US Navy, built up to a huge level, was now able to operate at will all up and down the South China Sea and against the remnants of the once all-powerful Japanese fleet in the home islands. At the Battle of Leyte Gulf the mighty battleship *Musashi* had been pummelled and pounded by the Helldivers and riven and torn open by the Avengers' torpedoes until she finally sank. This proved that even the mightiest ships could succumb to the scale of attack now available to the American fleet.

The Americans were continuing to expand their dive-bomber arm in the Navy, so that, by the autumn of 1944, it was easily the largest such force of this type in the world, coupled as it was by a similar expansion of the US Marine Corps air strength. Although the steady shift to the fighter-dive-bomber was apparent in the Pacific war zone, the great influence that the traditional dive-bomber had meant that trials were continuing with new and even more potent types of dive-bomber for future requirements.

The bulk of the design and experimental work in this field was described to me by Rear Admiral Paul Holmberg:[26]

The US Navy Air Test Center at Patuxent River, Maryland, was commissioned in early 1943. It was formed from the aircraft test unit that was stationed at Anacostia, DC, which dated back to the twenties, and the aircraft Armament Test Unit that was stationed at Norfolk, Virginia. Other test activity was set up, such as 'radio test' and 'tactical test', so that, when I was there a year after it started, the population of the Center was perhaps 3,000 military and civilians. I conducted 'Board of Inspection' tests and evaluations of dive-bombers and their related armament systems from the standpoint of determining of the aircraft manufacturers had complied with the specifications during manufacture. I tested late models of the SBD Dauntless with its various 'improvements', the SBA built by Brewster, the SB2C Helldiver and the AD, the successor to the SBD [which later became the Skyraider]. The Martin Mauler did not show up until after I had left the station. I understood that it was nearly as good as the AD [its low speed characteristics were not as good, so it eventually lost out to the AD].

Events that stick in my memory include every flight I made in the SB2C Helldiver! We had three aircraft of that model to use in testing. Of the three, two had their wings come off during recovery after a dive. My good fortune was that my assistant dive-bomber pilots were flying the aircraft on these occasions. We rotated these aircraft flights between the three of us. I was fortunate as the other two lost their lives. The early-model Helldivers had a fatally deficient dive-brake flap design that sometimes wouldn't close correctly on pull-out. This would put enormous forces on one wing that caused it to fail structurally. (It was a sort of Russian-roulette game to fly these particular aircraft.) Later, 'fixers' were installed to prevent this type of failure.[27]

*   *   *

Meanwhile the US Army ashore conducting the long drawn-out campaign to liberate the Philippines had become increasing reliant on the close air support given to them by the US Marine Corps dive-bombers, the old SBDs, now operating from shore bases. Like the RAF Vengeance units in Burma, the US Marine Corps dive-bomber pilots had a hard job to convince the doughboys that they were capable of hitting the enemy and not their own men. Bitter experience with traditional USAAF fighter-bombers and medium bombers had made them very reluctant to call in air strikes, no matter how dire the situation. As in Burma, the soldiers on the ground had to be shown that the SBD operated at a different level of competence.

Marine Air Group 23, commanded by Colonel H. Meyer, supplied this skilled and accurate support, building on its already considerable expertise in this field. The group was joined by MAG-32 and an extensive course of study and training was put into effect. The duties of the seven Marine Corps dive-bombing squadrons were formally set out by Lieutenant-Colonel McCutcheon in a personal monograph, which stressed they were to concentrate

> ... against targets that cannot be reached by his weapons or in conjunction with the ground weapons in a co-ordinated attack. Close support should be immediately available and should be carried out deliberately, accurately and in co-ordination with other assigned units.[28]

This monograph, Close Support Aviation, was to become the Marine Corps flyers' textbook during their subsequent perfection of the technique. During the Lingayen landings in January 1945, Major-General Mudge paid the Marine flyers the following tribute:

> I cannot say enough in praise of these men of the dive-bombers for the job they have done in giving my men close support in this operation.[29]

Such tributes continued to flow until the campaign was brought to a victorious conclusion.

*   *   *

At sea, as the net closed in upon Japan herself, the last great exploit of the Navy dive-bombers took place on 7 April 1945, when the largest battleship ever constructed, the Japanese *Yamato*, sailed on a one-way suicide mission to attack the American invasion fleet lying off the island of Okinawa. She had sufficient fuel only to reach her target and inflict as much destruction as she could with her nine massive 18.1-inch guns, before beaching herself. She was accompanied on this mission by the light cruiser *Yahagi* and eight escorting destroyers. She relied on evading detection, but in the event she was quickly spotted and plotted, and on 7 April was set upon by an unprecedented air armada: wave upon wave of US Navy dive- and torpedo-bombers subjected the force to attack after attack and simply swamped her defences. The Navy flew no fewer than 386 sorties, losing just ten aircraft to the ships' gunners. This proved to be the final great dive-bomber attack on warships at sea.

Bombing Squadrons 9, 10, 83 and 84 flew Helldivers in the action that followed from the carriers *Yorktown-II, Hornet-II, Essex, Intrepid* and *Bunker Hill*, a total of forty-nine SB2Cs. They made dive-attacks against both *Yamato* and *Yahagi*, and from their combat reports the young flyers recorded for posterity the last moments of the giant.[30]

Bombing Squadron 83 approached the target from the south-east at 6,000 feet, picking up the Japanese force at a range of 30 miles on the ASH radar scan as a single large blip. At 24 miles, this blip began to break up and at 19 miles nine individual ships could be counted. Lieutenant Berry reported this fact to the Task Group Strike Co-ordinator, who told VB-83 to wait. The squadron therefore circled the Japanese ships at 6 to 10 miles' range for about forty minutes, while another group prepared to attack. From time to time *Yamato* fired her main battery at this squadron, though without coming close. There was heavy cloud and visibility was poor.

At about 1250 hours the *Hornet* group attacked, followed by the *Essex* group, the dive-bombers leading in from 6,200 feet. The *Yamato* was tracked in by radar to a range of 1 ½ miles, and 'window' was used by all flights to confuse the enemy radar, with considerable effect. About thirty seconds before the first attack *Yamato* turned starboard into the attack.

Lieutenant-Commander Berry led in for VB-83 from the starboard quarter, with the following dive-bombers 'rosebudding' around to dive on the battleship's starboard bow. Dives varied from 45 to 70 degrees, only one Helldiver using flaps. Lieutenant Mitchell scored a hit amidships near the bridge tower structure, diving at about 65 degrees without flaps and releasing at 1,500 feet, pulling out at around 850 feet. An Avenger reported that the tower structure had blown up a few minutes later. Ensign Samaras, with a similar dive, hit her forward, near 'A' turret, and two other hits were also claimed by this squadron.

Anti-aircraft fire of all types was intense. The heavy bursts were usually black, but about ten per cent were white phosphorus. A few dirty yellow bursts were observed and there were a few that shot out flaming red balls about an inch in diameter. Throughout the attack the Japanese ships maintained excellent formation discipline and kept closed up, even after hits. Fire was concentrated on the attacking planes, rather than on those retiring or preparing to attack.

'It is believed, from the above indications, that the commander of the Japanese Task Group was an unusually capable officer.' The report also added that, 'It is notable that the pilots whose bombs hit, dove low to make them ....'

The two other hits claimed were by Ensign Wellen and Lieutenant Goodrich respectively, both of whom had steep, no-flap dives. Wellen released at 2,000 feet and Goodrich at 1,500 feet. Their hits were one slightly forward of the bridge, and one forward of the after turret. After all their dives, all planes retired low over the water under fire from the screening destroyers. When last seen, the *Yamato* was still under way, smoking slightly.

VB-84's report commenced:

> Reports that the target would be warships of the Japanese Fleet made this mission one that all pilots wanted to fly. There had been some juicy targets in Kure harbour about three weeks previously, but the current operation was the first for the squadron against enemy warships under way. The composition of the enemy force was fairly well known. Rounding the southern end of Kyushu during the night, they had been sighted by a scout plane and the word was given to go in for the kill. Principal warship and pride of the fading Nipponese Navy was the battleship *Yamato*. Around her was a screen of about eight destroyers and a light cruiser of the 'Agano' class.

With this information, VB-84 rendezvoused with other planes of the group, which in turn joined up with other groups in the force and headed from the south-west of southern Kyushu. Course was set to the north-west, across the Ruyjus. Overcast at about 7,000 feet kept the formation low as it passed over the rock Amami O Shima and sped over the water of the East China Sea. Blips were first picked up on the radar in the squadron commander's plane at a range of 32 miles, altitude 6,500 feet and, by the time the formation was 20 miles away, the composition of the Japanese formation was well defined. Their account continued:

> Despite the knowledge of the whereabouts and composition of the Japanese force, it was still surprising to look over the sides of cockpits and actually see it below. Reports were accurate; there was the *Yamato* with her screen of one cruiser and eight

destroyers. But even more surprising was the absence of opposition. The entire formation of more than 300 planes flew directly over the Jap force at 6,500 feet and did not draw a shot.

Following the lead of the other groups, these dive-bombers circled north of the force awaiting orders, but after some time, no direct word having been received from the strike leader, and mindful of the critical fuel situation, Lieutenant-Commander Conn decided to attack. When the decision was made a destroyer was seen speeding below the squadron and it was selected as their target. The ship was apparently one of the force's pickets as it was several miles from the battleship and her screen, but at the time of the attack the thick cloud prevented this fact from being realised.

The Helldivers flew in for their attack under the clouds at 3,500 feet, approaching from the starboard side of the destroyer's wake. Several hits were scored in the first run and the heavy flak that had first met them ceased abruptly, the second run meeting no opposition, nor did subsequent attacks by fighter-bombers later. By this time the target, wrecked from stem to stern, lay dead in the water with white smoke pouring from the fore funnel for several minutes. Soon after the second run this smoke ceased and a terrific explosion took place aft of No. 3 turret.

> First there was a red-orange blast, then the fantail seemed to heave and shudder. Immediately afterwards black smoke billowed upward and the destroyer sank by the stern.

Their victim turned out to be the 2,033-ton destroyer *Hamakaze*, built in 1941.

VB-9 sighted the Japanese ships some time later, at 1325 hours, dead ahead. The *Yorktown* group, which included twenty F6Gs and thirteen TBMs, veered to the north to skirt the ships out of gun range, and prepared for the attack. The light cruiser was seen stopped dead in the water surrounded by oil slicks, with a destroyer alongside its starboard quarter but with no obvious damage topsides. About 6 to 10 miles north of these ships the *Yorktown* force circled, waiting for the other groups' attacks to cease and for their target assignments.

The *Yamato* engaged them with her main batteries, and at 1345 hours, the group commander ordered the Helldivers to attack the cruiser. Lieutenant Schneider led the Helldivers in a climb into the clouds, spreading out in loose formation and proceeding south to swing into position for a fore-and-aft run. 'The 4,000-foot cloud ceiling prohibited the 70-degree split flap dive the pilots had so arduously practiced in view of such a target and necessitated glide bombing runs breaking through cloud cover.'

Heavy, medium and light AA was being fired by the two Japanese ships with some accuracy, although only minor hits were taken by the two lead planes at this stage. Lieutenant Worley broke his section from the main flight approximately abeam of the cruiser, and these three dive-bombers made their attack, coming in on the port beam. The reason for this is not known, as Lieutenant Worley was subsequently lost, but these three planes, diving without flaps at a 35-degree angle, scored no hits. Meanwhile, the Avenger torpedo-bombers had commenced their runs and requested flak suppression to cover their approach. Worley immediately turned back towards the destroyer, firing his 20 mm guns, and thus drew the bulk of the ship's AA fire on himself. Heavily hit and on fire, Worley broke his glide attack and put his flaming Helldiver into a 60-degree dive, aiming straight for the destroyer, but missed her by 10 feet and smashed into the sea off the vessel's bow.

Revenge for his sacrifice was soon extracted by the rest of his unit. Bomb hits were recorded near the cruiser's bridge, while Ensign Greenwell followed these up with more on the cruiser's fantail. Lieutenant Durio, leader of the last division, attacked from the starboard quarter in a steep glide, hitting close aboard the starboard side with one of his bombs. Ensign Hanawalt hit her amidships on the port side with one SAP. Lieutenant Martin and Ensign Sigman placed their bombs forward and aft of amidships. After the first hits were made, explosions and fires were seen on the deck of the cruiser, several fighters made strafing runs at the same time as the bomber attacks, and 'the cruiser appeared to be covered by smoke and flame …. During the attack a lifeboat was lowered, as the ship was obviously being abandoned.'

After the rendezvous was effected to the north of the stricken target ship some ten minutes after this attack, she rolled over and disappeared. Again the Helldivers returned and bombed and strafed the 50-foot motor launch and the survivors in the water. Again re-forming to the south-east, VB-9 witnessed the *Yamato* explode and roll over at 1425. Their own victim had been the light cruiser *Yahagi*, 6,652 tons, completed in 1943.

VB-10 had been launched at a range of 270 miles from the last reported position of the Japanese fleet, again picking up the target through the murk by radar plot. They had made their approach under 3,000 feet in order not to lose visual contact, so thick was the cloud cover. *Yamato*, when first seen, was on a southerly course, making about 10 knots' speed and turning to the right, with four or five destroyers in close formation on her. Bombing Ten was ordered to take the battleship as its target, approaching her from the east and co-ordinating its attack with the torpedo-bomber section.

Lieutenant C.D. Rauch Jr, leading the dive-bombers, circling under the cloud base, led one division of Helldivers into a glide-bombing attack over the bows of the battleship. The second division of seven, led by Lieutenant Jacobbsen, circled to the north and came in over the battleship's stern at 190 knots, angle of dive between 30 and 40 degrees.

Bombs were released at 1,000 to 1,500 feet, at which level the huge ship presented a beautiful target. 27 bombs were dropped with excellent results, due to a combination of the great size of the target, its slow speed, the low altitude and well-planned approach of the planes.

All the Helldivers strafed *Yamato* on the way in and the destroyers on the way out. Four of the dive-bombers were hit by flak, but all returned safely.

Yamato was, in total, hit by no less than four bombs in the first attack, up to thirteen torpedoes and many more bombs in the second attack. It was a great achievement.

Notes

1. Harrington, Captain, to the Author, op. cit.
2. Pete C. Smith, *Skua!*, op. cit.
3. *Memorandum*, ACAS (T) to CAS, dated 17 March 1942 (National Archives, Kew, London, AIR 8/631).
4. *Memo* on the Barracuda Aircraft, undated (National Archives, Kew, London, AIR 20/1873).
5. *Report on Operation Tungsten*, Appendix II, to 2nd BA, 128/026. Appendix I of *Victorious* Letter and *Air Crew Reports*, 0137/6206, dated 5–10 April 1944 (National Archives, Kew, London, ADM 199/941).
6. *Ibid.*
7. *Ibid.*
8. Halliday, Captain, DSC, RN, interview with the Author, at RN College, Greenwich, London, 1968, and quoted in my book *Task Force 57*, Crécy, Manchester, 2000.
9. See Peter C. Smith, *Curtiss SB2C Helldiver*, op. cit.
10. See Peter C. Smith, *Task Force 57*, Crécy, Manchester, 2001.
11. The Chesapeake (V156F) briefly formed one squadron, which was evaluated as an anti-submarine aircraft, for which purpose it was found, not surprisingly, as it was a dive-bomber, to be unsuitable. It was used as a target tug!
12.
13. *Letter*, Air Council to Secretary of the Treasury, dated 27 April 1943 (National Archives, Kew, London, AIR2/25504).
14. *Memorandum*, Air Council to War Office, dated 7 April 1943, CS.18666/S.6 (National Archives, Kew, London, AIR2/25504).
15. *Memorandum*, War Office to Air Council, dated 30 April, 1943, D. Air to DMC/43-RAF/646 (Air I) (National Archives, Kew, London, AIR 2/25504).
16. *Memorandum*, DMC to War Office, dated 1 May 1943, CS.18666/DMC (National Archives, Kew, London, AIR2/25504).

17. Arthur Murland Gill, series of taped interviews with the Author at his home in Llanwarne, Herefordshire, 1986. See extracts reproduced in 'Deadly Diving Accuracy', article in *Military History*, June 1988 issue, Leesburg, VA.

18. *Ibid.*

19. Wing Commander Arthur Murland Gill, RAF, to Anthony Gray, QPM, Royal Scots Dragoon Guards Association, in *Scorpion News*, Issue No. 36, dated August 2004.

20. Memorandum, War Office to Air Ministry, dated 4 August 1943, 43/RAF/646 (Air.I. (National Archives, Kew, London, AIR 2/5504).

21. DCAS to PS of S-of-S Air, dated 9 September 1943 (National Archives, Kew, London, AIR 2/5504).

22. *Memorandum*, DCA to S-of-S Air, dated 17 September 1943 (National Archives, Kew, London, AIR2/5504).

23. *Letter*, from Air Council to Secretary of the Treasury, *op cit.* (National Archives, Kew, London, AIR2/5504).

24. As these words were being typed in January 2007, the British government was announcing it had just paid off the very last payment of the nation's wartime debt!

25. George M. Lane to Don Cooney, 18 February 1998, and made available to the Author.

26.

27. *Ibid.*

28. Sherrod, Robert, *History of Marine Corps's Aviation in World War II*, Armed Forces Press, Washington, DC, 1952.

29. *Ibid.*

30. *Action Reports and War Diaries* of major US Naval Commands involved in the sinking of IJN *Yamato* and ships operating in company, viz: TF.58 (First Carrier Task Force, Pacific), dated 18 June 1945; TG.58.1 (Carrier Division Five), Rear Admiral Clark, dated 5 May 1945; TG.58.3 (Carrier Division One), Rear Admiral Sherman, dated 18 June 1945; TG. 58.4 (Carrier Division Six), Rear Admiral Radford, dated 25 May 1945 (NRS-1971-7). Report of the sinking of *Yamato* (ACRSs, AR-165-77). Microfilm copies in Author's collection.

CHAPTER FOURTEEN

'Lobbing bombs into tunnels'

W
ith the termination of hostilities in 1945, there seemed little or no future for the specialised dive-bomber in the major air fleets of the victors. Save for the Soviet Union, which viewed the coming of peace as merely a breather before getting on with her declared aim of world domination, defence spending in the other nations plummeted sharply. Not only was this drastic cut in all defence spending a major blow to follow-up developments in every field, but the switch-over to the fighter-bomber concept was by now almost universal, and there seemed no need for further study. Moreover, technical advances in all fields relating to dive-bombing and precision attacks seemed be ruled out with regard to any future warfare of the major kind with the advent of the Atomic Bomb. Events were to prove otherwise, so let us examine briefly why this was so and why the dive-bomber in fact received a further extension of life in the post-war era.

For a start, the major wars that took place in the first decade after the end of the Second World War did not take place against technically efficient opposition, but, in the main, against Communist-inspired and -backed anti-colonialists' nationalist uprisings. The strength of the enemy was mainly in its ability to subvert, by stealth or propaganda, and where that failed, by the overwhelming commitment of expendable foot soldiers. With their lack of sophisticated weaponry these forces relied on fifth-column activities and the general war-weariness of the West, which eroded the will of their peoples to resist. In view of the bankruptcy of the most of the 'victorious' nations, the emphasis on what resistance there was became, and has remained outside the United States, defence on the cheap. If little money was to be made available, then, quite obviously, if a piston-engined aircraft could dive-bomb effectively, it was cheaper all round than a highly advanced jet plane performing the same function, but less precisely.

And so, strangely, the dive-bomber story did not quite end in 1945.

Only in tiny neutral Sweden had the research work continued into the perfection of dive-bombing through the development of a highly

215

specialised dive-bombing sight. Although this AGA sight was adopted pre-war by the Swedish Air Force, and was considered advanced for its day, far more, indeed, than anything developed outside Germany during the war, Sweden remained the only nation to try and refine further this art to its ultimate logical development in the post-war years. As already commented upon, British dive-bombing research was stifled early on and never ever given a high priority. Even in the United States, lack of interest prevailed, for, even when such sights were developed, the pilots themselves invariably rejected them and continued to rely on eye-shooting right through the Korean War.

In Sweden the story was very different, and two former *Flygvapnet* pilots, Erik A. Wilkenson and P. Torsen Faxén, continued their studies into the theoretical problems throughout the war years and beyond. The inventor told me that:

> Dive-bombing became my greatest interest from 1940 onwards. As a matter of fact we had a flying test model of our equipment as soon as nine months after the original idea, i.e. we flew and made test bombing in August 1940. From late 1942 all aircraft from Saab were equipped. It is true that we were very isolated from foreign developments in dive-bombing, not only during the hostilities but for a long period after 1945.
>
> A period of experimenting began in summer 1940, with the definite object of building a trial model of the bombing instrument. In a small laboratory which had been equipped for the purpose, we studied the possibilities of carrying out the various suggestions for the solution of the technical detail problems, and under Mr Faxén, the designing of the trial instruments began.
>
> Many difficulties were encountered. The rapid change of altitude and speed in the dive made great demands on the immediate reaction of the instrument. Various causes for time delays were therefore carefully studied, but only after producing a few interesting inventions of details did we obtain the basic conditions for achieving accuracy in spite of temperature changes, vibrations and external acceleration.
>
> From the outset the air tests proved that the fundamental idea was correct, namely, that the pilot could accurately and easily direct his aircraft towards the target in a medium-steep dive and that the pull-out from the dive could be made in the calculated manner. Until these preliminary tests had been made, it was of course impossible to determine whether this bombing method would be practicable. The functioning of the trial instrument was first checked by electric measuring devices and lamps, which registered the bomb-release during pull-out. When the results

appeared favourable, the first releases of practice bombs were begin. The results showed well-concentrated hits, which promised well for the future.

Their work and findings was backed and developed by Saab Aircraft Company at Linköping, and finally adopted in 1947 by the *Flygvapnet*. Between 1942 and 1977 the various marks of his invention, from the BT2 to the BT9H, were fitted to all Swedish Air Force aircraft with ground-attack missions, from the twin-engined B17 through to the A-32.

The inventor published a detailed study of his theory and work that year, in which he described the basic principle involved in solving what his RAF contemporaries had always regarded as the unsolvable:[1]

An attack according to the new method would be as follows. The pilot dives the aeroplane straight toward the target, aiming by means of a fixed sight approximately in alignment with the direction of flight. He presses a button and begins the pull-out, i.e. recovery from the dive. An automatic instrument measures the various factors influencing the proper release and gives the impulse, which releases the bomb at just that moment in the pull-out when the aircraft attains the correct altitude for release. The pilot is the only person concerned in the process and it is easy for him to align the sight because it is approximately in the direction of flight toward the target, and then to end the dive with a sufficiently correct pull-out. The instrument can be designed to cope with wide variations of diving angle, height of release, speed, etc., which also facilitates operation for the pilot. The possibility of variation in the choice of elements of air is also advantageous from the point of view of tactics, as is also the fact that the time required for aiming can be very short, can be preceded by evasive manoeuvres, and is also automatically followed by an evasive movement, the pull-out.

The curvature of the bomb trajectory is compensated for by the change of direction of motion of the aircraft during the pull-out. The pilot's view forwards and downwards, which is often very limited by the structure of the aeroplane, does not need to be utilised for a movable sight line, and the pilot accordingly has a good field of view round all sides of the target at the moment of attack.

Brilliant theorising, of course, but never put to the hard practical test of actual combat conditions, when the pilot's reactions, co-ordination and responses, which would always vary with the individual, would be distracted by heavy flak incoming, target evasion and, ultimately, guided missiles, which had a range far exceeding the maximum bomb-release height. But this final attempt to resolve the dive-bombing dilemma was overtaken by events. None the less the Americans were interested enough at the time to purchase the patent for their own further evaluations. The Wilkenson BT9B sight, directly purchased, was fitted to 250 of the USAF's F84-F86 aircraft between 1952 and 1953, and licences to manufacture in America ensured its continuation in that service.[2] Other foreign air forces which adopted it were the French Navy, the Swiss Air Force in its Hawker Hunters and the Danish Air Force for its F100D/Fs.

And so the dive-bombing story was to end, for all practical purposes, as it had begun, with young men in fighter planes using their own judgement to achieve an accuracy that still eluded the machine.

It was the French who first demonstrated the validity of the dive-bomber concept in the post-war world and the continued usefulness of the old traditional type of dive-bomber in their colonial wars, especially in what was then French Indo-China in the years 1946–9.

The surviving SBDs soldiered on, the two *Flotilles* becoming 3F and 4F respectively and embarked aboard the light carrier *Arromanches* and the escort carrier *Dixmude*. With the advent of the Communist Viet-Minh insurgency, both ships, which the French had made ready to take part in the closing stages of the Pacific War, were sent east. Here they found ideal employment. The Viet-Minh were the classic guerrilla formations that fought fierce hit-and-run battles against traditional land forces, dropping their hoes to pick up their machine-guns, slaughtering quickly, then resuming hoeing, a type of warfare now commonplace, but then a revelation. Initially they avoided direct confrontations with traditional French forces, but General Giap, prematurely over-confident, expanded to the stage of all-out war very quickly and thus presented more worthwhile targets for the French Navy flyers. Thus the Dauntless proved effective in pounding enemy concentrations, and many such dive-bomber strikes were flown in the period 1946–8 in the coastal plain around Hanoi, then still a French bastion.[3] Not until July 1949 were the last SBDs retired from combat, a fact totally ignored in many histories of this remarkable aircraft.[4]

Two fresh dive-bomber flotillas were formed to replace them in 1949, 3F and 9F, equipped with forty-eight SB2C Helldivers, purchased from the United States, and these units left France aboard the *Arromanches* at the end of 1952. They carried out a total of 824 war combat missions, representing some 2,000 hours of battle flying, during which they dropped 1,442 tons of bombs on Communist targets. 9F finally returned to France in 1953 and the remaining Helldivers were used as training and liaison aircraft.

In Britain, the fighter aircraft of the Royal Navy had proved adaptable for dive-bombing in the closing stages of the Pacific War for want of anything better, and this trend continued post-war.

I arrived in the Pacific Theatre – too late for operational duties – in command of No. 1850 Squadron equipped with Corsairs aboard the light carrier HMS *Vengeance*. We had practised a certain amount of dive-bombing with practice bombs, the angle of dive being about 65 degrees. I seem to remember the approach level was about 8,000 feet. We were told, however, that if employed against the Japanese this would be suicide, and I gather the Pacific technique established in combat was a very fast, shallow dive and hope for the best! 250 lb or 500 lb were used.[5]

Another British FAA pilot recalled to me:

The Hellcat was a rugged, formidable and flexible fighter from which the then new rockets could be fired, and napalm plonked into an enemy nest. It was a great fighter but, of course, had no form of dive-brakes or speed spoilers. This meant you had to have a lot of airspace to be offensive with a dive-bomb attack: even this was at the expense of accuracy and real effectiveness.[6]

Experience in this technique was very patchy, and yet another FAA veteran told me how 'the only dive-bombing I ever actually undertook was in the SNAW course at St Merryn in 1946, on Seafires'.[7] This is confirmed by an eyewitness:

One naval pilot gave some Russian top brass a demonstration with a Seafire and his second bomb actually went into the hatchway of the tank target! This was Lieutenant-Commander R.T. Leggott MBE, while at St Merryn, Cornwall, in 1944.[8]

The visitors were, no doubt, suitably impressed, but the Royal Navy still had no real dive-bomber aircraft to back up the skills of her young pilots. There were some new aircraft under development for the Fleet Air Arm at the end of the war and these were subsequently tested and evaluated, but only a few of them ever saw service afloat or were further fully developed for dive-bombing. Among these was the Fairey Spearfish, designed as a replacement for the Barracuda, and three prototypes and one production model actually flew, before the programme was cancelled under the inevitable post-war defence cuts. The other major naval aircraft of this type in the immediate post-war era was the Blackburn Firebrand. Originally designed as a fighter, its specification changed several times between 1940 and 1945, finally emerging in May 1945 as the Firebrand V. This was a single-seater (at last) with a top speed of 350 mph, and although dive-bombing was still not considered her principal function, she was equipped with dive-brakes under her wings and could carry a useful bomb-load of two 1,000-pounders. The first squadron formed in 1945, and she continued on in penny packets until 1947, but mainly as a torpedo-bomber.

Across the Atlantic, the new fighters followed the Corsair and Hellcat tradition in dive-bombing capability, with the development of the Grumman Bearcat. But, as might be expected, the US Navy still had more specialised dive-bomber designs in the pipeline in this transitory period.

The most formidable to see brief service was the Martin AM-1 Mauler. She could carry seven tons of hardware to the target zone and was fitted with slotted dive flaps. She had a top speed of 367 mph and a range of 1,300 miles. Over one hundred were built, enjoying a brief period of front-line carrier deployment between 1947 and 1950.

One US Navy pilot who flew the SBD, the SB2C and the AM-1 was Charles Shuford, and having this unique experience he kindly gave me the following comparison views on all three dive-bombers:[9]

> I flew the SBD Dauntless until advancing to the SB2C. Our introduction to fleet-type aircraft consisted of formation flying in groups of six, twelve, eighteen and twenty-four planes and an opportunity to gain experience as a Squadron Leader. We practiced procedures for making entrance to the landing pattern for final approach to land aboard a carrier.
>
> The majority of our time was spent on bombing technique. Approaches to the target; breaks; dive angle and rendezvous after the pull-out consumed several hundred hours of flight. Some of our land targets were manned so as to give us dive angle, range and deflection. We dropped cast-iron bombs that contained an elongated shot-gun shell so the puff of smoke would mark our drop.
>
> At this stage, we were flying three-plane sections and six-plane divisions. We usually broke from an echelon. Later we went to two-plane sections with four-plane divisions. I found this to be more desirable, especially when tight turns and evasive action was required, We tried to perfect our accuracy of bomb drops and obtain a dive angle of 65 or 75 degrees (although it felt as if we were perpendicular).
>
> The SBDs we flew had the telescopic bomb sight, which restricted your sight and sometimes resulted in late and low pull-outs. The reflective sight was a great improvement and also served as a gunsight.
>
> I received orders to go to San Diego, California, to check out in the SB2C. Upon arrival I was sent to Oxnard NAS, which was

nothing but a motel with a landing strip. We had all types of fleet aircraft there. My CO was Lieutenant Louis L. Bangs, fresh off the *Enterprise* and Bombing Ten. The senior officer on board was Lieutenant-Commander J.D. Ramage, also of Bombing Ten. Ramage eventually made Admiral.

After reading the handbook I flew the SB2C for several hours, both solo and then in formation with other pilots. After practicing field carrier landings (FCLP) in a farmer's pasture, we were ready to try our luck at landing on a real carrier. We had done our practice over land at 2,000 ft altitude with wheels and flaps down at a few knots above stall speed. We were careful to monitor our cylinder head temperatures so as not to exceed 269°C.

My group did not have any accidents during our land practice nor on the CVE we landed on off the California coast, although the 'Beast' as she was known, was a much heavier plane than any we had flown previously. Prior to going aboard the CVE *Takanis Bay*, we had a couple of land catapult shots at NAS Los Alamitos.

In my contact with senior pilots who were still flying the SBD, I found that many did not like the Curtiss Helldiver and had no desire to change over to it. There were a lot of horror stories floating around about the aircraft and, no doubt, *some* of them were true!

I flew the 'Beast' from the fall of 1944 until the spring of 1947 and it seemed to be reliable (although it had its faults) if you had respect for its limitations. I personally liked this plane for shipboard use. It was heavy and stable in the groove and had good rudder control. Tailhook bounce was a problem in the early models, but was corrected later. I was landing on the *Saratoga* (CV-3) and got a bouncing hook and ended up in the barrier. An engine change was necessary, but I was launched the next morning in the same plane. I was not injured in the barrier crash but I certainly was embarrassed. Night landings were no problem since it was so dark you had no distractions and relied 100 per cent on the landing signal officer.

With the introduction of the perforated flaps, the dive characteristics were much improved from the early models. The 'Beast' had a series (3) of valves on the floorboard of the pilot's compartment that controlled the hydraulic systems of the aircraft. Under certain conditions you were to turn off certain valves to control the functions of each. I'm not certain that anyone ever understood the entire procedure. Operating in extremely hot regions produced a world of hydraulic leaks, but our aircraft mechanics were proficient in overcoming these problems.

According to the aircraft manual, the propeller was supposed to go into the low pitch position if it were to malfunction, but this did not always happen in reality. In the fall of 1945, while making an approach to *Wake Island* (CVE-65), Lieutenant (jg) John Olson of VB-80 experienced propeller failure and the prop went into the high pitch position. With wheels and flaps down, Olson was unable to maintain flying speed and made a water landing. He was rescued by an escorting destroyer with no harm to himself.

My experience with the R-2600 engine was generally good. While I was attached to VB-80, we had one complete engine failure over water at night. Pilot and aircrewman baled out. The pilot survived but the aircrewman was never found. The pilot swam 10 miles to the island of Maui, Hawaii, and was found on the beach the following morning.

I personally experienced engine trouble off the California coast in 1945. While practicing dives on an armoured boat, one of my engine cylinders swallowed a valve and I subsequently lost another cylinder. The resulting explosion blew most of the engine cowling off the engine. I was able to return to base and make an emergency landing.

Prior to my joining the squadron there were several fatalities due to engine failure. These occurred during the squadron's formation on the East Coast.

VB-80 commissioned 1 February 1944 at Wildwood, New Jersey. Aircraft consisted of SBDs, which were later replaced with SB2Cs. The squadron lost five SB2Cs with pilots prior to their first combat flight.

Having switched to the 'Beast' from the Dauntless, I found the aircraft to be much to my liking as a dive-bomber. Most of the problems had been worked out before my first flight. I especially liked the reflex gunsight.

With the perforated flaps I had better control in a dive. With time in aircraft I found that my accuracy in bombing improved. Pull-outs required a higher altitude than with the SBD.

As a general rule (weather permitting) we usually approached a target at an altitude of 18,000 feet or 20,000 feet and made a high speed run-in down to 15,000 feet before making our break. During the run-in the divisions would take their interval on the lead so as to prevent overrunning and so as to accomplish a rendezvous after pull-out. Flap degree was agreed on at the pre-flight briefing. On low-altitude dives, we might not use any flaps.

After the squadron returned from its first Pacific tour in early 1945, it was re-formed in California. At this time we were assigned SB2Cs fitted with a bombing device that we experimented with. It was apparently the system you describe developed by the Saab Aircraft Company. We did not have much success with this program and we reverted to our 'Mark 1 Eyeball' system.

Prior to deploying to the Far East in 1946, we did a lot of night dive and glide bombing on an ocean target. Flares were dropped by a designated pilot to give us light. The rendezvous was a little nerve-racking to say the least.

Our group had one incident involving structural damage to an SB2C. While making a dive on a water target off the California coast, the pilot, Ensign Thomas Perry, made a low pull-out and recorded about 13 Gs. The skin on the wings was wrinkled so bad that the plane was scrapped.

Speaking of high 'G' pull-outs, frequently the wheels of the 'Beast' would extend partially, and then return to the wells upon level flight. I believe this was because the wheels were not locking in the up position. So much for maintenance.

After so many years of flying attack aircraft, I have come to the conclusion that each pilot develops his own style of making his dive to get the maximum result. After the formation break, your own particular style takes over. After operating in a squadron for a period of time, you become familiar with each fellow pilot and know exactly what they will do in a given situation.

The Martin AM-1 Mauler was satisfactory in our operation as an attack squadron. With the 3,000 hp Pratt & Whitney Wasp Major 28-cylinder four-row radial engine, it was fast. The bubble canopy provided excellent visibility and the dive-brakes were very good. Only around 160 of these dive-bombers were ever manufactured. They were not satisfactory for the fleet and therefore were handed down to the Reserves.

Some of the planes assigned were equipped with Curtiss Electric Propellers and some with Hamilton Standard Propellers.

My Reserve Squadron had poor experience with the AM. We had a number of complete engine failures. Most of them resulted in fatalities. The engine had a habit of 'coughing' on the climb-out and the momentary silence was absolutely frightful.

The Douglas AD was probably the better of all the propeller-drive dive-bombers that I flew. Excellent for dive- or glide-bombing, it was able to carry a heavy load. It was comfortable to fly and had a good auto-pilot. Good for instrument flight.

Indeed, by general agreement with Charlie, the ultimate in dive-bomber design proved to be the replacement for the SBD, the Douglas SB2D Destroyer. A two-seater dive-bomber double the weight of the Dauntless, she had an internal bomb-bay, a range of 1,490 miles and was powered by a 2,300 hp engine. A modification of this design resulted in the XBTD, a single-seater plane with bomb-bay stowage of 3,200 lb and a top speed of 340 mph. Dive flaps were fitted operating from the sides of the fuselage. Some 358 were ordered in April 1942, but all were cancelled in 1944.

During the Korean War, when the United Nations for the one and only time in its history operated in unison to oppose the unprovoked Communist invasion of a neutral sate, the Royal Navy performed the last of its true dive-bombing missions and the aircraft it used to do the job were still the piston-engined developments of old Second World War designs.

The Fairey Firefly Mk V was an old friend in modified guise, for earlier marks had served with the British Pacific Fleet in attacks on the Japanese home islands in 1945, more commonly in the rocket-firing configuration, however, than as a dive-bomber. The Firefly appeared during the war in the Fulmar tradition, but early versions had been fitted with the Fairey-Youngman flaps, and the Mk 1 went aboard the carrier *Indefatigable* with No. 1770 Squadron as early as 1944, being later joined in service by No. 1771 Squadron aboard the carrier *Implacable*. Although famed as a rocket-firing attacker, the Firefly *could* carry a pair of 1,000 lb bombs under her wings for shallow dive-bombing if called upon.

The development of this aircraft continued as the Mk V, which joined the fleet with No. 814 Squadron at Yeovilton in January 1948. She was a two-seater, with a maximum speed of 386 mph, and some 160 were built.

The other mainstay of the Fleet Air Arm in Korea was the Hawker Sea Fury. This beautiful and powerful piston-engined aircraft had its origins in a 1942 specification calling for a long-range, high-performance fighter for Pacific warfare on the lines of an improved navalised Tempest, but all orders, save for a hundred or so, were ultimately cancelled. The first Sea Fury prototype flew on 21 February 1945, undergoing trials in 1946–7. A third prototype featured a Centaurus XXII engine, and fifty-six Sea Furies were eventually built of various marks for the Royal Navy to replace Lend-Lease aircraft returned to America or dumped to save money.

The first production Sea Fury X flew on 30 September 1946, and the first squadrons soon began equipping. No. 807 at Eglington was followed by Nos 778, 802 and 805 Squadrons later that same year. By this time the Seafire 47 was in service, but despite proving too fragile for naval operations, carried on as fighter defenders, and so the Sea Fury was modified as a fighter-bomber, to become the FB Mk 11, the first of which joined the fleet with No. 802 Squadron, in May 1948. For the next three years this delightful aircraft served with the 1st, 11th and 21st

Carrier Air Groups in Nos 801, 803, 804, 805, 807 and 808 Squadrons embarked aboard the light fleet carriers *Glory*, *Ocean* and *Theseus*, all of which were rotated in Far Eastern waters during the Korean conflict. With this machine the Fleet Air Arm re-established a formidable reputation for accurate dive-bombing well into the 1950s.

The Sea Fury FB II had a 2,550 Centaurus 18 engine, which gave her a top speed of 460 mph, combined with a range of 700 miles. She could carry two 1,000 lb bombs beneath her wings and had four fixed 20 mm cannon for strafing.

In the United States, the dramatic and skilful design work of Ed Heinemann modified his twice-aborted Destroyer design as the XBT2D, and this time he came up with a winner. The Destroyer had originally featured a faired cockpit, but this now became a 'bubble' canopy, and the faired tailplane was elongated and curved into the fuselage. The inverted-gull-wing configuration of the Destroyer's wing was abandoned and changed from a midwing feature into a straight, low-wing type as of old, which provided valuable additional lift.

The last modification enabled the Dauntless II, as she was originally termed, to take off from existing carriers with ease, whereas the Destroyer would have been restricted in this vital requirement. Altogether a ton was removed from the aircraft's all-up weight and the bomb capacity was at the same time increased to 5,000 lbs, a remarkable achievement. Her speed was increased as well by 30 mph to 375 mph.

The new deign, the XBT2D, first flew on 18 March 1945, and immediately won a substantial Navy contract, 548 Dauntless IIs being initially ordered. With the end of the Second World War, naturally, came the inevitable cut-back, to just 277 machines, and when these aircraft joined the US Fleet they marked the end of an era for specifically designed dive-bombers for the Navy.

The dive-bomber *par excellence* had now become an all-round stable, reliable weapons-delivery system, cheap to build and run, easy to maintain and fly, and she could carry any combination of bombs, torpedoes and rockets into action with ease. She duly served her appointed span of time in the post-war American fleets, but even more remarkable than this was the come-back that this by then ageing workhorse was to achieve many years later.

Finally christened the AD Skyraider, coded A-1, she was one of the very great piston-engined post-war aircraft success stories. It proved to be one of the military surprises of all, as most people had forgotten, if they ever knew, of the linger and exploit features of the old Junkers Ju 87 in influencing battlefield decisions, that such an anachronistic aircraft proved herself still more effective in some roles that the jets which now dominated all the air forces of the world. The military aviation world had to take on board, yet again, that speed was not, actually, the final arbiter of everything and that there was still a place for accuracy. In this aspect of fighting values, the old Skyraider proved herself far more reliable and credible than all the newer alternatives.[10]

Initially, it was the abandonment of the rival design, the Kaiser Fleetwing XBTK, coupled with the strictly limited orders for the Mauler, which only saw service with four squadrons, VA-44, VA-45, VA-84 and VA-85, that left the post-war attack aircraft category wide-open for the Skyraider.

On changing her designation in February to AD, she survived the initial reductions in orders, and even the reduced programme ensured that she remained a viable proposition while the worsening situation *vis-à-vis* the Communist aggression plans were finally digested in the complaisant West, and further expansion of her numbers was belatedly called for between 1946 and 1948, as the AD-2 and AD-3 variants. AD-8s first joined the fleet with VA-3 and VA-4 in April 1947 and conducted deck trials aboard the escort carrier *Sicily* that spring. That same autumn the AD joined front-line squadron service aboard the carrier *Midway* in the Mediterranean. A year later, the AD-1s were in service with no fewer than eight attack squadrons.

The AD-2 joined the US Fleet in 1948, and after 178 had been accepted, the AD-3 series took their place, featuring minor modifications to the cockpit and undercarriage. By 1950, production, having passed with minor improvements through AD-4 and AD-5, along with an infinite number of variations for anti-submarine, radar, air picket and target-towing duties, was beginning to taper off, with an end in sight. But, with the invasion of South Korea on 25 June that year, things changed dramatically, and the waning Skyraider received the first of her many rebirths.

Thus dive-bombing and the dive-bomber, written off as done in the summer of 1940, was again in full usage, re-emerging like the legendary Phoenix, a decade later.

*   *   *

During the Korean War, the Royal Navy light fleet carriers, *Glory*, *Ocean*, *Theseus* and the Australian *Sydney* (formerly HMS *Terrible*), with their respective air groups, worked off that barren and hostile coast for four long years of the conflict, and the reputation which their aircrews attained was of the highest statue, and comparable with anything that had gone before in dive-bomber history. It was the last time that dive-bombing, as such, was to be featured by the Fleet Air Arm, and as such, is deserving of detailed examination, for it has been ignored by most aviation historians.

Captain Eric M. 'Winkle' Brown RN gave the Author his description of Fleet Air Arm methods at this period:

> I trained a squadron before it set off for Korea and they were highly successful with 30-degree and 55-degree dive-bombing. The 30-degree technique was more accurate, basically because the release height was lower, but of course it was more vulnerable to the ground defences. The 55-degree technique was used against well-defended targets, and in Korea key targets were very well defended, particularly bridges, and even if they had not been bristling with ack-ack, a 55-degree dive would most often have had to be used because of the hilly terrain.[11]

In some cases, 65-degree dives were conducted, and Captain Brown recalled: 'Dives up to 65 degrees were also tried, as the Korean anti-aircraft fire was so accurate, but as the Sea Fury had no dive-brakes it accelerated so rapidly at this angle that the release height had to be high to allow sufficient pull-out space, and the bombing accuracy suffered.'[12]

Different methods were, naturally, utilised for the more docile Firefly, for she and the Sea Fury varied enormously in performance and capability. Captain Brown again described them thus:

> The technique used for the Firefly was basically simple: the aircraft flew in at right angles to the target and let it run along the port wing or the engine cowling. When it met the leading edges of the wing, for a 55-degree dive, the pilot winged over almost inverted, so that he could keep his eye on the target as he let the nose drop and pulled through onto it at right angles to his original line of light. Sighting during this manoeuvre was done by using the top of the engine cowling as a datum and then transferred to the gyro gunsight fixed ring. Adjustments in the dive for crosswind effect had to be made by aileron and for dive-angle change by elevator. Rudder was used only to eliminate skid effect.
>
> The dive was normally entered about 6,000 feet and pull-out initiated immediately on bomb-release at 1,000 feet. The pull-out had to be made with at least 4 G steady pull to avoid one's own bomb burst and to give a rapidly changing angle to the ground defences.
>
> For a 30-degree dive, a steep turn was made into the dive rather than a wingover. The release height was about 800 feet, and the pull-out was usually a steep, climbing turn.
>
> The Sea Fury, whose cockpit was over the trailing edge of the wing, used the 'Double the Angle' method of turning in. For example, when it was desired to carry out a 65-degree dive to port on a line of attack of 090 degrees, the approach was made on a

track of 220 degrees at 8,000 feet. When the target began to disappear beneath the leading edge of the wing close to the fillet, the pilot eased the nose down to keep the target in view. When at about 7,000 feet, the pilot pulled the nose up into a steep climb. The target would then appear behind the trailing edge of the wing, and the speed would be about 124–140 knots. The aircraft was then rolled over and turned 130 degrees (i.e. double the 65 degrees) toward the target, which was kept in view at all times. The aircraft would have to be aileron turned through approximately 100 degrees to get onto the line of attack. A speed of 360 knots would be reached in both 65-degree and 55-degree dives.

For 30-degree dives, the approach height was normally 5,000 feet, and the speed of release was 330 knots for the Sea Fury and 290 knots for the Firefly. The Firefly normally made 50-degree and 60-degree dives, i.e. 5 degrees shallower than the Sea Fury, and the speeds at release were 320 knots and 350 knots respectively.

Captain G.B.K. Griffiths RM served with the Air Operations Staff in Korea, and he gave me this description of how they functioned:

I selected targets, briefed and debriefed, built up intelligence and did photo interpretation. I knew the methods of attack, and since neither the Sea Fury nor Firefly had dive-brakes and were carrying 2,000 lb of bombs, an almost vertical dive would build up too much speed so that accuracy would fall off. The pilots used their experience, after training, from each mission, still using the gunsight to aim off, but now the gunsight was a GGS gyro-stabilised one.

All the bombing was dive-bombing, very accurate, all on land targets of course, even lobbing bombs into tunnels in which enemy trains took cover. I remember bridges that we dive-bombed, then rebuilt by hordes of Koreans slaving overnight, until five or six routes had been blasted, and *still* they came on if it was an essential route.[13]

This latter comment indicated the non-stop nature of the work required by the carrier aircrews at this period, and it also gave some indication of the tenacity and ruthlessness of a totally indoctrinated and fanatical enemy in achieving their ends, almost incomprehensible to the Western mind. Although Korea was to be the only time the United Nations stood up to aggression until the Iraqi invasion of Kuwait four decades later, the actual effectiveness of the action it took depended then, as now, almost entirely on the armed services of the Western Democracies, and in particular the United States and, decreasingly as her defence capability remorselessly declined, Great

Britain. In particular, the ability of these two nations to deploy their aircraft-carriers throughout the world's oceans, immune from nationalistic embargo, proved crucial. This is a lesson that, until recently, had been forgotten or discarded by successive British governments, both left and right. The strongest of these contributions was, of course, the US 7th Fleet, and in particular, the Skyraiders embarked thereon, being the only dedicated attack aircraft on hand.

The first attack in which the AD participated was in a strike against Pyongyang airfield, VA-55 under Lieutenant-Commander D.E. English, with sixteen AD-3Qs being launched from the carrier *Valley Forge* at 0540 on 3 July 1950, the first dive-bombers of the American forces to see combat action since the Second World War. They were accompanied by Corsairs fulfilling the same role they had done five years earlier, and all given the protection against the intervention of Communist MiG-15s by the jet Panthers. The combined striking force duly achieved surprise and, after initial strafing runs by the Corsairs and Panthers, the Skyraiders flattened the airfield and left it inoperational, despite heavy flak defence.

This first strike set the pattern. Skyraider bomb-loads varied enormously, with mixes of 1,000 lb, 500 lb or up to a dozen 100 lb bombs being carried, according to availability. Apart from airfields, the classic targets were those of the extended lines of communication of the invading army, which was by now deep into the South's hinterland, in the same manner as described for the Fleet Air Arm flyers, railways, road and rail bridges, supply columns and ammunition dumps. In addition to bombs, of course, each AD could pump twelve 5-inch rockets into the target area, which proved highly effective. Thus, on the same day as the first attack, the Skyraiders were back attacking the rail marshalling yards at Pyongyang and the rail bridge over the River Taedong, which was finally destroyed on 4 July, an appropriate enough date. But, as the British pilots have recalled, this was to prove itself to be an open-ended task. No ADs were lost in these initial attacks, although four were damaged by flak.

After some doubts as to whether the old traditional dive-bombing attack still had any validity in the jet age, combat experience soon demonstrated that it really did. Orders for additional ADs soon began to reach the Douglas factory, and within months over three hundred extra dive-bomber orders were on their books. During the first months of the conflict, the 'Able-Dogs' covered the landings at Pohang and the defence of Pusan, as well as participating in round-the-clock bombing strikes along the coast. In August, the carrier *Philippine Sea* arrived in support, with VA-15 aboard, and the combined squadrons concentrated their efforts against the vital Koehang bridges (which they destroyed with three direct hits) and other vital communications links.

By March 1951, when they were rested, the AD squadrons of the fleet had carried out 4,000 combat sorties and proved their worth, and that of the prop-driven dive-bomber, beyond dispute.

Missions of this nature continued throughout the war, the last squadron serving over Korea being VA-45 flying from the carrier *Lake Champlain* in June and July 1953 with AD-4s. Not only front-line squadrons were deployed in Korea, but also many reserve units were commissioned with the Skyraider and saw active service, with the veterans of the Second World War being recalled to duty and conducting dive-bomber missions with VA-702, VA-728 and VA-923. Ashore, the US Marines again renewed their long association with both dive-bombing and close-support aviation when VMA-121 equipped with AD-3s moved into Korea under command of Lieutenant-Colonel P.B. May in October 1951. This unit, the 'Heavy Haulers', thus known because of their massive bomb-loads, won great acclaim as part of MAG-12.

As much as her accuracy and great lifting power, along with the diversity of weaponry that the old dive-bomber could tote, the AD won the praise of the troops on the ground in Korea for her ability to 'loiter' over the battle area for extended periods, in strict and striking contrast to the quick 'in-bash-out' sweeps and long absences of the jet aircraft employed by the USAF Thunderchiefs and the like. The very presence of the AD, continually on call whenever required, and its comforting ugly shape roaring down on the enemy with her side-mounted 'barn-door' dive flaps fully extended, were worth their weigh in gold for morale. German veterans of the Second World War could have related to *that* reassuring feeling which only the reliable Stuka had matched.

As testimony to her battlefield value, production was again stepped up, with the development of the AD-5, which was adapted for the whole spectrum of air-support roles. Small wonder, then, that Rear Admiral Hopkins of the 7th Fleet was to firmly declare, 'I believe that the Skyraider is the best and most effective close-support airplane in the world.'

With the stalemate in Korea and the end to active fighting in 1953, it was to be expected that the old workhorse, already long past retirement age, would finally be put out to grass, but, again, this just didn't happen. Skyraiders soldiered on in the US Navy in a huge variety of roles, while the Royal Navy bought fifty of them, albeit for an ASW role, selling some of them to Sweden when their day in this guise was finally done. In America, the AD was yet further developed, through the AD-6, no longer a true dive-bomber, but able to deliver tactical nuclear weapons in the LOB manner from low level. The final configuration was the AD-7, with an R-3350-WB engine, the last aircraft leaving the factory in February 1957, after being in production for twelve years to close a run of 3,180 Skyraider aircraft.

Foreign governments continued to find employment for the Skyraider; the French Navy used 100 during the Algerian conflict in the late 1950s and early 1960s, handing over the survivors to Cambodia in 1965. With the US Navy, the numbers steadily declined over the decade, and when the Vietnamese War went 'hot' in August 1969, only twelve units were still flying them. Two were with the 7th Fleet and operated from the carriers *Constellation* and *Ticonderoga* in the combat strikes made against invading North Vietnamese armies soon afterwards. Skyraiders also equipped the South Vietnamese Air Force in increasing quantities, and finally even the US Air Force, for so long a stout opponent to dive-bombing and close support, realised just what a valuable tactical weapon she still remained, even in the 1970s, for this type of warfare, and took over a large number.

No longer a true and pure dive-bomber, of course, but a general-purpose support aircraft of great versatility that *could* dive-bomb when the occasion demanded it, her proved attributes of accuracy and battlefield endurance saw to it that the AD continued in service in Vietnam right up to the grisly end of that terrible war. Even after the American pull-out, a few Skyraiders flew on during the closing stages of the defeat as the victorious Communist North Vietnamese Army surged southwards, overwhelming the South Vietnamese, Cambodian and Laotian forces. It was the Skyraiders' final contribution, and with the passing of these three nations under the control of Pol Pot and his ilk, there passed the final link in the true dive-bomber story, a story which had started over sixty years earlier in an equally terrible war fought with the same objective, the upholding of freedom against tyranny, but fought then with ultimate success and a happier conclusion.

Dive-bombing, as an art, relying on the individual skill of each pilot, has, of course, long since had its day with the rapid development of electronic warfare, the final outcome of which is, perhaps the 'Smart' bomb or laser-beam riding, sea-level cruise missile launched at long range 'over the horizon' far away from what had always been the dive-bomber's main enemy, heavy anti-aircraft defences. Such weapons can now find their way unhesitatingly to the target with the same precision and deadly result as once only the dive-bomber had been able to achieve.

Thus passed a unique era in the history of aerial warfare.

Notes

1. Erik A. Wilkenson, *Dive-bombing: A theoretical examination of ballistic and aeronautical problems connected with precision dive-bombing. Especially with release of the bomb in the*

pull-out from a dive and based upon atmospheric and mechanical measurements, AB Seelig & Co, Stockholm, Sweden, 1947, signed English-language copy presented to the Author by Erik Wilkenson, 25 March 1986.

2. Lennart Larsson, *Svesnk salde bombsikte till Pentagon! (Swede sold bomb sights to the Pentagon!)*, article in *Flyghistoriskt Manadsblad*, Stockholm, 1978.

3. O'Ballance, Edgar, *The Indo-China War 1945–54: A Study in Guerrilla Warfare* (Faber, 1964).

4. For full details see Peter C. Smith, *Douglas SBD Dauntless*, op. cit., and *Jungle Dive-bombers at War*, John Murray, London, 1987.

5. Horndern, Lieutenant-Commander Mike, RN, to the Author, 29 May 1977.

6. Cheesman, Major V.B.G., RM, to the Author, 12 April 1977.

7. Harrington, Captain T.W., DSC, RN, to the Author, op. cit.

8. Monk, Lieutenant-Commander H.A., DSC, RN, to the Author, 27 March 1977.

9. Charles R. Shuford, to the Author, 26 January 1998.

10. A fact impossible for most to accept, including Hollywood. When the famed James A. Michener novel of the Korean War, *The Bridges at Toko-Ri*, came to be filmed it was Panther jets that were featured in the admittedly beautifully filmed battle sequences, when, in truth, it was the unacknowledged (and unglamorous) Skyraider that had done the job.

11. Brown, Captain E.M., RN, to the Author, 5 May and 21 June 1977.

12. *Ibid.*

13. Griffiths, Captain G.B.K. to the Author, op. cit.

Glossary

AA	Anti Aircraft
ACTS	Assistant Chief, Technical Services
AD/RDA	Assistant Director, Research Directorate Armament
AP	Armour Piercing
ATC	Air Training Corps
BAC	British Aircraft Commission
BDU	Bombing Development Unit
BuAer	Bureau of Aeronautics
BuArm	Bureau of Armament
BuOrd	Bureau of Ordnance
BuSup	Bureau of Supply
CAS	Chief of the Air Staff
C-in-C	Commander-in-Chief
DAF	Desert Air Force
DCAS	Deputy Chief of the Air Staff
DDRD	Deputy Director Research and Development
DDTD	Deputy Director Technical Development
DMC	Dirtector Military Construction
DNAD	Deputy Director Naval Air Division
DTD	Director Technical Development
DTS	Director Technical Services
FAA	Fleet Air Arm
FF	Fleet Fighter
GR	General Reconnaissance
HE	High Explosive
MAG	Marine Air Group
MAP	Ministry of Aircraft Production
MAW	Marine Air Wing
NBC	National Broadcasting Company
NCO	Non-Commissioned Officer
ONI	Office Naval Intelligence
OR	Operational Requirement
PS	Private Secretary
PM	Prime Minister
RAE	Royal Aircraft Establishment

RAF	Royal Air Force
RAAF	Royal Australian Air Force
RD(Arm)	Research and Development (Armaments)
RFC	Royal Flying Corps
RM	Royal Marines
RN	Royal Navy
RNAS	Royal Naval Air Service
SAC	Senior Aircraftsman
SAP	Semi-Armour-Piercing
SASO	Senior Armaments Staff Officer
S-of-S	Secretary of State
SEAC	South East Asia Command
TSR	Torpedo Spotter Reconnaissance
TV	Terminal Velocity
USAAC	United States Army Air Corps
USAAF	United States Army Air Force
USN	United States Navy
USNI	United States Naval Institute
VB	Bombing Squadron
VF	Fighter Squadron
VS	Scouting Squadron
VCAS	Vice Chief of the Air Staff

Bibliography

Other published works recommended for further study

Air Ministry – *Notes on Dive-bombing for the Information of Designers of Aeroplanes for the R.A.F* (London, 1936).

Air Ministry – *The Theory of Dive-bombing* (London, 1936).

Air Ministry – *Dive-bombing* (London, 1940).

Borelli, G.; Borgiotti, A.; Caruana, R.; Pini, G.; and Gori, C. – *Junkers Ju 87 Stuka* (Stem Mucchi, Modena, 1975).

Borgelli, A. and Gori, C. – *Gli Stuka Della R. Aeronautica 1940–45* (Stem Mucchi, Modena, 1978).

Brutting, Gerog – *Das Warren die Deutschen Stuka Asse, 1939–45* (Motorbuch Verlag, Stuttgart, 1976).

McGee, Captain Vernon E. – *Dive-bombing* (Washington DC, 1937).

Mizrahi, J.V. – *Dive and Torpedo-bombers* (Sentry Books, 1978).

Overfield, Lieutenant David B. – *Dive-bomber compared with bombing from level flight* (Washington, DC, 1939).

Obermaier, Ernst – *Die Ritter Kreuz Trage Der Luftwaffe 1939–45 Band II Stuka und Schlachtflieger* (Verlag Dieter Hoffmann, 1969).

Parson, Major C.S., BSc, *Dive-bombing* (London, 1942).

Parson, Lee M. – *Dive-bombers – The Pre-War Years* (Washington DC, 1949).

Royal Aircraft Establishment, Farnborough – *Dive-bombing as practised by the German Air Force and a Comparison with proposed British system* (London, 1940).

Smith, Peter C. – *Dive-bombers in Action* (Blandford Press, London, 1988).

Smith, Peter C. – *Stuka Volumes One & Two – Luftwaffe Ju 87 Dive-Bomber Units 1939–41 & 1942–45* (Classic, Shepperton, 2006 & 2007).

Winston, Robert Alexander – *Dive-bomber: Learning to Fly the Navy's Attack Planes* (Harrap, London, 1940).

Wilkenson, Erik A. – *Dive-bombing – A Theoretical Study* (Norrkpings Tidningars Aktiebolag, Stockholm, 1947).

Index

Ships

Military Units